BREW
BRITANNIA

Jessica Boak and Ray Bailey have been blogging about beer at boakandbailey.com since 2007, inspired by an eye-opening trip to Nuremberg. They have written articles for the Campaign for Real Ale and the Brewery History Society, among others. They live in Penzance, Cornwall.

JESSICA BOAK & RAY BAILEY

BREW
BRITANNIA

THE STRANGE REBIRTH OF
BRITISH
BEER

Aurum
Press

Brimming with creative inspiration, how-to projects and useful information to enrich your everyday life, Quarto Knows is a favourite destination for those pursuing their interests and passions. Visit our site and dig deeper with our books into your area of interest: Quarto Creates, Quarto Cooks, Quarto Homes, Quarto Lives, Quarto Drives, Quarto Explores, Quarto Gifts, or Quarto Kids.

First published in 2014 by Aurum Press
an imprint of the Quarto Group
The Old Brewery
6 Blundell Street
London N7 9BH
www.QuartoKnows.com

This paperback edition first published in 2017 by Aurum Press

A catalogue record for this book is available from the British Library.

ISBN 978 1 78131 715 0
eISBN 978 1 78131 271 1

1 3 5 7 9 10 8 6 4 2
2017 2019 2021 2020 2018

Typeset by Carrdesignstudio.com
Printed and bound by CPI Group (UK) Ltd, Croydon, CR0 4YY

CONTENTS

PROLOGUE

Half a century ago, the last rites were being said for British beer.

In 1965, Christopher Hutt arrived in Norwich as a new student. He had grown up in a village in the North West of England, where good beer was a part of everyday life, and had learned to drink in the pub on the green with his cricket team, enjoying jugs of traditional draught ale. But he realised with growing horror that, in the city where he was studying, it was almost impossible to find anything worth drinking.

In East Anglia, Hutt found that the three local breweries were in the process of being taken over by a national giant – Watney's – and that, in all of the city's beautiful medieval streets, there was only one pub selling what was then known as 'traditional draught beer'. Hutt is an important character in our story, but in 1965 he was just a young man who appreciated a decent pint. The village idyll back home, it turned out, was atypical: elsewhere, Britain's traditional beer culture was already starting to decay.

'Trad draught' – more often called 'real ale' – was sufficiently bitter that acquiring the taste took effort, becoming something of a rite of passage into adulthood. Ideally such beer was served at 'cellar' temperature (around 12°C to 14°C), so that the subtle flavours of the ingredients, for better or worse, could make themselves known. Contrary to popular belief, it wasn't 'flat', but was only gently carbonated, meaning that there was little to distract from the essential quality of the product. It *tasted* of something.

The new type of 'keg' beer that had taken over in Norwich was the opposite of an acquired taste: it pandered to the palates of those brought up on white sliced bread and processed cheese, being relatively sugary, pricklingly fizzy, chilled and pasteurised. Though it had its defenders, it seems that no one loved keg beer, and plenty of people hated it. Hutt certainly did.

Informed by his experiences in Norwich, Hutt would go on to write a book with an apocalyptic title: *The Death of the English Pub*.

In 1970, another large brewing company, Bass Charrington, announced plans to close at least eight local breweries across the UK, concentrating production at a vast new computer-controlled facility near the ICI chemical works in Runcorn, Cheshire.[1] One of the casualties was Joule's in the market town of Stone, Staffordshire. Founded in 1780, after nearly 200 years Joule's ceased brewing in 1974. As its doors slammed shut awaiting the arrival of demolition crews, redundant brewery workers filed into a local pub, the Red Lion, where they held a wake, led by a local beer enthusiast, Rod Tolley, dressed as an undertaker. Wreaths were laid and messages of condolence from beer lovers across the country read out. The beer they drank, though still labelled as Joule's, had actually been shipped in from out of town. Before long, even the brand name had gone. As local historian Philip Leason put it: 'The history of Joule's is so much more than just that of another industry; it weaved in and out of everyone's lives. Whole families were employed.'[2]

Not only were drinkers being deprived of the opportunity to partake of distinctive local beers, but entire historic styles of beer were disappearing. On its last legs for decades, porter – a black beer on which the British brewing industry had been built in the eighteenth century – finally became extinct in 1973, when Guinness ceased production of the last remaining example. Stout, which had evolved from porter, was becoming rather inbred, with only Guinness and a few other breweries' bottled efforts left on the market. And hardly anyone drank mild any more.

By 1976, there were just 147 breweries in existence in the UK owned by 82 companies, and barely any beer on sale that wasn't one of a handful of near-identical bitters.

And yet, though the cover of Christopher Hutt's book showed a funeral wreath placed over a pair of hand-pumps, he had also sounded a note of hope: 'This is one corpse that can still be revived.'

Bristol, 27 December 2013

Even in the post-Christmas doldrums, and despite the weather, the city-centre streets of the 'capital of the West Country' are busy with evening drinkers. Many, including us, are converging on cobbled King Street. Just 200 metres long, it has traditionally been home to a run of drinking establishments, but over the last year it has undergone a marked change.

What was previously a nightclub has become 'The Beer Emporium'. Housed in a Victorian industrial building, it has an atmospheric vaulted cellar bar of exposed brick. When we first visited in August, we found it crammed with earnest twenty- and thirtysomethings drinking expensive imported American India pale ale by the half-pint, or locally produced Belgian-style sour beer from champagne glasses. It boasts twenty-four taps, as well as fridges crammed with bottled rarities from around the world. Fifteen years ago, this might have been the most remarkable selection of beer on offer in any pub in the British Isles. Now it isn't even the best on the street, and we walk on by.

A few doors down, The Famous Royal Navy Volunteer has known various incarnations. An old maritime tavern, in the 1970s it was a hangout for young people, with 'Barry White on the juke box',¹ before reverting to brown beams and 'traditional real ale'. Once again it has changed, and is newly refurbished with stripped wood and bright lighting. On the bar there are eight pumps for 'real ale' but, behind it, mounted on the wall in the fashionable style, are twelve gleaming steel taps for more expensive and exotic kegged beers. There are forty or so bottles on offer, too, their brightly coloured labels exhibiting cutting-edge illustration and design. So dazzling is the choice, and so rapidly does it change, that a menu is displayed using pieces of paper slipped into the slots of a repurposed church hymn-board. India pale ales, 'double' India pale ales, 'saisons', 'sours', lagers, wheat beers and stouts vastly outnumber anything resembling traditional British bitter, but everything on sale is made in the United Kingdom, and much of it is brewed in Bristol or in one of the surrounding counties.

But there is more. We are heading for the end of the street where, on the site of what was previously a shots-'n'-lager party venue, a third 'craft beer' place has just opened. Its name is Small Bar (tagline: 'Big Beer') and it is by far the trendiest of the three locations. A local 'street food' vendor is in residence, selling burgers in 'artisan buns'. What looks like a hundred retro light bulbs dangle on cords from the ceiling, their coiled filaments casting a gentle orange glow over the unpainted brickwork and reclaimed furniture. The beer menu here is made from old wooden transport pallets with each brew's name, origin and alcoholic strength chalked onto interchangeable black planks and hooked in place.

We choose a locally made Flemish-style sour brown ale and a strong, American-style India pale ale from Derbyshire. Neither beer is remotely designed to appeal to a broad audience. Both beers are served in dainty stemmed glasses printed with the bar's logo. Taking a seat on tall, wobbling stools apparently constructed from bicycle seats with slender fashion models in mind, we peruse the list of bottled beers available, which is, of course, housed in a carved-out child's encyclopaedia.

Around us are parties of bony young men with towering quiffs, tattoos and Edwardian facial hair comparing notes on what they are drinking. There are no old boys propping up the bar with jugs of mild, and not a beer belly in sight.

We shake our heads in disbelief and ask, 'How the hell did beer get so hip?'

In 2012, for the first time since before the Second World War, the number of breweries in Britain exceeded 1,000, a number that continues to climb.

Many of the new breweries founded since the 1970s are small – Nigel Poustie of Sunbeam Ales in Leeds brews in his kitchen in his spare time, and makes around 150 bottles, or two casks, per week.⁴ Others barely exist at all, operating as 'cuckoos', using other brewers' premises at weekends and overnight. The longest-established are more than thirty-five years old and are still going strong, while others, such as BrewDog, which opened in 2007, are on the cusp of becoming high-street names with branded bars in every major city.

As for the *types* of beer on offer, there has never been more choice. Between them, the 1,000-plus breweries produce everything from straightforward lagers to beers flavoured with fruit; from the very palest session bitters to pitch-black export stouts. And some strange avenues are being explored: Huddersfield's Magic Rock, for example, have experimented with an almost extinct type of beer from Saxony known as 'Gose', which is flavoured with salt and coriander. As if that wasn't weird enough for the English palate, they've also brewed lurid versions, with pink grapefruit juice, gooseberry and lime.

With the new breweries have come new outlets, even against a prevailing narrative of a collapse in the number of 'community pubs'.⁵ Some have spun out into ever-growing chains. When Westfield built a shopping centre at Stratford, east London, in time for the 2012 Olympics, they invited tenders to run a small brewery on site – a sign that the trend is not confined to the backstreets, the urban 'creative' quarters.

Pubs and bars are no longer the only places to find good beer, either. Supermarkets devote aisles to beer from small breweries and from around the world, their level of commitment varying in response to fluctuations in demand. There are independent shops specialising in carefully 'curated' selections of rare and interesting brews, all of which have opened in the last forty years, but most noticeably since the Millennium. Latterly there has been a proliferation of internet-based mail-order services, which, for a fee, will deposit on your doorstep mixed cases of bottled beer from every corner of the globe.

There are new beer festivals, too, often featuring bottled and kegged beer from newer breweries, thus complementing the established events run by the Campaign for Real Ale. The Birmingham Beer Bash, which took place for the first time in 2013, was organised and run by volunteers from across the country, many of whom had met online through blogs or on Twitter. For people like these, beer is a hobby, perhaps an obsession, and in some cases, almost a religion: they feel the urge to go out and spread the good word.

This 'alternative' scene is a niche representing a small segment of those who drink beer. Whether they identify as enthusiasts for 'real ale', 'craft beer' or both, or for something else altogether, what they have in common is a contrary desire to drink anything other than the dominant product – the mass-market 'commodity' beers produced by international companies with maximum efficiency but at the cost of flavour.

This book connects events that have occurred over the course of half a century, in every corner of the country, to tell the story of how the new beer culture came about. Throughout, we have tried to question the received wisdom, glib assumptions and established mythologies that have grown up around organisations such as the Campaign for Real Ale, and around specific influential beers and breweries. Some diehard CAMRA supporters will no doubt feel that we have failed to give them enough credit for 'saving British beer'; others might be surprised at our suggestion that CAMRA, to a great extent, has created the modern 'craft beer' scene, viewed by many as the antithesis of the 'real ale' culture.

There is no getting away from it, though: however 'cool' beer has become, the story of this remarkable pushback begins in 1963 with a group of Pooterish, middle-aged men in the Home Counties who drew a line between 'good' and 'bad' beer, and so became unlikely rebels.

PRESERVATION ACT

Upon this new Britain the REVIEW bestows a name in the hope that it will stick – SUBTOPIA. Its symptom will be . . . that the end of Southampton will look like the beginning of Carlisle; the parts in between will look like the end of Carlisle or the beginning of Southampton . . . Subtopia is the annihilation of the site, the steamrollering of all individuality of place to one uniform and mediocre pattern.

Ian Nairn, 1955[1]

Epsom is in Surrey, just south-west of London, and is part of what is sometimes called 'the stockbroker belt'. In every general election since 1885 it has elected a Conservative MP. In the post-war period, however, even conservative (small c) suburbanites were becoming 'bolshie' (small b). As the 1960s began, a spate of middle-class strikes led young journalist Michael Parkinson, later to become the famous chat-show host, to write this:

> Suburbia, 6.25 p.m. The trains chase each other's tails into the station. The passengers, crumpled by rush-hour travel, pour out from the compartments . . . Bank clerks, office workers, 'something in the City' alike as soldiers in their uniform of sober suit, bowler, rolled umbrella. A new revolutionary army – the militant middle class.[2]

One such City clerk was Arthur Millard. He was born in 1916,[3] educated at Bancroft's, a private school in Essex, and joined the Bank of England in 1934. Like many young men of his generation, his career was interrupted by the Second World War, and he served with distinction in the Western Desert Campaign in North Africa. On his return, he achieved a position of responsibility in the bullion department at the Bank, but still referred to himself as a clerk, considering it a perfectly honourable title and anything grander to be pretentious.[4] He was broad-shouldered, tall and lean – athletic despite his pipe and horn-rimmed glasses. He laughed loudly and certainly liked a drink – five or six pints on a normal day by his own reckoning, going up to perhaps fourteen 'on an outing'.[5] Millard was also a 'joiner-in', revelling in the organisation and bureaucracy of clubs and societies. He was a star of the rugby team at school, vice-captain of the Bank of England First XV, secretary and treasurer of the United Banks Rugby Football Union, and so on.

One club that would, in a small way, make Millard famous had its origins in a letter he read in the *Financial Times*. Like everyone working in the City of London, he was an avid reader of the *FT*, which had always provided generous coverage of beer and brewing, including stories about the decline of 'traditional' draught beer. In the issue of Saturday, 30 November 1963, another suburbanite, Mr E.A.H. Cross of Uxbridge, set out in six paragraphs what now reads like a proto-manifesto. He bemoaned the 'swallowing up' of small breweries by larger ones, and the subsequent turn to keg beers 'blown up out of sealed dustbins', and went so far as to propose

Arthur Millard of the SPBW pictured in 1971.

nationalising the brewing industry, saying that, under such an arrangement, consumers might complain to their MP if they could no longer find beer they liked in their local pub. While they were at it, Mr Cross went on, they might also suggest to their MP 'that he had some nice draught beer drawn from the wood'. In that single letter was encapsulated the whole story, and all the tensions, of British beer in the post-war period.

During the 1950s, coverage of the brewing industry in the financial press seems to have consisted of three basic stories recycled at intervals: 'profits falling', 'costs rising' and 'consumption down'. Drinkers were abandoning draught bitter and mild at an alarming rate, choosing bottles instead – if they drank beer at all. Though brewing businesses had long been predatory, the climate of decline accelerated the tendency and around half the country's breweries were closed or taken over. From a total of 567 at the start of the decade, fewer than 360 independent breweries remained in operation by 1960.[6]

It was in this context that a kind of arms race got under way. Brewers competed to maintain profits by running the most efficient operations, the most effective distribution networks and the biggest, glossiest advertising campaigns. Giant national brewing concerns began to emerge, until Ind Coope and Taylor Walker, Watney Mann, Courage and Barclay, Bass Ratcliffe Gretton, Whitbread and Scottish Brewers came to be known collectively as the 'Big Six'.[7]

As well as takeovers within the industry, there were also outsiders on the prowl, among them Canadian E.P. (Eddie) Taylor, of Carling lager fame, who began acquiring small British breweries in 1959 with a view to building an empire. Taylor in particular rattled the close-knit brewing aristocracy represented by the Brewers' Society. For smaller brewers, the choice was this: bet everything on expansion, in the hope of becoming a national concern too big to be taken over; or allow the company to find safety under the protection of one of the new brewing giants, who were at least home-grown predators.

What happened to the West Country brewers Starkey, Knight and Ford is typical: struggling financially, in 1960 they signed a pact with the much bigger Whitbread. That friendly arrangement would see Starkey, Knight and Ford distribute some Whitbread beer in their estate of pubs, while Whitbread helped them modernise their brewing facilities. Whitbread's offer of friendly 'assistance' became a takeover in all but name when a 'merger' was announced in 1962. Before long, the smaller brewers had become 'Whitbread Devon', and its beers and prancing-horse trademark were snuffed out of existence.

Across the country, many favourite local beers – those on which parents and grandparents had been nourished – went the same way, replaced with nationally distributed and marketed brands such as Watney's Red Barrel, the original 'keg' beer.

Kegs had been in use in a limited way since 1930[8] but really took off with a specific brand, Flowers Keg, launched in 1955,[9] whose name would become the generic description for this type of beer. Whereas 'traditional draught' (cask) beer often went bad in the hands of careless publicans, keg was much easier to look after. Brewers liked the new method of dispense because, with their pasteurised beer and airtight seal to prevent spoilage, kegs reduced wastage at a time of heightened, almost desperate competition. It was also hoped that keg might win back some of the punters who had defected to bottled beer, as it was of a consistent quality, if perhaps lacking in complexity. Traditionalists, however, saw it as a mere shadow of 'the real thing'.

Arthur Millard had a small circle of regular drinking partners, most of them former military men – Dougie Chamberlain, Boyes Lee, Gerry Smith, Penri Thomas, John Gore and John Keeble[10] – whom he knew either through playing golf, the Bank of England, or both. All were bankers except Thomas and Keeble. Over the course of a week, they discussed Mr Cross's letter.[11] In it were echoes of something they'd all been feeling – an anxiety that was part of a wider apprehension in British society in the post-war period as progress rubbed up against tradition.

Along with various other types of building, from music halls to ornate Victorian public lavatories, pubs became the focus of an urge to preserve. In a 1947 Introduction to Richard Keverne's *Tales of Old Inns*, novelist Hammond Innes suggested one reason why veterans like Millard might have become rather sentimental about them:

> During the war, [pubs] played their part and there were few soldiers overseas who, when they thought of home, did not also remember some snug bar or quaint little roadside inn with affection.[12]

Pubs had even been the focus of a 1945 propaganda film for British troops stationed abroad, *Down at the Local* (directed by Richard Massingham), intended to remind them of why they were fighting and what awaited them when the job was done.

German-born architectural critic Nikolaus Pevsner, famous for his series of guides to the buildings of England, was a particular devotee of the Victorian pub and its embodiment of an 'overwhelming' Englishness. Many of his peers agreed, and in 1946 the head office of the *Architectural Review* even had an idealised period pub built in its basement.[13]

There is a general sense in books and articles from this period that, especially in cities, historic pubs and inns which hadn't been done for by the Luftwaffe would soon enough fall foul of the 'vandalism' of ambitious town planners. As for the 'modern pub', it was considered by most to be a contradiction in terms. In a 1949 book review, poet and architectural writer John Betjeman, a founder member of the preservationist Victorian Society, wrote:

> There is ... the unselfconscious cottage character of an old-fashioned country inn and the drunken glory of a London gin-palace with its engraved glass and polished bars, both types of building fast disappearing as the brewers hygienise the interiors with tiled floors, chromium bars and polished plywood walls.[14]

He would return to the theme in his 1950 poem 'The Village Inn', in which a brewery public relations officer convinces a wine-drinking cynic to visit the 'old village alehouse' at the heart of public life. He finds it crudely refurbished, its thatched roof gone, and capped with a neon sign 'visible for miles':

> *Our air-conditioned bars are lined*
> *With washable material,*
> *The stools are steel, the taste refined,*
> *Hygienic and ethereal.*

One outcome of this unease over the disappearance of Old England was the founding of a series of preservation groups. The Talyllyn Railway Preservation Society was founded in 1951,[15] inspiring the 1953 Ealing comedy *The Titfield Thunderbolt*. The Sailing Barge Preservation Society was launched in 1956,[16] followed, three years later, by a similar group dedicated to paddle steamers.[17] Betjeman and Pevsner were both founder members of the Victorian Society, whose members, from 1958, dedicated themselves to saving buildings of all sorts, including pubs, that were scheduled for demolition. (The foundation of a Music Hall Society, with the aim of preserving Victorian popular theatres, was announced with great fanfare in November 1963,[18] only days before Mr Cross's letter about beer appeared in the *Financial Times*.)

Dougie Chamberlain called the first 'formal' meeting for the Society for the Preservation of Beers from the Wood for Friday, 6 December. It was to be held at the gang's usual haunt, The Rising Sun, known as 'the Riser', on a backstreet a few minutes from the station. It met the ideal, being a Victorian pub converted from a slatted cottage in the nineteenth century,[19] with public and saloon bars as well as two 'snugs', perfect for intimate meetings. It served 'traditional' beer, too – the perfect accompaniment to Millard's billowing pipe.

The meeting commenced with a rousing speech from Chamberlain which summarised Mr Cross's letter and, in the process, transformed several of its more emotive turns of phrase into campaign slogans, as recorded in the minutes (our emphasis):

> He soundly deplored the monolithic policies of the brewers which, accepted with a spineless lack of gumption by the bartenders guild, were forcing the sale of beer from *sealed dustbins* thereby depriving discerning drinkers of their traditional tipple, which was, and had been for centuries, *beer drawn from the wood*.

After cheering and applause, Arthur Millard was elected the first chair of the SPBW, the name being agreed unanimously. Its aims were recorded as follows:[20]

1 To stimulate the brewing and encourage the drinking of beers drawn from the wood.

2 To denigrate the manufacture and sale of beer in sealed dustbins and to discourage its consumption.

John Keeble, the only surviving founding member, told us in a letter that they did not take themselves at all seriously – an assertion supported by the minutes of that first meeting:

> After a confused debate, during which the chairman called the meeting to order and demanded to know whose round it was, the following orders were laid down:

> All members shall, at all times, eschew the consumption of dustbin beers during public-house licensing hours. Dispensation from this order, which is otherwise mandatory, shall be granted only in the following cases:

> a Unavoidable hospitality.

> b Non-availability of beer from the wood within a radius of half a mile if on foot, and one of five miles if travelling by car.

> c Those members over fifty years old.

That last dispensation meant, of course, that most of the founder members could drink whatever was convenient: from day one, the SPBW was anything but hard line.

It was not only with the seven founder members of the SPBW that Cross's letter hit a nerve. The next Saturday, 7 December, the letters page of the *Financial Times* was all but taken over by supportive responses from beer-drinking readers. Picking up on this outpouring of frustration, and further fuelling the debate, the following week the paper ran a substantial article on sales figures for draught and bottled beers. An accompanying graph showed consumption of mild collapsing and sales of keg on the rise, and concluded: 'There is no doubt that the sales of draught under pressure will spread.'

In truth, despite their strident rhetoric and doom-laden prophecy, Millard and his colleagues had much in common with a string of earlier, more obscure drinking societies, such as the Ancient Order of Froth Blowers (1924–31),[21] the National Society for the Promotion of Pure Beer (c. 1923)[22] and the Black Pig Society, formed in Derby c. 1959.[23] There was also the Pub Users' Protection Society (c. 1946),[24] which, though it was small – really a one-man operation – was more than a drinking society, with a mission to protect consumers from short measures.

Millard liked good beer but scoffed at anyone who appreciated it with too straight a face, and rejected anything that resembled the snobbery of the 'wine buff'.[25] He was no dogmatist, either, happily drinking keg beer when it would be churlish to do otherwise, or when the alternative was – horror! – to drink nothing at all.[26] The joke ran on, however, and the society grew. John Keeble:

> [We] encouraged the formation of SPBW branches and got as much publicity for our campaign as possible. The press got hold of it, and the *Daily Mail* wrote about it at some length,[27] which helped the campaign considerably. We had monthly meetings which were both humorous and serious and we encouraged branches to visit The Rising Sun, which they did in great

numbers, including a coachload from Yorkshire, to sign the
visitors' book and visit the 'mecca' of the SPBW.

They did very little to recruit new members. Rather than advertise,
they simply waited for people to hear of them on the grapevine[28]
or, on occasion, tipped the wink to a likely-looking fellow in the
City of London. Alan Risdon, who worked in the City in 1965,
recalled entering into conversation with a stranger in the queue at
a dry-cleaner's. On correctly identifying the stains on the stranger's
dress shirt as Worthington's bitter, he was handed an SPBW application form and instructed to complete and return it care of the
Bank of England. That stranger was Arthur Millard.[29] There was
no membership fee, but aspiring members were obliged to pass a
test (Risdon's form was returned stamped 'APPROVED – Office of
the Chairman'[30]) and to buy a specially designed tie – mourning
black, decorated with brown beer barrels – the wearing of which
was obligatory every Friday.[31] Risdon once forgot to wear his tie
and, on running into a group of fellow SPBW members, was bayed
at and berated until he had paid the penalty of buying a round of
drinks.

Although The Rising Sun in Epsom continued to be described
as the SPBW's national headquarters, it was a City pub, Ye Old
Watling on Watling Street – one of a number of narrow, Dickensian
passageways filling the block between Cannon Street, Queen Victoria
Street and Cheapside – that became a centre for 'meetings' and was
later generally recognised as SPBW Central.[32] Here's how it was
described in a 1973 City pub guide:

> The ceiling has massive beams, worn by the ravages of time.
> The considerable quantity of wood is all dark, and the furniture
> is plain, comfortable and perfectly in keeping with the
> surroundings. In one corner a snack bar nestles unobtrusively,
> and a door opposite leads to the small Wren Bar and an almost
> unnoticed dartboard.[33]

As is often the case with such groups, the SPBW were much clearer about what it opposed than what it supported. Though keg beer and 'top pressure' – what founder member Boyes Lee called 'dull and gassy conformity'[34] – remained the avowed enemy, those involved in the SPBW slowly began to accept that the wood part of 'beer from the wood' was too much to ask, and, in the late 1960s, reluctantly declared metal containers acceptable, if not desirable.[35]

In the early years, the Society found brewery visits an effective way of combining social activity with the application of gentle pressure on the industry. Delegations from the SPBW toured several breweries, and Millard had a reputation for 'sales-manager baiting'. As hapless public relations people attempted to convince the group that the latest keg or top-pressure beer was every bit as good as the traditional 'draught' version, Millard would slap them down with a blunt dismissal: 'Then why does it taste so bloody awful?'[36] Marketing people too were seen as the enemy, and symptomatic of the priority given to advertising over the quality of the beer.[37]

As it became more widely known, the SPBW also became the butt of jokes. It was referred to as 'The Flat Beer Society' – a sly comparison with the Flat Earth Society, which also lampooned their obsession with 'fizzy beer'. It was gently mocked for its 'numerous and voluble spokesmen' (there was no 'message discipline'). It even inspired a lyric in The Kinks' satirical 1968 song 'The Village Green Preservation Society' in which, among such hopeless causes as 'The Custard Pie Appreciation Consortium', is listed 'The Draught Beer Preservation Society'. They were held up as examples of English eccentricity, and were the stuff of the 'weird and wacky' columns in the papers.

By the mid-1960s, while Millard was nominally the president of the national SPBW, such as it was, there was very little central control or bureaucracy. John Keeble noted that, in fact, the founder members began to lose interest, as the Society gained a momentum of its own:

> I think we were getting bored with the campaign and had other things to do . . . In spite of the headquarters at The Rising Sun

closing down, our branches carried on the good work and
refused to quit. I think we were all quite amazed and delighted at
the continuation of the Society and its expansion.

In 1967, the SPBW embarked on its first real attempt at political
lobbying, with efforts to convince the Department of Trade and
Industry to regulate the application of the term 'draught beer'
by breweries. To many people, it was growing to mean anything
dispensed into a glass from a tap – the opposite of bottled beer –
regardless of the method of its manufacture or dispense. As the
SPBW saw it, this made it easier for breweries and publicans to sell
keg beer to people who might think they were buying 'the real thing',
especially as many were presented with ceramic or plastic replicas
of wooden barrels. At first, they were fobbed off, being told that
'anyone who believes the term "draught" has been applied in a false
or misleading way may institute proceedings himself or complain to
the Food and Drugs or Weights and Measures Authority in the area
in which the alleged offence has taken place'[38]. This vexed the SPBW.
How could they prove the term had been misapplied without a legal
definition against which to measure it?

After plugging away for several years, in 1971 they changed the
angle of their attack[39] and, with the help of new members employed
in the legal profession,[40] set about writing to the Secretary of State for
Trade and Industry, John Davies, proposing three categories of beer:[41]
draught, meaning drawn from a cask; *top pressure*, meaning filtered
and with added gas; and *keg*, meaning pasteurised, filtered and with
added gas.

They were, once again, unsuccessful, apart from making it into the
papers, but the proposal represented a significant early attempt to
distinguish between 'good' and 'bad' beer – a battle that others would
later continue and go on to win.

Such serious campaigning attracted support. By the beginning of
the 1970s, despite the withdrawal of many of the founding members,
despite the embroidered ties and entry test and a shambolic approach

to public relations, the SPBW had around twenty branches and more than 1,500 members.[42]

At some point in 1971, Terry Pattinson, a young journalist from Gateshead in the North East of England and industrial correspondent at the *Daily Express*, became an executive member, with responsibility for press and marketing. The energy and expertise he and other new members brought created a brief upsurge in their profile. Millard was pushed further into the spotlight, even in the absence of his fellow founders. He was treated to a full-page portrait piece in the *Guardian* in the same year, being encouraged to give full vent to his spleen. 'Fuming', he dismissed keg beer, the people that sold it and those who drank it, with characteristic bluntness:

> It tastes nasty, it blows you up like a balloon and it costs too much. In a lot of pubs nowadays one's dealing with just autom- atons behind the bar. They only need an ignoramus with a spanner to stock it and serve it . . . The younger generation grow up knowing no different, having been introduced at an early age to the clear stuff with bubbles in it.[43]

When he suddenly and unexpectedly retired from the Bank of England in December 1971, the notice in *The Old Lady*, the Bank's staff magazine, made light of his recent fame: '[He] has appeared on TV, spoken on the radio and . . . he seems to be fast becoming Fleet Street's favourite pin-up boy, and nowadays can hardly take a pint in his hand without the photographers popping up all round him with their flashlights.'

It was also in 1971 that London brewer Truman ceased brewing 'draught beer', prompting an attention-grabbing, theatrical response from the SPBW, as described by writer Christopher Hutt:

> A wreath was taken to the London Stone [on Cannon Street] and placed over the last barrel of the real stuff. At the aptly named Who'd a' Thought It [a pub on Plumstead Common], a mock funeral service was held. A thirty-six-gallon barrel was interred

in the back garden of the pub by the local branch chairman, dressed up as a vicar.[44]

The 'vicar' was probably a younger member, Howard Purdie, and his 'sermon' raged at Truman: 'They have visited us with the curse of the Demon Keg'. The lowering of the barrel into its grave was accompanied by a lone trumpeter.[45]

In September 1972, frustrated by the slow and unhelpful response to their requests for a legal definition of draught, the SPBW planned to lay on yet another piece of street theatre, this time outside the offices of the Ministry of Agriculture, Fisheries and Food (MAFF) on Whitehall Place in Westminster. This so-called 'Down With Keg demo', the centrepiece of which was a barrel of beer to be given away to civil servants, generated yet more headlines.[46] In practice, though, it achieved nothing: we have not found any evidence that it actually took place.

What might arguably be called the SPBW's greatest achievement on the campaigning front came just a week or so after their Whitehall ale-tasting protest, by which time membership had risen to around 2,000.[47] The Society had booked a stand at a privately run beer festival scheduled for 21 to 28 October 1972,[48] at which the only beers would be keg bitters and lagers supplied by members of the Big Six and a handful of larger regional brewers. The SPBW intended to distribute leaflets and sell or give away samples of 'real beer' in an attempt to convert keg-drinking heathens. Presumably they also planned, in line with their founding charter, to 'denigrate the manufacture and sale of keg beers' in some more or less disruptive, attention-grabbing manner.

Fearing the worst, the big breweries threatened to pull out unless the SPBW was excluded. John Robinson, managing director of Trade Aids, who were organising the event, said: 'The brewers objected to our giving the Society a free stand when they have to pay for theirs, and they thought that these people would start up a petition at the festival against the breweries.'[49] Though Trade Aids presented their decision as the withdrawal of an offer, the SPBW seized on the opportunity to spin it as something more sinister: OLD-STYLE BEER BANNED was the headline in the *Daily Mirror* of 19 September 1972. This fitted perfectly with the SPBW's narrative of 'the tyranny of the big breweries'[50] and is a good example of how taking action to avoid negative publicity only draws more attention to an issue, which might otherwise have generated none.

Further capitalising on Trade Aids' capitulation, on 20 October the SPBW organised a photo opportunity, with members marching from Wood Green to Alexandra Palace holding placards – 'KEG IS KID'S STUFF', 'A FISTFUL OF FIZZ' – and rolling before them a wooden barrel of 'the real stuff'.[51] They set up pickets outside the festival, and more column inches followed, with stories casting big beer as the bad guys and the SPBW as the plucky underdogs.

Even Lord Mancroft, president of the London Tourist Board, could not resist giving them a supportive mention in his speech opening the event: 'I have nothing against keg beer ... I completely understand its merits and economics, but there are people like myself who still prefer to drink beer from the wood.'[52]

The text of a flyer handed out at this event gives a flavour of the SPBW's campaigning tone. Titled 'Festival of Fraud: Facts you should know', it is peppered with exclamation marks, and concludes: 'UNITED ACTION NOW can save TRADITIONAL BRITISH BEER from extinction. The battle against the BIG BROTHER BREWERS has begun.'

That mention of 'united action' is telling. Ally Pally, though it was the SPBW's great moment centre stage, spelt the end for the Society as a major campaigning force. For, alongside it on the picket line that day was a newer, more efficient, downright sexier protest group: what was then known as the Campaign for the Revitalisation of Ale (CAMRA).

THE CAMPAIGN FOR THE ... SOMETHING ... OF ALE

An unassuming character like the beer drinker, with no union, no trade association, no press agent and no lobby, can get kicked around.

LIFE magazine, 4 April 1949[1]

By the dawn of the 1970s, preservation societies seemed very quaint. The model for the next stage in the consumer revolt against the big brewers would be that of the protest group. The Campaign for Nuclear Disarmament was founded in 1957, the Homosexual Law Reform Society in 1958 and the Campaign Against Racial Discrimination in 1967. In 1970, several more high-profile groups appeared almost at once, including the Gay Liberation Front, Friends of the Earth and the National Women's Liberation Conference.[2] Beer drinkers were about to demand their rights, too.

On 20 March 1971 in Chester, in the North West of England, four young men gathered at The Ship Inn for a Saturday-night pub crawl as a warm-up to a lads' holiday in Ireland on which they were due to embark the next day. One of them was Michael Hardman, a twenty-four-year-old journalist and former grammar-school boy from Warrington.

When we met him in November 2012, he was in his sixties, semi-retired but smartly dressed, and still had the look of a schoolboy in his wide eyes, with eyebrows permanently arched in an expression of good humour. 'Founding CAMRA is the thing I'm mostest proudest of in my whole life,' he told us. 'That's an old in-joke we used to have,' he explained, but it was clear that, self-deprecating humour aside, the statement was sincere. As he told the story, punctuated with amusing anecdotes, some of which he asked us not to record, one thing became clear: if the Campaign for Real Ale is today seen as rather earnest and geeky, that's certainly not how it started out. He mentioned love affairs – 'We had a couple of women with us, of course' – and nights of drunken debauchery; he said a few words in Spanish, learned from a Mexican girlfriend, and conveyed just how much *fun* it all was.

In 1971, he was living and working in Birmingham, but trouble with a girlfriend brought him back to his youthful stamping ground and the company of old friends. Bill Mellor was also a journalist, and also from Warrington; born three years later than Hardman, he was the youngest of the group. Graham Lees, tall and hawkish with substantial sideburns and Harry Palmer glasses, had grown up in Salford, near Manchester, and worked for the *Chester Chronicle*. It was he who brought along the odd man out, Jim Makin, who was not a journalist but a clerk in the offices of Threlfall's Brewery.

That night in Chester, they visited several pubs and a private club.[3] They were not exactly beer snobs, but they certainly preferred some to others. Hardman was in the habit of ordering whichever was the cheapest, as he had worked out that that would usually result in a pint of 'proper' draught bitter. In the absence of 'decent' beer, though, he would drink whatever was on offer. The aim was, after all, to get drunk and have a good time. But as the evening passed, he and his friends found themselves increasingly irritated by the appalling quality and limited range.[4] Several pints the worse for wear, they finished the evening with a curry, over which they talked about the bland, expensive, rather weak big brewery products they'd endured.

Even on holiday, their irritation continued to grow, as Irish beer, they discovered, was worse still. Guinness stout, especially that brewed and sold in Ireland, had a certain cult following, and they enjoyed it, but Smithwick's draught beer was 'rancid' and offered a nightmarish vision of what might come to pass back home:

> Stout served us well that week, but we did miss the more refreshing qualities of beer and our conversation occasionally switched from the merits of the local ladies and the lack of Indian restaurants to the plague which had not only swept Ireland's ale into oblivion but was also threatening to wipe out the national drink in England.[5]

They began to talk about a campaign. They were joking, of course, just as the founders of the SPBW had been almost a decade before, but it can be fun to take something absurd seriously, and so they deliberated over a suitably grand name for their newly conceived organisation. First, Lees suggested the word 'ale' because it seemed solidly Northern and down to earth – less pretentious, he felt, than 'beer'. It was regarded, then, as 'a manly, vigorous'[6] synonym. Hardman has claimed that he was inspired by the sight of Mellor and Lees grappling with a camera and pronounced the word aloud, as if it were already an acronym: 'CAMERA'. The Campaign . . . something . . . Ale. As they walked across the yard at the Guinness Brewery at St James's Gate in Dublin, they entertained themselves by finding words to fill in the gaps. The Campaign for the Restoration of Ale was suggested by Mellor, prompting Lees, a few days later, to proffer an alternative: 'No, Revitalisation of Ale . . . it's more of a laugh.'

They decided that they ought to have at least one formal meeting. That took place at the 'mostest westernmostest' pub in Europe, Kruger Kavanagh's[7] in Dunquin, County Kerry. It was described by American travel writer Paul Theroux in a contemporary account as 'a friendly, ramshackle place with a dark side of bacon suspended over one bar

The founder members of CAMRA in Ireland, 1971 (right to left): Graham Lees, Jim Makin, Bill Mellor and Michael Hardman, with an unknown Irishman at far left.

and selling peat bricks, ice cream, shampoo and cornflakes along with the Guinness and the rum'.[8] The date of that first CAMRA meeting was probably 23 March 1971.[9] They amused themselves with the pretence of bureaucracy, inspired by Lees's experience of involvement with the National Union of Journalists. Hardman became the Campaign's first chairman, because he volunteered; Lees, the secretary, because he had a pen; Makin, the treasurer, because he worked in an office and Mellor, the event organiser, because he was the only candidate left. They decided to go along with Lees's suggestion and call themselves the Campaign for the Revitalisation of Ale, dropping the superfluous E to become CAMRA.

As Hardman has repeatedly said, at this stage it was a joke, a game, a laugh: 'Apart from scrawling the word CAMRA on a deserted beach and annoying innumerable locals by chanting: "We're only here for the ale", there was little further reference that week to the Campaign for the Revitalisation of Ale.'[10] On the flight home, however, the sense that something was in the air was underlined when Bill Mellor looked up in frustration from a double-page spread in his copy of the *Sunday*

Mirror[11] and said, with some bitterness: 'Special Mild and Watney's Red Barrel, it's so weak you could serve it to children.'[12] The article that prompted his comment detailed the strength and price of beers from every brewery in the country under the headline THE SOBERING TRUTH ABOUT THE BRITISH PINT. It was the potency as much as the quality of their pints that bothered the founders of CAMRA.

In their disorganised, barely post-adolescent way – 'We were four daft lads!'[13] – they came home and promptly forgot about the whole thing. 'We were among the cynics,' said Hardman in a 1975 newspaper column, sounding like a religious convert. 'We did absolutely nothing to fight the brewers' policies, believing that no one would listen to us.'[14] This was a retrospective gloss: in fact, they had better ways to spend their time.

But Graham Lees could not bring himself to drop it, not quite. Obviously attached to the idea, he acted on his own initiative and printed membership cards, which he sold for five pence each. When a colleague with a printing business on the side badgered him to have some Christmas cards done, he gave in. The verse inside said:

> *Whether in city bar you sup,*
> *Or in village vault you get tanked up,*
> *Be on your guard against bad ale,*
> *Or you'll never live to tell the tale . . .*
> *Of CAMRA.*

He sent them out in December 1971, and the cryptic signature encouraged a few more people to 'join', though membership, at this point, made about as much demand on anyone's time as being part of the *Beano* fan club.

During 1972, the gang drifted further apart, with Lees moving to the South East; Mellor to Nuneaton in the West Midlands, where he worked on the *Coventry Evening Telegraph*; Hardman sticking in Birmingham and Makin remaining in Salford. It was only some months later,[15] when Lees and Hardman found themselves once again in Chester on yet another pub crawl, that Lees brought up the subject of CAMRA and suggested making a real go of it as a consumer campaign. Not only had the beer in Chester not improved, but, as both had spent several months living and working in other parts of the country,[16] they'd tasted worse. Hardman's turn of phrase in recalling this conversation is telling: he was 'stunned' at the idea that CAMRA should now 'pass itself off' as a serious consumer group.[17]

When pressured to explain how they could go from 'having a laugh' to taking themselves seriously, Hardman protested: 'We started to take the Campaign seriously, but not ourselves. We never took *ourselves* seriously.'

Lees was persuasive, however, and a grandly titled annual general meeting was scheduled to coincide with the approximate anniversary of the Irish holiday. Its venue was to be The Rose Inn in Nuneaton, in the West Midlands. Mellor had been living above the pub in a rented room[18] and was a regular, and the town was conveniently connected to Manchester, London and Birmingham. It is for this reason that some sources[19] erroneously imply that Nuneaton was where CAMRA was born, and why some who attended this meeting have themselves claimed to be founder members, much to Michael Hardman's irritation.

The prospect of explaining the purpose of the Campaign in concrete terms forced the founders (Hardman and Lees, primarily) to think harder about exactly what it was they were campaigning for.

> We started by talking to publicans about the difference between what we liked and disliked, and were invited down into cellars to find out that the stuff we favoured was cask beer and the newfangled gassy liquid was keg beer. That was, though we didn't realise it, the moment when we identified our cause for the first time. Our mission would be to save and promote cask beer.[20]

Hardman recalled the Nuneaton AGM as a drunken affair lasting some three hours. In attendance, along with the four founders, were twenty or so friends of Lees and Mellor. As it became more raucous,

Hardman was required repeatedly to bang his glass on the table and call for order.[21] The tone of the AGM and the credibility of those in attendance might be judged by the reaction of the Warwickshire press; the local newspaper implied that a group of con artists had tricked the landlord of The Rose into believing they were a national body called 'CAMERA' and giving them the run of his pub. It quoted Mellor as saying that the group had 'up to ten thousand members', but observed that 'fewer than two dozen had turned up'.[22]

What emerged was an executive committee of seven[23] and a written constitution, of sorts, full of secret language and wilfully arcane turns of phrase, such as 'slutching' for drinking. In the cold light of day, Hardman and Lees edited this, along with the minutes of the 'AGM', to make it more businesslike and to clarify CAMRA's objectives.

Bill Mellor's last significant contribution to the establishment of CAMRA was suggesting *What's Brewing* as a title for a monthly newsletter, which Hardman was to edit.[24] After Nuneaton, he dropped out of active participation in CAMRA's leadership. Makin withdrew too, because his job in the industry (Threlfall's was part of the Whitbread empire) presented a conflict of interests.[25] That left only Hardman, Lees and a handful of the new recruits who were seriously engaged. Little more than a year into its existence, CAMRA already needed new blood.

On 20 April 1972, the beer trade journal the *Morning Advertiser* ran a substantial article on CAMRA. The headline CALL GOES OUT TO SERIOUS DRINKERS announced CAMRA's presence to the beer world. It also grabbed the attention of a young man who was both a 'serious drinker' and, more importantly, a serious thinker.

In March 2013, at The Royal Oak in Borough, south London, not far from London Bridge, Christopher Hutt sipped at a half of Harvey's Old Ale. White-haired, softly spoken and thoughtful, with a mild Northern accent that came and went, he chose his words carefully. 'I was born in 1947, in Cheshire, near Stockport,' he began.

I started drinking beer in 1963, when I was sixteen. I played for the village cricket club and the bar always had good beer; and, playing away, I got to drink quite a good range of beers from various breweries. Without knowing it, I got used to good beer because it was ubiquitous in Cheshire. There was a wide choice and a general interest in which was best. People had their preferences – favourite beers and breweries – and we would talk about it.

In 1965 he went to the University of East Anglia, and was struck at once by the enormous contrast between the quality and variety of beer in the North West and what he found in Norwich.

It had three breweries – Bullard's, Steward and Patteson and Morgan's – but they were in the process of being taken over by Watney's, who soon had a complete monopoly. Watney's didn't care about beer ... Eventually, Norwich had just one pub still serving real ale.

While this set him thinking critically about beer, he was also making a name for himself as a member of the Young Liberals,[26] which he recalled as 'a training ground for politicians'. Labour Prime Minister Harold Wilson had been a Young Liberal and future Labour leader Michael Foot was another, as was anti-apartheid campaigner and later Labour minister Peter Hain – a near contemporary of Hutt's. For his part, Hutt learned how to convey an authority beyond his years and to hold a crowd with impassioned, persuasive speeches.

After university, he joined the graduate trainee scheme at Ford Motor Company in Dagenham, Essex, but continued to think about pubs and beer. Eventually, after three and a half years, he realised that he did not want to work in a large organisation, slogging his way up the ladder, and began to talk about dropping out to write a book. Those he spoke to were encouraging, and so, in 1972, he left Ford and started work on what would become *The Death of the English Pub*.

At the age of twenty-six, Hutt set about building his case in the most emotive terms possible, while also gathering evidence from trade journals. It was while scouring the *Morning Advertiser* that he came across the article about CAMRA and decided he had to meet its leaders: 'That I happened to write a book about beer just as CAMRA was emerging was an accident – just very good timing. There was something in the air, clearly.'

As part of his research, he called Hardman, who was then working at the *Evening Standard* in London, and introduced himself. They met at The

Christopher Hutt as drawn by CAMRA cartoonist John Simpson in 1973.

Flask in Hampstead, then regarded by those in the know as one of the city's very best pubs. 'My immediate impression was that here was a fellow who might be of considerable help to us,' recalled Hardman. 'He knew much more about the brewing industry and licensed trade than Lees and I.' They got on well – though Hutt was more studious, introverted and earnest than Hardman – perhaps united by their shared roots in the North West of England. Hutt joined CAMRA immediately, introducing a certain gravitas and helping to form Hardman and Lees's passions into something like an ideology, while he continued to work on his book.

If Hutt brought intellect, Hardman and Lees brought journalistic savvy and a can-do attitude, and one indication that CAMRA might have a greater impact than the SPBW was its newspaper, *What's Brewing*, first published in June 1972.[27] A single-sheet tabloid, printed on both sides, it had eye-catching, muck-raking content a world away from that found in the usual deadly dull club newsletter or the industry-friendly *Morning Advertiser*. That first edition featured a *Daily Mirror*-style exposé of Dirty Dick's, a famous London pub that had been caught serving pressurised Bass pale ale through fake barrels on the bar top; it included a promotion for a four-day trip to Munich for Oktoberfest, at a cost of £35 for flights and hotels and embryonic plans for *The List*, a publication set to detail the country's best pubs and which would cost no more than 25p. The newsletter also gave an address for the Campaign office: 207 Keats Court, Salford[28] – actually the home of Mary Lees, Graham's mother, from where she despatched mail to members of the executive around the country.

The Alexandra Palace Beer Festival in October 1972 brought CAMRA to the attention of those members of the SPBW who hadn't previously been aware of the more youthful, more media-aware organisation. The collaboration was carried out in the name of a temporary alliance, The Beer Campaign.[29] Given their many shared aims, there were talks about a more permanent merger, but it wasn't to be. On the one hand, Millard couldn't commit to it: to him, CAMRA seemed rather ambitious and serious-minded, and therefore at odds with the SPBW's drinking-club ethos.[30] On the other, Graham Lees recalled that CAMRA's leadership were unimpressed with their fellow travellers: 'The SPBW was a defeatist group, retreating every time a pub stopped selling beer from the wood.'[31]

Hardman and Hutt did go along to an SPBW meeting, but though Hardman in particular liked a joke, both men were irked by running gags about turning the kitty into 'liquid assets' (pints of beer). 'We couldn't get past reading the minutes of the last meeting without getting a round in,' said Hardman, still annoyed by it even today. As for Christopher Hutt, when we asked him if, had CAMRA not come along, he might have joined the SPBW and led them to victory, he shook his head before delivering an uncharacteristically blunt judgement:

> The SPBW were nice people, but they were piss artists, not
> boat-rockers. Their angle was essentially wrong. They wouldn't
> have ever been organised or pushy enough to stand up to the
> Big Six, and, if CAMRA hadn't succeeded, the course of events
> would have been very different.

All that the Beer Campaign achieved in its short existence was the transfer of power from one campaign group to another: CAMRA decided to do its own thing and, quietly, the SPBW, a drinking society with a campaigning problem, shrank back to make way. 'The battle's lost. We know this perfectly well,' said Millard, referring to the big brewers,[32] though it might as well have been a declaration of surrender to CAMRA. 'We in Epsom had had enough,' said another founder member, John Keeble, 'and were pleased to hand on the baton to CAMRA.'[33] Many SPBW members went on to join the newer organisation – including Millard, who became a passive part of CAMRA's rank and file as he entered old age.[34]

✿

Meanwhile, it was becoming apparent that the CAMRA leadership structure settled upon in the spring of 1972 was all but collapsing, and had achieved little. A special general meeting (SGM) was scheduled for 28 October 1972, the last day of the Alexandra Palace Beer Festival, to start afresh. It was at this point that things got really serious. First, in line with recent resolutions,[35] no one drank at the meeting, which meant that business got dealt with more efficiently and without raised voices or fits of passion. A new executive was elected and plans for a 'National Guide to Good Beer' discussed.

In the same month came the earliest example of what would prove to be an important campaign tactic when the Bystanders Society of Norwich – a regional beer fan club along the lines of the SPBW and with links to CAMRA – boasted that its festival would offer what was, at that time, unprecedented choice: TWELVE DIFFERENT BEERS AT REAL ALE FESTIVAL, announced *What's Brewing* proudly.[36]

Other important developments soon followed. Various 'big hitters' joined the Campaign, most notable among them being Frank Baillie, another writer, who was working on a book called *The Beer Drinker's Companion*. The first technical definition of 'real draught ale' was published in *What's Brewing* in November 1972, based on discussions at the SGM:

> [Real ales] are living beers, kept in their natural conditions and not pasteurised ... they are dispatched and kept in casks and barrels without the addition of extraneous CO_2 ... they are drawn

from casks or barrels by methods other than those requiring CO_2 pressure . . . they should taste pleasant and wholesome.

Branches of CAMRA began to appear around the country, each with its own local chair and programme of activity. The Hertfordshire branch claims to have been the first, meeting in November 1972 at the Farriers Arms in St Albans, but the credit is sometimes given to West Yorkshire, whose founder, John Brearley, was killed by a tram on holiday in Munich in October 1972. Soon, many branches had more members than CAMRA itself at the time of the first AGM. By the second full AGM, which took place at 3.30 p.m. on 17 March 1973, there were almost 1,000 CAMRA members nationwide, sixty-six of whom attended the even more professionally run meeting in London.[37]

Hardman and others have always taken pains to emphasise CAMRA's Everyman appeal – 'There were bus drivers, licensees, teachers, graphic artists, librarians, brewers' – but, in those early years, they often faced the accusation that CAMRA was a nest of mischievous urban sophisticate journalists who 'had it in' for the big brewers without in any way speaking for 'the common man'. Other critics, especially within 'the Big Six', suggested that they were really a bunch of dirt-digging journalists trying to stir up something to write about.[38] It is true that there was a relatively high proportion

Terry Pattinson (left) chats to Minister of Defence Roy Mason, 1975.

of journalists, writers and broadcasters in the upper echelons of the Campaign, including former SPBW spokesman Terry Pattinson. And this brought an obvious benefit: they knew what journalists wanted and could provide ready-packaged stories, getting them into the hands of the right people. Graham Lees has admitted that there was something of a hype machine in operation:

> Having journalists involved was a great help. They weren't great campaigners, but they were looking for a story and we provided it – and you know what journalists are like, they began to over-exaggerate what we were about and how big we were and that perhaps made the breweries take more notice than we deserved.[39]

It is certainly telling that the March 1973 AGM took place at the London Press Club on Wine Office Court, just off Fleet Street – home turf, either literally or spiritually, for many key players, and also handy for Ye Olde Cheshire Cheese, one of London's best-known pubs, a short walk from Dr Johnson's house.

Several other important events occurred at this meeting. It was here that Christopher Hutt formally succeeded Michael Hardman as chair – arguably the point at which CAMRA ceased to belong to its four founders and became a living, breathing entity in its own right. It is also the occasion on which the name changed to the one we know today. Initially, 'The Beer Drinkers' Union' was decided upon, but, as Terry Pattinson told us, that raised some hackles.

> [One member] objected and left in protest. It turned out he was very opposed to unions on principle, and it dawned on us that we might alienate 50 per cent of our potential membership, and so we had another think.

A further motion was proposed by Midlands campaigner Peter Lynlie,[40] who had recently 'come over' from the SPBW.[41] 'Revital-isation', Lynlie argued, was hard to say after a few pints and, frankly, sounded pompous; instead, he suggested employing a phrase used in *What's Brewing* from time to time that would allow them to retain the catchy acronym. And so CAMRA became The Campaign *for Real Ale*, a decision that would prove to be both a stroke of marketing genius and a cause of strife.

The next major contribution to CAMRA's rapid rise was yet more media coverage. Among those elected to the National Executive was the late Jeremy Beadle, best known now as the grinning host of various Saturday-night entertainment shows on ITV throughout the 1980s and 1990s. But back then he was known for having organised two large rock festivals and, in his own words, as a 'happy hippy'.[42] Terry Pattinson recalled him as a disruptive presence, interrupting constantly:

> Michael Hardman eventually said, very frostily: 'Mr Beadle, since you have so many ideas, perhaps you should join the National Executive.' So he did. He always seemed bored, like he had better things to be doing.

But Beadle made two notable contributions to CAMRA during his time with them. First, he pointed out that the 'frothing pint' logo looked like 'fizzy' keg beer. It was changed. Next, he used his connections in broadcast media to secure CAMRA its first radio coverage, on *Platform*, a two-hour-long show on BBC Radio London in which voluntary organisations were given the opportunity to make their case. In May 1973, thanks to Beadle, Hardman, Hutt and CAMRA secretary Valerie Mason were given the chance to discuss 'The Battle for Better Beer' with John Young (eccentric chairman of the south London brewery Young and Co.), Labour MP William Wilson and other guests.[43] Sadly, no recording survives, but the broadcast seems to have been closer to propaganda than to debate.

There was also newspaper coverage, this time by non-affiliated journalists who wrote not for local papers, but for the nationals. The double-page spread in the *Sunday Mirror* that had caught Bill Mellor's eye in March 1971 had garnered plenty of attention, even prompting lengthy debates in the House of Commons[44] and leading to a follow-up in the *Daily Mirror* on 10 July 1972. Perhaps that, and the increase in coverage of beer in other newspapers, helped to make the editor of the *Guardian* receptive to this letter from 'Stephen Edwards' (in truth probably written by either Cambridge-educated, left-wing anarchist wit Richard Boston or his friend, Michael McNay[45]), printed in the newspaper on 14 July 1973:

> Sir, I have read with interest your correspondence on the subject of beer. It has always been a matter of wonder to me that while the novice in wine-drinking can undergo his novitiate guided by the discriminating palate of John Arlott through your columns, the . . . beer drinker is left to sup his pints with no more guidance than the advertisers' blurbs. It seems to me that it is this refusal to take beer as seriously as wine that has allowed the development of a brewing industry which cares little . . . for quality and even less for variety. Perhaps the occasional newspaper column by a discriminating beer drinker might help to bring the brewers to their senses?

And so, less than a month later, on 11 August 1973, a new column made its debut appearance: 'Boston on Beer', written by Richard Boston, who was once described by a colleague as looking like an idealistic curate and talking like Patrick Moore.[46] It took Boston three weeks to get around to mentioning CAMRA, but when he did so, he was generous with it. He began with a critique of 'dead beer' (pasteurised, filtered keg); set out the benefits of 'well-kept traditional draught bitter' and then devoted several paragraphs to explaining the

Richard Boston pictured in 1994.

Campaign's purpose, how to join and where to send your 50p membership fee. CAMRA could not have paid for better publicity. 'We got a thousand applications that week,' said Hardman.

When Christopher Hutt's long-awaited book finally emerged in November 1973, it too caused a stir. The cover of *The Death of the English Pub* showed a funeral wreath wrapped around two handpumps. Aberdonian photographer Iain Macmillan was then best known for taking the

The Death of the English Pub by Christopher Hutt, 1973.

cover shot for the Beatles' *Abbey Road* album, but, for Hutt's book, he provided a series of brilliant, evocative, deliberately poignant monochrome images. They showed brewers, publicans and working-class drinkers staring glumly or, worse, with pathetic smiles, into the camera, like abandoned dogs in a charity appeal. It spoke of beer in more general terms than cultural commentators had been doing since the 1950s: it was collapsing into one grim, homogeneous product; pubs were turning into branded, plastic monstrosities or, worse, were simply disappearing:

> [It] is this attitude that is wreaking havoc in the English pub . . .
> It is this attitude that has led many brewers to throw hundreds
> of their tenants out in the street for the crime of building up a
> successful business; that has led them to gut some of their finest
> pubs on the advice of market research men and accountants who

are more interested in fashion and a fast buck than the tradition
of centuries; that has led them to shut down hundreds of country
pubs leaving villagers with nowhere to go for a drink.[47]

The book attracted warm reviews from Richard Boston in the
Guardian[48] and from Edmund Penning-Rowsell in the *Financial
Times*, who called it a 'fighting paperback'.[49] Perhaps more importantly, though, it provoked bad reviews from 'the enemy', in the form
of an anonymous editorial in the *Brewing Review*, the trade journal of
the Brewers' Society, which was dominated by the Big Six:[50]

> The appreciation of beer is . . . very much a personal matter.
> This, unfortunately, is what Mr Hutt and members of CAMRA
> generally, carried away by their enthusiasm, seem to overlook
> or, for purposes of publicity, disregard . . . The fact is that, faced
> with a wide range of choice throughout the country, the vast
> majority of pub-goers do not share their faith. It is . . . an unedi-
> fying spectacle when CAMRA . . . tries to push its pet likes and
> dislikes down other people's throats, good copy though this may
> make for those of its members who are engaged in . . . finding
> something to write about in newspapers.[51]

In Hutt's book, CAMRA had a manifesto. With *What's Brewing*
and the constant flow of newspaper stories, it had a voice. Its growing
network of branches gave it access to, and intelligence on, pubs and
breweries in every corner of the country. The phoney war was over: it
was time for battle to commence.

THREE

CAMRA RAMPANT

I always saw CAMRA as political, as a radical movement, challenging entrenched and powerful interests.

Christopher Hutt, 2013[1]

Under the leadership of Hutt and Michael Hardman, CAMRA set about irritating the Big Six with gusto, and Watney's became, in Cold War terminology, 'the main adversary'. Hutt's experiences in Norwich, where every pub had been painted red and adorned with a dangling plastic barrel, no doubt laid the groundwork for enmity between the two organisations. *The Death of the English Pub* had shown that Watney's were no more acquisitive or aggressive than, say, Bass Charrington, but their unabashed, unapologetic approach seemed especially to annoy 'real ale'. Hutt: 'It's hard to overstate how complacent and arrogant they were.'[2]

Facing up to CAMRA on behalf of Watney's was the brewery's Public Affairs Group, led by E.C. Handel, known as Ted. Born in 1916 in the East End of London, Handel was a veteran of the Second World War and had worked in advertising before joining Watney's in the 1950s. His son, Nick, recalled that he was 'not at all combative',[3] but in 1973, having tried to 'keep a dialogue open', he finally decided to tackle CAMRA head on.

The trigger was a letter from Keith Watkins of the North Midlands branch of CAMRA which appeared in the *Financial Times* on 16 June. Responding to an article about Watney's plans to move into the German market, Watkins derided them, before giving details of CAMRA's aims and how to join. These days, a big company would either ignore such a letter or respond with carefully measured comments about valuing their customers, listening to criticism and perhaps slip in a few words about products they hoped the correspondent might enjoy if he were to give them a second chance. Ted Handel, however, issued what reads like a sarcastic put-down.

> Sir, May I answer, please, what looked very much like a classified advertisement gone astray and carried gratis in the correspondence columns . . .? Most of your readers will probably not have heard of CAMRA . . . so I should explain that it is a group that includes in its small membership (about 1,500) a number of journalists who see in the 'ancient v. modern' beer situation a golden opportunity for 'controversial journalism' . . . we have always taken the trouble to answer letters from CAMRA and to point out the inaccuracies of the arguments they produce so monotonously.

'Ted Handel at Watney was completely hapless,' said Christopher Hutt. 'They really didn't like their world being turned upside down and reacted very badly.' Given that the breweries were already often locked in battle with their own pub tenants, represented by the National Federation of Licensed Victuallers, as well as with their own unionised brewery workforces, it is easy to understand why they reacted with frustration to yet another interest group demanding appeasement. Handel's letter kept CAMRA's name on the letters page of the *FT* for a second week, and prompted a further flurry of membership queries. Hutt seized the opportunity to prolong this valuable line of free advertising by responding himself.

> Mr Handel speaks of our small membership . . . It is, in fact, 2,500, and these members have been recruited in the last year from a standing start. The monthly rate of increase in our membership is well over 300 . . . Mr Handel refers to the 'sour tone' of earlier

letters printed in your columns from disgruntled beer drinkers.
This debate is not about the sour tone of anybody's prose style,
but about the sour taste of pressurised beer.

Handel did not back down and wrote another letter which, this
time, began 'Mr Hutt is at it again ...' It appeared on 21 July 1973
surrounded by correspondence broadly supportive of CAMRA. 'He
kept responding to my letters, drawing out the argument, and after
every letter, we got hundreds if not thousands of new members,' Hutt
told us, shaking his head in disbelief and perhaps in sympathy.

Cloak-and-dagger methods were also employed. Terry Pattinson,
a Fleet Street journalist used to 'playing dirty' to get stories, recalled
hanging around in pubs near the Watney's brewery in Mortlake,
luring off-duty brewers into criticising their own product: 'It's fizzy
shite – we'd drink anything but Red Barrel.' CAMRA used similarly
underhand methods to get information on the strength of beers
available on the market. Christopher Hutt:

> [It] was almost impossible to find out how beer was brewed,
> kept, dispensed, or even its strength. They absolutely refused to
> publish the gravities of their beers. I suspect the big breweries
> had cynical motives, and that the small ones were bullied into
> compliance.

With the industry tight-lipped, Hardman instead made contact
with a sympathetic chemist who worked at one of the biggest
breweries. He joined CAMRA's technical committee and began
to sneak a few CAMRA samples in among his regular workload.'
Though the resulting database would eventually be published in full,
the results began to trickle out in *What's Brewing*. The first 'CAMRA
Test' article appeared in June 1974, referring, rather grandly, to
'CAMRA's analysts' as if there were an entire laboratory at work. It
included a table of the original gravities of ten beers from independent
regional breweries – 'OG' then being the most popular indicator
of a beer's strength, indicating the amount of sugar present before

fermentation. Those figures demonstrated that the products of the smaller producers were superior to the Big Six keg bitters, details of which had been published by the *Daily Mirror* and *Which?* magazine in preceding years. This was a direct challenge to the brewers' right to keep such information from the public, and it put them under pressure to be more open with consumers.

Meanwhile, CAMRA's ever-growing membership (9,000 by the beginning of 1974) became a news story in itself, generating more coverage, bringing the Campaign to the attention of new members, making the statistics even more remarkable and prompting further press interest. As a result of this rolling story, in June 1974[5] the papers were suddenly flooded with writing about CAMRA. Eric Wainwright began writing a column in the *Daily Mirror* under the title 'The Good Beer Spy', kicking it off with a mention of CAMRA and what had now become 10,000 members. Wainwright was no Richard Boston, and seems to have struggled to find enough material to fill a page every week: the column was full of fluff ('which pub has the nastiest pet'), appeared at irregular intervals and each time got smaller and nearer to the seedy classified ads in the back pages. It was, nonetheless, among the first really supportive coverage for the Campaign in a popular tabloid newspaper.

Further evidence of beer's new-found status as a cause célèbre came the same month when the 'Angry Young Man' architectural and cultural critic Ian Nairn cited Christopher Hutt in a long piece for the *Sunday Times*. Nairn used this essay, entitled 'The Best Beers of Our Lives',[6] to announce that he was a member of CAMRA, and also applied his theory of Subtopia to beer in explicit terms for the first time:

> Because of the hops we use and the way we brew, British beer is unique . . . to extinguish a local flavour, which is what has happened a hundred times in the last ten years, is like abolishing the Beaujolais: it is red and alcoholic, might as well make it in a Eurocity to an agreed Common Market recipe . . . the peasants wouldn't know the difference . . . but the peasants are fighting back.

Nairn was, by this time, a household name, with several TV shows under his belt as well as a series of popular books on architecture. His interest in 'ale' wasn't entirely a surprise: his 1966 paperback, *Nairn's London*, listed almost thirty pubs among the overlooked and threatened architectural gems of the city and, unusually for such a book, took the trouble in most cases to mention the quality of beer on offer. He was a passionate, somewhat erratic character, famous for his unkempt appearance and fluent, almost hectoring style. He was also a chronic drinker, and his attachment to beer would eventually be his undoing: when he died in 1983, at the age of fifty-two, he had become too unreliable for TV, had been sacked from his job at the *Sunday Times* and was reported to be drinking fourteen pints every lunchtime.

At the height of his fame, however, he did CAMRA a huge favour: having, via Richard Boston, captured readers of the *Guardian*, where the leadership's youth and rebelliousness played well, Nairn presented CAMRA to a rather different audience. 'It was perfect,' Michael Hardman told us. 'Boston appealed to the socialists, Nairn to the capitalists.' CAMRA had set out on the road towards being a national institution.

Watney's attempts to counter this positive coverage, and to fight back against CAMRA's 'dirty tricks', were clumsy. First, realising that Terry Pattinson's work with CAMRA wasn't his day job, they appealed to his employer:

> They rang up my editor, Ian McColl . . . and said: 'Are you aware that a member of your staff is saying nasty things about the brewing industry?' But he approved of what I was doing, and said: 'I know, he's my consumer affairs correspondent. I'm very proud to have him.'

Next, they tried to launch a smear campaign, approaching a freelance journalist to place critical stories in the press.

> The freelancer they chose, Charles Lyte, they hadn't realised, also worked at the *Express* and knew me. He took me to one side

and said: 'Terry, there's something you need to know. Watney's have been in touch offering me lots of money to write and place stories critical of CAMRA, and you in particular.' So that went straight onto the front page of *What's Brewing*.

Watney's denied it, of course, but who would believe them? The following month, CAMRA's investigators managed to prove that two articles placed in the trade press that were critical of the Campaign had been written by a freelance copywriter who had worked for both Bass Charrington and Watney Mann.[7] It did not look good: Watney's had cast itself as the sinister dictator. When CAMRA fought dirty, it was the underdog biting back. When Watney's did so, it was big business throwing its weight around.

In 1974, the sparring reached new heights with the publication of CAMRA's first book – the bestselling *Good Beer Guide*. 'There was certainly no information about pubs,' Christopher Hutt told us, bemoaning the scarcity of guidance available to beer drinkers in the 1960s and early 1970s. 'You just stumbled across one you liked, with decent beer, and remembered it.'

According to Michael Hardman, the guide idea was partly inspired by Young's Brewery who, from the early 1960s, published a comprehensive list of their own pubs under the title *Real Draught Beer and Where to Find It*. It tapped into a completist, obsessive tendency which CAMRA was to find both useful and a burden in later years. When CAMRA members began to compile and share 'The List' among themselves – a record of their combined knowledge of where decent beer was to be found – it was given the title *Where to Find Real Draught Beer*, in homage to Young's.[8] It wasn't remotely complete, and was certainly weighted towards London and the South East but still, couldn't this, if polished up and printed, be a useful campaigning tool? And might it also bring funds into an organisation, which, at that stage, was spending more on enrolling each member than it was receiving in fees?[9]

To realise the idea of the *Good Beer Guide* proper, Hardman turned to an eccentric beer and pub enthusiast who just happened to be the head of a small publishing company. Beric Watson was born in Leeds in 1931, the grandson of the founder of Waddington's, and one of the first people in Britain to play the board game Monopoly as a small child.[10] By the early 1970s, Watson was the head of Waddington's printing arm, through which, in 1971, he had published his own guide to pubs in Leeds, under the unfortunate title *Hand-Pulled Beer and Buxom Barmaids*. In 1973, Hardman telephoned him to fix a date and time for a meeting.

The 1974 CAMRA *Good Beer Guide*.

I agreed to meet him at the Guinea [pub] in Berkeley Square, and he told me I'd know him by his broken nose. We hit it off straight away, and he agreed to back and print the publication of the first commercial edition of *The Good Beer Guide*. He was interested in beer, but he was a businessman, and saw the potential in it to make some money.

According to *What's Brewing*,[11] a team of eighty volunteer inspectors spent months touring the country inspecting pubs. John Hanscomb, then a printworker in his mid-thirties, upon whose original notes 'The List' was largely based, acted as editor. Its ninety-six pages included every single pub in the country *known* to be selling 'real ale'.

In the draft text, sent to Waddington's for printing early in 1974, there were two digs at Watney's. The first appeared in the Introduction, entitled 'The quest for a decent pint', making reference to the brewing giant's dominance of Norwich and the surrounding area:

> The big brewers say there is plenty of choice – more than 1,500 brands of beer currently available in Britain. But this is no consolation for the man in the little Norfolk town who can find nothing but the fizzy products of one big group within a ten-mile radius of his home.

The second, however, named names, and was to be the cause of considerable controversy. On the back flyleaf, under a list of every brewer in the country (which then required just two pages), came this entry:

> **Watney:** Mortlake, London; Norwich; Whitechapel, London.
> *Avoid like the plague.*

The question that managers at Waddington's asked themselves on seeing that text was: 'Is it libellous?' CAMRA had considered this and were more than willing to take the risk. 'We wanted the bastards to sue us!' said Terry Pattinson. Waddington's, though, did *not* want to be taken to court, and had a sudden change of heart. Trevor Unwin, then a young CAMRA member, told us what happened next:

> The plague edition *Guide* was delivered to the De Grey Rooms in York, which was the venue of the 1974 Annual General Meeting ... We had started to unload when we received word that the printers had got cold feet over the Watney comment and wanted a less inflammatory substitute. Waddington's had apparently agreed to reprint at their expense. Would we mind awfully just loading them all back onto the van again so that they could be sent back to Leeds for pulping?[12]

The *Daily Mail* quoted an incensed Chris Hutt: 'Mr Watson has sabotaged two years' work. I am sure his expulsion will be proposed at our next meeting . . . It's a disaster for us, but we refuse to have the remarks censored.' Watson replied: 'I thought our job in CAMRA was to persuade people to brew better beer, and this isn't the way to do it.'[13] A compromise was eventually agreed, but Trevor Unwin is one of a handful of people who, thanks to a box that got 'accidentally' damaged, has an uncensored edition of that first *GBG*. The revised text, hardly less complimentary, said: 'Avoid at all costs.' Watney's expensive, heavily marketed brand was taking a hammering, as Terry Pattinson told us:

> Even Watney's admitted, eventually, that 'real ale' had become a brand. They'd invested a fortune: all their pubs were painted red and white, with the plastic barrel over the door, the plastic barrel on the bar, with the idea being that they'd be easy to spot for a mile off. Then we ruined all of that for them – we nicknamed them 'Grotney' and it stuck. They eventually went out of their way to make their pubs hard to spot.

Another key campaign tactic, for a short while at least, was the protest march. Evoking the spirit of the Tolpuddle Martyrs, the Jarrow March of 1936 and the Campaign for Nuclear Disarmament's marches to Aldermaston in November 1973, Terry Pattinson led over 600 CAMRA members from around the country, and a handful of locals, in protest against the closure of Joule's Brewery at Stone, Staffordshire by its owners, Bass Charrington.[14] With a little stage management by Pattinson and his colleagues ('Form into a thinner line – it will make it look longer'[15]), there were several hours of banner waving and slogan chanting led by the twenty-five-piece town brass band.[16] The procession finished with a gathering at the cinema on the High Street, where Christopher Hutt delivered a rabble-rousing speech decrying the Big Six as 'feudal barons'.[17]

As CAMRA considered the march a success, the same approach was chosen when, a year later, the Barnsley brewery came under threat of closure from its owners, Courage, by now part of Imperial

Tobacco. Terry Pattinson was again given the job of organising the protest. The Minister of Defence, Roy Mason, who was Labour MP for Barnsley as well as a CAMRA member, gave the Campaign a huge boost when he announced his support and agreed to join the march, although on the appointed day, Saturday, 7 September 1974, Terry Pattinson arrived in rainy South Yorkshire to hear that the minister was not coming due to 'urgent ministerial business'.[18] Pattinson led the march himself, insisting that there were something like 2,000 CAMRA members in attendance, but the local newspaper, under the headline BAD WEATHER WATERS DOWN BITTER PROTEST, quoted an estimate of half that number.[19] Their banners read 'KEEP BRITAIN TIDDLY' and 'BARNSLEY BITTER: WHAT MY RIGHT ARM IS FOR!'

Some CAMRA members found the tactic embarrassing. On the one hand, it compromised the Campaign's political neutrality, allying CAMRA with trades unions, because the Transport and General Workers' Union (TGWU) was also opposing the closure of the brewery, where around a hundred of its members were employed. On the other, it was seen as ineffectual.[20] Ultimately, the reason CAMRA gave up on marching and protests of this sort was because they did not work. Joule's closed at the end of 1974, and Barnsley followed soon after. If they achieved anything, it was media interest, though the coverage did not always do CAMRA any favours, as Terry Pattinson recalled:

> I got interviewed by the *News at Ten* – it was their lead item. I was there with my hair hanging down, soaking wet, like John Lennon in my round glasses ... I was in the pub the next day and someone I was drinking with said: 'Did you see the news last night? That CAMRA spokesman – what a dropout he was! What a total loser! What a fucking twat!' He didn't recognise me, and I kept my mouth shut.

At around the same time, CAMRA began to make more extensive use of a campaigning tool which would have remarkable popular appeal and longevity: the beer festival. Unlike earlier events, organised by private companies in vague imitation of Munich's Oktoberfest, the Campaign for Real Ale's festivals really were about the beer, offering the opportunity to drink rarities from the other end of the country and to mingle with fellow activists. After the success of the Norwich Beer Festival in October 1972, more CAMRA branches began to organise their own one-day 'thrashes'. It was perhaps one-upmanship between regions that led to the first large-scale event, held in Cambridge. Writing in *What's Brewing*, Michael Hardman described the four-day festival, which took place at the city's Corn Exchange in July 1974:

> A dedicated band of CAMRA members have proven that a highly successful beer festival can do without pressurised beer, high admission prices, or hordes of PR men . . . And they have provided a conclusive answer to the disbelieving brewers who have for years been claiming that traditional beer could not be served in good condition at an event staged over a number of days in a public hall.[21]

More than 6,000 people attended, and it made a small profit, thanks, in part, to the voluntary labour of CAMRA members:

> The original consignment of beer ran out halfway through the festival and reserve supplies had to be drafted in. Altogether, 12,000 pints were quaffed. One nine-gallon cask went in ten minutes . . . It can't be long before CAMRA stages a national festival.[22]

Sure enough, in early 1975 a committee was formed to discuss the possibility of a similar event in London. It took months of work to find suitable premises, and they eventually agreed with the Greater London Council to use the recently retired Victorian Flower Market, now the London Transport Museum, at Covent Garden, just outside the city's West End. They had to sign agreements with thirty-one breweries, and put in place a temporary infrastructure capable of receiving, storing and dispensing fifty different beers – twice as many as were at Cambridge the previous year. It was to be staffed by volunteers, who would need training and coordinating. At the last minute, there was a crisis when they realised the venue wasn't licensed to sell alcohol. Fortunately, London brewery Fuller's stepped in and secured a licence on CAMRA's behalf.

The hall had a glass roof supported by green-painted, cast-iron columns and had just ended its hundred-year life as a working flower market. It was rather tatty, grubby and austere, but attempts were made to brighten it up with a handful of colourful brewery banners and flags. Some breweries had also erected painted wooden signs at the ends of their 'bars', while others had hand-drawn efforts hung with string. Posters featuring the Campaign's soon-to-be-abandoned cartoon mascot 'Cheerful Charlie' were tacked to the peeling, painted walls.[23] Casks of scuffed metal and red-ringed oak were lined up on the counters of the old market stalls, which might have been constructed with a beer festival in mind.

With little experience and no previous 'good practice' to draw upon, miraculously the organisers pulled it off, and the Covent Garden Beer Festival opened, as scheduled, on 9 September 1975. But would anyone come? The organisers' concerns that the huge hall might be 'half full, or empty' proved to be unfounded, and the moment the doors opened 'all hell broke loose', as John Bishopp, a member of the organising committee, later recalled:

> Hundreds of people quickly overwhelmed the front-of-house staff selling beer tokens ... Many members, who had come as customers, found themselves press-ganged into service; not a few stayed and worked until the end on the Saturday.[24]

Understandably, perhaps, it didn't run entirely smoothly. Queues for entry went round the block, many people waiting for hours to get in, while others reached the door 'only to have it closed in their face'.[25] In the chaos, someone stole half the takings, and the key to the already oversubscribed gents toilet went missing for a time.[26] They sold all 15,000 souvenir glasses and eventually began to run out of beer, supplementing the former with plastic tumblers and securing emergency supplies of the latter from helpful breweries.[27]

Those drinkers who did get in – largely but not exclusively male – milled about between displays of beer and drank standing up, sitting on the floor or perched on any flat surface they could find, while CAMRA volunteers pulled pints direct from taps hammered into the fronts of the casks. Patrick O'Donovan, writing for the *Observer*, captured the atmosphere:

> Most of the 1,000 in the hall at a time were young. They seemed to belong to the fashionably unkempt, the set of rebels with pocket money . . . There were also gentlemen from the City and a few women. Some of the drinkers were a little elevated and were sweating in the cool pavilion. The noise of talk rose in a single unwavering chord of sound. But overwhelmingly it was a serious occasion. People would take a sip of their beer, raise it to the light and then drain it.[28]

He also noted that anyone showing signs of inebriation – 'verbal violence and slightly indecent behaviour' – was led from the premises by burly volunteer stewards. This was partly an effort to reassure the local authorities, but also reflected an increasing sense within CAMRA that there were two types of drinking, summarised by another correspondent: 'Real ale is not for contemptuous quaffing . . . It is for appreciating.'[29] The event was festive, certainly, but it was not a debauch: this was a new kind of fun that, to some, might not look like fun at all.

Organisational setbacks aside, the festival was considered a success. Eight hundred new members were signed up, £4,300 of merchandise was sold (books, T-shirts, ties), and every drop of beer was dispensed. It took the National Executive no time at all to decide that the pilot event had made the case for an even bigger festival the following year.[30]

Like the marches, festivals were partly a show of strength – rallies, almost – gatherings of the faithful. Like the *Good Beer Guide*, they represented a challenge to the authority of the big brewers. Watney's, Whitbread, et al. were not invited, and the festival showed that, even if the Big Six had a stranglehold on the majority of pubs, there were ways for determined beer enthusiasts to get around that obstacle. The beer festival became, and still is, a key part of the infrastructure of 'alternative' beer appreciation in Britain, and around the world, where the Great British Beer Festival, as it is known today, has several imitators.

Towards the end of 1974, with membership standing at around 25,000,[31] the *Good Beer Guide* having sold all 30,000 copies[32] of its first print run and Watney's in retreat, the Campaign for Real Ale seemed unstoppable. But what next? Christopher Hutt had a plan, as he told us:

> It wasn't, in my view, enough to sit on the sidelines, jeering and barracking. You've got to put your money where your mouth is. I wanted to prove that free houses, selling a variety of good beers, would be very popular, in response to industry naysaying.

His proposal was that CAMRA should buy and run a string of pubs around the country. But this decision would expose fault lines in the leadership of the Campaign, just as the big brewers mounted a cunning fightback. The late 1970s was to be a difficult time for CAMRA, even as a remarkable parallel development got under way: new breweries were beginning to appear.

FOUR

LILACS OUT OF
THE DEAD LAND

The faster keg covers Britain – true foggy dew – the
sooner we'll have real beer back again. Forward ye
brewers! Onward ye Tories! Build more breweries on
England's green and pleasant land, and distribute your
alcoholic gruel in giant petrol tankers to every corner!
And thank Ted for those gallant souls who'll soon arise
and brew for the few.

Letter in the *Guardian*, 26 September 1970[1]

In the 1950s and 1960s, British breweries were subject to the gravi-
tational pull of the Big Six. When brewing companies made the
news, it was because they were being shut down, forcibly relocated or
demolished. But the revolt against Subtopian beer wasn't just driven
by the complaints of consumers: away from the boardrooms, in the
remote corners of the country, a few people with malt and hops in
their blood began to push back. The first of these 'microbrewers' (a
term that did not enter the language until much later) worked in
isolation, hundreds of miles apart. They were of different generations, and from different classes and professions. Independently they
had identified the opportunity created for 'local' products by the Big
Six's abandonment of the market, further opened up by CAMRA's
high-profile campaigning, but apart from that, these pioneers had

little in common. Between them, though, they evolved a successful formula which set them apart from the 'big boys': they were local; they made pure, virtuous beer; and they had personality in place of corporate slickness.

The earliest potential claimant to the title of Britain's original 'microbrewery' appeared before the formation of CAMRA, and could not have been more isolated from, or indifferent to, what was 'trendy'. Until the beginning of the twentieth century, it was customary for country houses, castles, universities and other such institutions to have breweries on site.[2] Traquair House at Innerleithen, Peeblesshire, Scotland was no exception. Beer was being brewed there, probably in the old kitchen, long before a brewery was built. From around the 1720s, brewing was relocated to a former carriage house and stables in the south wing. In 1739, a hefty 200-gallon 'copper' (boiler) was purchased. In the nineteenth century, the house and estate fell into decline. It was probably in this period that the brewery was shut down, as the practice of paying part of the servants' wages in beer died out[3] and the number of staff dwindled. The room was used for storage and, slowly, the beautiful brewing vessels disappeared from sight under heaps of rubbish,[4] just waiting to be rediscovered.

Peter Maxwell Stuart was brought up in the South of England[5] and served in India during the Second World War. He married Flora Carr-Saunders, a socialist later known to her neighbours as Red Flora,[6] in 1956. He worked for the whisky distillers John Haig until, in 1962, his father died and, at the age of forty, he became the twentieth Laird of Traquair.[7] He was a tall, lean man with a high forehead and rather sunken eyes, his expression in photographs a touch mournful, even when smiling. 'My father was a perfect gentleman who charmed everyone he met,' his daughter, Catherine Maxwell Stuart, told us, 'but he was also very hands-on and down to earth.'

He realised that Traquair needed to become self-sufficient, and set about renovating it, intending to make it, as it is today, a successful tourist attraction. It was while doing so that, in 1965, he unearthed the three copper brewing vessels, dirty but otherwise intact. He

Peter Maxwell Stuart (right) with his young daughter Catherine, now lady Laird of Traquair.

decided without hesitation to bring them back to life, and it took only a little work to ready them for use. 'It was purely an experiment, really,' Catherine Maxwell Stuart explained, 'intended as an add-on to the visitor attraction.'

Maxwell Stuart approached the nearby Belhaven Brewery for advice and raw materials, including yeast. Alexander 'Sandy' Hunter, whose family had owned Belhaven for more than 250 years,[8] was a university-trained, hands-on brewer[9] and gave his personal assistance.

Traquair House Ale was based partly on old recipes from the family archive and partly on educated guesswork by Maxwell Stuart and Hunter as they sought to create a brand-new 'traditional' Scottish ale.[10] It was certainly an unusual variety for a beer being brewed in the mid-1960s – 7.2 per cent alcohol by volume, dark, sweetish and spicy and fermented in naked, 'Memel' (Prussian) oak.[11] The Laird hung up his tweed jacket to brew, as Catherine Maxwell Stuart recalled: 'It was always the guide at the front door in a kilt that was confused as the Laird of Traquair when my father would be seen running down to the brewery in his boiler suit.'

He worked more or less single-handed, with occasional help from someone from the estate and, from the 1970s onward, his young daughter. He even labelled the bottles himself, with a damp sponge and self-adhesive paper, once they'd been returned from the bottling plant at Belhaven: 'We had some antiquated machine that slapped on glue and that was about the worst job you could land at Traquair . . . for about twenty years, my father hand-wrote the brew number and bottle number. These beers are now collector's items!'

At first there were only around two one-hundred-pint brews per year, all of them bottled and sold in the house tea rooms, and things continued this way until the early 1970s. Maxwell Stuart had no ambition to expand or to 'revitalise' British brewing, so the influence of Traquair was limited. He was only inspired to increase production drastically, after a decade of quietly doing his own thing, with the appearance of several other new breweries and the formation of CAMRA.[12] But this in itself is telling: a crucial 'feedback loop' between the consumer campaigners and the emerging microbreweries was already having an effect.

The next of the new brewers was also concerned with his inheritance. Martin Sykes was a London-educated Oxford graduate who had grown up in Northampton, but whose family had its roots in Yorkshire.[13] On leaving university in 1968, he got a job teaching law: 'I had nowhere to live in Hull, but my uncle told me that there was an empty flat above the brewery office which I could use till I found somewhere.'

Martin Sykes as drawn by John Simpson in 1973.

'The brewery' had been bought by Sykes's grandfather, Lionel, in 1944. It had been ailing even then and, over the years, had struggled, eventually finding a niche bottling and distributing Guinness in the North of England. But not long after Sykes moved into what was known as 'the brewer's flat', his uncle made the decision to close the business down altogether and retire. Sykes persuaded him otherwise, 'mainly to safeguard my living accommodation', and, before long, was touring the area as a sales representative, looking for outlets for Selby-bottled Guinness. He knew that the brewery couldn't survive for ever on the paltry profits from this intermediary role, and, like Maxwell Stuart, could not resist the lure of the dormant brewing kit with all its potential:

> I began to dream about resuming brewing, especially after I'd had a pint or two. After all, I thought, the brewhouse was still there, even though most of the equipment was too dilapidated to use, and we had a regular set of customers for the Guinness. Surely it ought to be possible to persuade some of them to try a new draught beer?[14]

Like many who have dreamed of opening a brewery, or any other small business, Sykes was put off by the difficulties: finding capital, navigating government red tape and, on top of all that, learning how to brew. Instead, pre-empting the founding of CAMRA, he set about doing his bit for 'beers from the wood' by signing a distribution deal with Theakston's, then one of the handful of surviving regional family brewers.

Meanwhile, at John Smith's Brewery in Tadcaster some thirteen miles away, a twenty-nine-year-old chemistry graduate called Basil Savage[15] was working as a second brewer. The company, then the largest regional brewer after Scottish and Newcastle, was in the process of being taken over by Courage. Despite reassurances that there were 'no plans for rationalisation of the breweries',[16] the need for a denial in itself suggests that the threat was in the air. Savage heard somewhere that there was a functional but dormant brewery on the Selby site and, on 7 December 1970, wrote to the brewery. 'It was almost as an answer to prayer,' said Sykes:

> He introduced himself as a local resident who was working as second brewer at John Smith's in nearby Tadcaster, who had heard that we had some small-scale brewing equipment at Selby and 'wondered if some arrangement could be made whereby I could brew strong ale for what could be quite a lucrative market'.[17]

Sykes was excited by this development, which so neatly echoed his own ambitions. Then, only a short while later, he was finally pushed into a decision by a sudden glut of cheap, decent equipment on the market, caused by the closure of two old-fashioned pubs with their own in-house breweries: the Druids Head near Dudley and the Britannia in Loughborough. He and Savage spent nearly two years rebuilding the brewery, using a combination of second-hand kit and bits and pieces from John Smith's.

This was another side effect of the centralisation of the brewing industry into huge new 'mega-breweries': the availability of discarded kit, supposed obsolete, which determined new entrants could get free or cheap and fashion into functional, small-scale operations.

Sykes and Savage began brewing in November 1972. When their first batch was sold in the run-up to Christmas the same year, for the first time since the 1950s the Selby (Middlebrough) Brewery was no longer just an intermediary, but was now a producer of beer.

It sold, too. Cannily, they'd come up with a product that offered just what a certain part of the market was demanding, but which the Big Six had no interest in supplying. Its strength was one selling point, but what really set their beer apart was the 'purity' of the recipe. Very few beers then were made without the addition of cheaper, easily fermentable sugars to supplement what could be extracted from expensive malt, but Selby's first beer was made with only four bushels of standard pale-ale malt, a little darker malt for colour and flavour and four pounds of traditional Fuggles hops. 'The main reason that our beers were "pure" was to make the job simpler. Using sugars and other adjuncts involved complicated procedures to satisfy HM Customs and Excise regulations,' Sykes told us. 'It was simpler not to bother. The upside was that it made the product appear more "real".'

In the late hippy era, parallel to the debate around beer, a 'real bread' movement grew up, and books such as Edward Espe Brown's *Tassajara Bread Book* (1970) would influence later 'real ale' rhetoric:

> [...] 'whole' corn meal, which contains the germ, will have a
> greater life-containing, life-giving quality than the 'degermed'
> cornmeal found in supermarkets. Whole cornmeal is a 'live' food
> – it spoils when the oil in the germ becomes rancid. Degermed
> cornmeal is a 'dead' food, as it lacks the germ (of life). Hence,
> it can be kept on grocery shelves for months without spoiling,
> though like all milled grains it does become stale.

Presenting their beer as a kind of 'wholefood' was an almost accidentally brilliant marketing ploy on Selby's part. Combined with the brewery's small size, its Northern-ness and its independence, this prompted student bars to lap it up, showing far more interest than the working-men's clubs – much to Sykes's surprise – to which Selby had been selling bottled Guinness for so many years.

Though the brewery sprang into life independently of CAMRA, Sykes credits the rapidly growing campaign group with its lasting success: 'Our great good fortune was to have begun brewing at about the same time as CAMRA was born. A few years earlier and we probably would have failed completely.'[18] At this time, small brewers and campaigners were to a great extent fighting the same fight, and Sykes was himself elected to CAMRA's National Executive in March 1973, having been introduced to the organisation by Frank Baillie.

The third of our pioneering new breweries sprouted in the fertile soil of Somerset, in the South West of England, under the command of an eccentric former scientist turned snail farmer and restaurateur. Paul Leyton was born in Leeds in 1914, the son of a Methodist minister. He grew up on the Isle of Wight, was educated in Bath and, after an apprenticeship at Austin Motors, from 1931 drifted into teaching. He joined the Royal Air Force during the Second World War, later transferring into the Fleet Air Arm of the Royal Navy. He left the service in 1945 as a Lieutenant Commander and then became an engineer, working on missile technology, which in turn led to a role in the British space programme, overseeing several successful launches of the Black Knight rocket from the

Woomera Test Range in the Australian outback.[19] Frustrated at the programme's lack of ambition, in 1959 he left[20] to take a job as director of engineering at Black and Decker. At this point, the same unconventional approach to life that had drawn him to live for a time on a converted double-decker bus resurfaced,[21] and, in 1961, at the age of forty-seven, he left the world of industry behind and took on the running of an experimental restaurant, the Heston Blumenthal of his day.

Despite the name, the rather tumbledown Miner's Arms, high up in the Mendips in the remote village of Priddy, Somerset wasn't a pub and hadn't been licensed to serve alcohol since 1913.[22] Leyton, with no experience but plenty of energy and intelligence, quickly turned it into a success, organising it, according to John Arlott, 'with the neatness of a scientist', with 'tables ... booked, and mealtimes arranged, in advance'.[23] It was an outpost of urban sophistication with rural trappings, such as a roaring log fire. Leyton seems to have had more than a touch of the Basil Fawlty about him, if a somewhat self-mocking letter to the *Guardian* about customers dressing inappropriately for dinner is anything to go by:

> On a recent occasion when ... I rejected what the wearer describes as a 'four-guinea orange slubbed silk Cecil Gee roll-neck shirt' we were not only assailed verbally but were subsequently treated to a closely typed two-and-a-half-page letter of abuse. This sort of distressing incident benefits no one, but short of total permissiveness can only be avoided by the general acceptance of some sort of convention. Those who reject the confinement of convention must expect the occasional unpleasant incident.

Despite his eccentricity, or perhaps because of it, the restaurant became fashionable, and Egon Ronay listed it in his *Guide to British Eateries*. By 1965, the Miner's Arms was on the trail for hip travellers. American poet Ronald Johnson visited with his travelling companion Jonathan Williams, searching Britain for whatever was 'most rich, most glittering, most strange', liked the menu with its 'Priddy Oggies' and 'Mendip Wallfish', and thought Leyton a marvellous character.[24] (A Mendip Wallfish, by the way, is a garden snail: ever the engineer, Leyton turned a disused swimming pool into a farm, ringing it with an electric fence to confine 100,000 or more snails at any time. He also became a renowned pioneer in freezing food, and also made ham by hanging legs of pork in the chimney.[25])

After more than ten years, the restaurant business had begun to wind down, but Leyton couldn't stop experimenting and, in 1973, decided to add beer to his list of home-made products. Much like Peter Maxwell Stuart at Traquair, Leyton had no apparent intention of joining a cultural trend or of kicking against the big breweries. His son, Julian Leyton, recalled receiving a home-brew kit as a gift. He had little interest in it, so his father borrowed it and established what he believed was the smallest licensed brewery in the country,[26] capable of producing five gallons (forty or so pints) every few weeks. Richard Boston visited not long after brewing commenced:

> When Mr Leyton showed it to me he led the way with a magni-fying glass. It's not quite that small, but it is small. The equipment consists of odds and ends like milk churns and a washing-machine engine, but though it looks Heath Robinsonish, it's all quite practical and seems to work.[27]

He brewed on Sundays, starting at ten in the morning and often working through the night.[28] Leyton's 'Own Ale' was put into tiny 'nip' bottles and sold exclusively to accompany meals in the restaurant. Considering the remote location, the small volume of production and the limited distribution, it generated a lot of interest. Later, Leyton would complain about eager CAMRA members turning up to try his beer only to be turned away – rather brusquely, perhaps – because he couldn't serve them unless they stayed for dinner.[29]

One new brewery was notable, two distinctly so, but three represented something that might be called a beginning. It also hinted at the possible revival of a particular type of brewery, which, from 1971 onward, seemed suddenly to be on a crash course to extinction: the 'home-brew house'. In the twenty-first century, pubs that produce their own beer for sale on the premises are usually known as 'brewpubs', borrowing an American term to avoid confusion with domestic home brewing. In 1970, according to Frank Baillie's *Beer Drinker's Companion*,[30] there were nine brewpubs, including Traquair; by 1973, as elderly owners and brewers passed away or retired, the number dropped to five. The emergence of the Miner's Arms bumped it back up to six.

The next new brewery to appear, only months later, was the first to be run by a bona fide professional career brewer – a veteran who had most recently worked for none other than the dreaded Watney. If Traquair could be dismissed as a mere novelty, Selby as a reopening and Priddy as a kitchen brewery, it was with the opening of the Litchborough Brewery in 1974 that the tide really started to turn, not least because of the personal influence of the owner and brewer, Bill Urquhart.

William Blackie Morrison Urquhart was born in Torryburn, Fife in 1916 and worked as a shipping clerk in Scotland in the 1930s. At some point, he took night classes[31] and qualified as a chemist, which led him into brewing, working at William Younger's and Archibald Arrol and Sons of Alloa[32] before being called up to fight in the Second World War.[33] He married Agnes 'Nessie' Noon in Inveresk, near Edinburgh, in 1941, and then served in India and Kashmir.[34] After the war, he lived for a time in London[35] until, in the late 1940s, he was taken on by the Tollemache Brewery of Ipswich, at around the age of thirty. There, he studied for his diploma and degree in brewing,[36] graduating in 1950.[37] From Ipswich he went to East Anglian Breweries in Ely, Cambridgeshire and believed he was being groomed for the role of head brewer,[38] though he was to be disappointed. A takeover by Steward and Patteson led to a brief period at their brewery in Norwich before they in turn were taken over by Watney, beginning Urquhart's association with the brewing giant. It was they who sent him to Phipps Northampton Brewery Co. (Phipps NBC) in 1964, where, from 1966, he was 'second brewer'.[39]

Those who knew him describe a softly spoken man with a gentle accent and something of a resemblance to a schoolteacher, an Oxbridge don[40] or Mr Mainwaring from *Dad's Army*.[41] That scholarly, authoritative manner carried through into an active approach to membership of the Institute of Brewing, in whose journal he published several articles from the 1950s onward.[42] The earliest photograph we have seen shows a gathering of Phipps brewery men, half-pint mugs in hand. Urquhart stands to the right, the shortest of the group, a slightly detached expression on his face, as if he would rather be somewhere else.

In 1968, production of cask-conditioned beers at Phipps ceased and the brewery was renamed Watney Mann (Midlands). Their replacement was a keg bitter – Mann's Northampton Draught.[43] Phipps, as a brand name, was being phased out. Then, in 1970, the decision was made to close Phipps's Bridge Street brewery and build a new Carlsberg lager brewery on and around the site. In 1973, in the run-up to the closure, the head brewer left to become deputy at the Carslberg plant – in effect, a demotion. In his absence, for a short time, and at the age of 57, Urquhart finally got to be the boss. With his little remaining hair now grey, wearing horn-rimmed glasses and with a hearing aid on his belt, he found himself in charge of a skeleton crew of old-timers and part-timers at the creaking,

Bill Urquhart pictured on the cover of *The Brewer*, February 1976.

labyrinthine nineteenth-century brewery. 'It was a very sad time,' he later recalled. 'I had to sort out the men into rejects and possibles for another job.'[44] On 26 May 1974, he oversaw the final brew and then left Watney's employment.[45]

With fewer breweries, there were fewer jobs for brewers and, despite his technical expertise, in an age of vast, shining, industrial mega-breweries, Urquhart faced stiff competition from a new crop of slick, industrial graduate brewers. He pondered a change of career, even considering becoming a blacksmith at one point, but when push came to shove, he wasn't ready to give up brewing and throw away years of experience.[46] In fact, that much-begrudged training in economics and budget management had laid the groundwork for his next move, as had conversations with a colleague, Peter Mauldon, in their shared office at Phipps, as Mauldon recalled:

> One day, and for the want of something better to do, I was playing with some of the figures, and I worked out the ratio of barrels-per-man out of the gate at Northampton. This brought me to the conclusion that a small brewery could compete easily on this ratio. My words to Bill were: 'You know, Bill, one day some silly bugger is going to set up a mini-brewery and have a bit of fun.'[47]

Urquhart would almost certainly have been aware of the grumbling discontent from Northamptonshire drinkers and pub landlords when Phipps IPA disappeared from the market, not least because a group of publicans paid a visit to the Bridge Street brewery to protest.[48] Urquhart was one of the first British brewers to recognise the commercial value of 'localness' at a time when generic national brands were on the rise and, in the months before his redundancy, he worked with another colleague, chief chemist Mike Henson, to brew illicit test batches of what would become Northamptonshire Bitter.[49]

Urquhart lived in the village of Litchborough, at 2 Northampton Road, in a house converted from a former Phipps pub. The Fox and

Hounds had been a coaching inn, and was a large, stone-built house with a yard surrounded by stables and a barn. He set about turning that barn into what we would now call a microbrewery.[50] There was no option, as there is today, of calling a specialist and having a cheap-and-cheerful brewery fitted for about the price of the average redundancy pay-off but, fortunately, Urquhart had the know-how and, as regional breweries closed or were modernised, they made not only brewers redundant but also the brewing equipment. Consequently he was able to find, more or less on the rubbish heap left after the demolition of the Phipps brewery, everything he needed to construct a cramped, rather ramshackle miniature version of Bridge Street in his own backyard. He had spent plenty of time daydreaming, planning just such a brewery, thinking through how the kit from the larger brewery could be cut down to size, repurposed and reused.

When it was finished, with the help of a young neighbour, engineer Frank Kenna, the sealed steel fermenting vessels with their rivets and portholes gave the place a certain H.G. Wells feel, 'more like a museum than a working brewery', according to George Jenkinson, who visited as a child.[51] Urquhart himself took to sporting a white coat and flat cap – a homely British version of the eccentric scientist – and prepared to be his own boss, outside of the institutional comfort of the Watney empire.

Mick Bolshaw, on-and-off chair of the local branch of CAMRA throughout this period, recalled that the brewery's launch was low-key: 'Bill had already got his plant together and into production before going public . . . it came as a huge surprise to have this happening on our doorstep.'[52] Peter Mauldon first heard that the project had turned from daydream to reality when, lying in bed one morning, he opened the newspaper to see Urquhart's smiling face under the Watney-parodying headline WHAT THEY WANT IS BILL'S BEER.[53]

Elspeth Urquhart, Bill's daughter, told us it was plain sailing. Nessie Urquhart supported his efforts and ran the brewery 'office', handling paperwork and accounts, managing stock and receiving visitors. She also looked after the 'works canteen', keeping staff and visitors fed and watered.[54]

The first outlet for Litchborough Brewery beers was Urquhart's own golf club at Farthingstone, followed shortly by a pub in a village on the other side of Northampton, The George Inn at Maidwell.[55] Did the drinkers who tasted Northamptonshire Bitter in July 1974 realise how significant those first pints were in the context of the history of British beer? Probably not. Mick Bolshaw remembers it as 'quite middle-of-the-road', and CAMRA described it as an 'imitation of the Northampton bitter produced by Phipps'.[56] Bolshaw told us that Urquhart denied this outright, but, as the beer was brewed 'to appeal to the widest range of palates', there was nothing to distinguish it noticeably from Phipps's product. Richard Boston described it as 'unfortunately . . . somewhat removed from traditional cask beer'.[57]

Given the choice, Urquhart would probably have preferred to produce nothing but 'real ale', as he had done for most of his brewing career, but this wasn't always practical, at least not in the first year or two. One of the reasons people such as CAMRA's founders and Christopher Hutt had felt so despairing on behalf of 'traditional draught' was that brewers across the country, including Phipps, had 'salted the earth', ripping handpumps and beer engines out of their pubs, meaning that, even those landlords who would have liked to buy cask ale had no way of serving it. As a result, Urquhart seems to have sold a substantial amount of beer under CO_2 'top pressure'[58] at least until 1978.[59]

Urquhart also filtered his beer[60] (a 'real ale' no-no). So he pitched it cannily as an 'upgrade' from the national keg bitters, rather than a radical, left-field alternative. He was, after all, a sensible businessman rather than a frustrated artist, and, according to Mick Bolshaw, though warm towards CAMRA, wasn't convinced it would really make a difference in the long run. There is further evidence of this attitude in his brief sojourn into lager brewing, with the wonderfully named Litchbrau. At any rate, Urquhart's instincts were right and he was soon able to make a living, producing around 350 barrels a year – enough, at least, to see him to retirement at sixty-five.[61] 'Really, the venture is getting out of hand,' said Urquhart at the time. 'It's fifteen hours a day, seven days a week. I'm working twice as hard as I did before.'[62]

Urquhart's success confirmed that some consumers valued products that had a tangible connection to the places where they lived; that the appeal of the underdog could not be underestimated; and that other beer drinkers simply craved something, anything, that was new, instead of the same old names.

More generally, the new brewery revival proved that there was demand for an alternative to the mechanised, centralised, processed-food approach of the huge brewing combines. National press coverage and reports in the CAMRA newspaper brought these new breweries to the attention of thousands of people, and a number of them were inspired to follow suit. Most commonly their founders were, like Bill Urquhart, former professional brewers for the Big Six, but some came via another route: *Good Life*-style amateur home brewing.

For decades, brewing at home required a licence, which generally cost between 25 and 50 shillings, depending on the rental value of your home, and which entitled you to make beer for your servants and farm labourers, as per legislation drawn up in 1880.[63] In his Budget of 3 April 1963, the Chancellor of the Exchequer, Reginald Maudling, abolished the home-brewing licence on the grounds that it cost more to collect fees than was being raised.[64] Of course, plenty of people had been brewing furtively without licences, safe behind their own doors from the Excise man,[65] but, after this point, anyone could do so without guilt. Shops selling brewing supplies experienced a sudden and welcome lift in business,[66] and newspapers were suddenly full of 'handy guides' and (slightly suspect) recipes,[67] with books arriving soon after.

At first, the motive for most people to start brewing at home was cost: as the price of a pint in the pub crept inexorably upward, and its strength down, the idea of 'beer at 3d a pint'[68] must have seemed very appealing at a time when a pint of bitter in the pub might cost 1s 7d (around 22p and £1.40 respectively in today's money).[69] From the start, however, there was an awareness that home brewing also offered the opportunity to make something other than the 'standard products' offered by the big brewers[70] – to create something super-local and, in all likelihood, unique from brew to brew, to put it politely. Before too long, alongside those brewing 'loopy juice' in buckets in the airing-cupboard with kits from high-street chemist shop Boots, some very serious hobbyists began to emerge.

The Durden Park Brewing Circle was founded in June 1971 in Southall, on the south-western fringes of London, by amateur winemaker Ted Hickson. It met at first in the tin hut that served as a changing room for players at Durden Park cricket ground. Fifteen people attended the first meeting, but the group's numbers rose to thirty within their first year, and membership has kept at around that size ever since.[71] Tony Badger joined the Circle when it was just a few months old. 'Our evenings consisted of one of us giving a talk and/ or demonstration about various aspects of our brewing knowledge,' he told us.

A while later, Dr John Harrison, sometimes mistakenly described as the Circle's founder, joined their number. He was a chemist who worked for the Post Office and became the driving force behind research, from 1973 onward, into old brewing logs mouldering in archives around the country, which led to a series of incredibly detailed 'how to' guides on brewing extinct varieties of British beer such as porter.[72] *Old British Beers and How to Make Them*, published in 1976, became a staple of brewers' bookshelves just as the late 1970s microbrewing boom took off.

Many of those brewers also had copies of a book by Dave Line called *The Big Book of Brewing*, published in 1974. Line was the quintessential amateur and apparently saw home brewing as an act of rebellion, a form of libertarianism in action:

> You can steal a man's wife, burn down his house, sack him from
> his job, but never should you deny him the right to sup good ale
> ... Gone are the days when you got a decent pint of acceptable
> strength in your 'local'. The present laws of the country penalise
> strong beer with heavy taxation, and with shareholders to
> please, the accountants in the big breweries seem to have more
> influence on the quality of the beer than the brewers themselves
> ... A good beer is rapidly becoming 'extinct' commercially; the
> only way to ensure a good supply is to brew it yourself.[73]

Line was born in Southampton in 1942 and, after grammar school
and an apprenticeship at the docks, joined the Central Electricity
Generating Board, where he became an electrical engineer. In 1967,
he and his wife Sheila had a small party to which someone brought
home-made elderflower wine. This inspired the Lines to begin making
wine themselves. Then, in 1971, Guinness, with a certain degree of
arrogance, ran a humorous newspaper advertisement giving away the
recipe for their stout, but with a disclaimer:

> This recipe produces a quantity of Guinness sufficient
> for 2,450,000 people. Should you require more, you can
> increase the amounts in proportion.[74]

The implication was that it wasn't worth attempting to brew at
home but, as Sheila Line told us, 'Dave liked a beer, but he liked a
challenge even more.' He scaled the recipe down and called his
version 'Romsey Stout':

> He wrote to Guinness to let them know and they invited him to
> the brewery. It was through that that he got to know so many
> people in the industry, such as hop growers, and Cyril Berry
> from *Amateur Winemaker* magazine. Cyril asked him to write
> an article about Romsey Stout and he eventually got a monthly
> column.

It was that column that led to the publication of *The Big Book of Brewing* in 1974 and *Brewing Beers Like Those You Buy* in 1978. Line preached obsessive cleanliness (the absence of which, with the resulting infection by bacteria, is one reason why so much 'airing-cupboard' home brew tasted foul) and coached against the use of kits and extracts. Instead, he urged home brewers to use whole malted grains and hops, and devised scaled-down versions of industrial processes using easy-to-build, improvised kit. His recipes were thoughtful and inspiring, too, offering amateurs the opportunity to 'clone' commercial beers. For example, his 'Goodness Stout' is accompanied by a description of Guinness and notes on how to recreate the characteristics of Dublin water.

'He eventually started travelling all over, giving talks. He was scheduled to visit Dallas, Texas,' said Sheila Line, 'but died a couple of weeks before the trip.' He was thirty-seven. Having been unwell for months, doctors misdiagnosed him with mumps, only confirming that he had cancer two weeks before he died in early 1980. A final book, *Beer Kits and Brewing*, was published posthumously later that year. 'I think he'd be amazed if he could see that his books are still in print and that he's been so influential,' Sheila told us.

Whether committed, after the manner of Line and the Durden Park Circle, or casual, buying kits from Boots, plenty of people took up brewing. Enough, in fact, for the *Daily Mirror* to declare the advent of 'the brew-it-yourself booze craze' – a market, they claimed, that in 1978 was worth £9 million a year.[75]

Several amateur brewers went professional during this period. Cliff Davies' garage home brew went on sale at the Miskin Arms in Pontyclun, Wales in 1976. Chiltern, founded in 1980 in Aylesbury, Buckinghamshire was the conclusion of several years of home brewing by its founder, Richard Jenkinson. The York Brewery, a spin-off from another home-brewing supply shop owned by John Boothroyd, began selling bottled beer brewed on site in 1976. John Payne began in modest circumstances what became Smiles Brewery at Bell's Diner, Montpelier, Bristol in 1977: 'It began as a plastic-bucket effort . . . I ran a vegetarian restaurant with my girlfriend, and we thought we might as well sell decent beer with the meals.[76]

Some years later, when customers started to demand more variety in their beer, many professional brewers would also turn to Durden Park and Dave Line for inspiration – putting to use techniques and recipes that had long been lost and forgotten.

In 1977, two more significant breweries began trading. The first was a real landmark, bringing the 'real ale revolution' to London, where no new brewing company had opened 'since the turn of the century'.[77] It offers a case study of how enthusiastic amateurs could build a brewery from nothing; and, later, lose it just as easily. The story begins thousands of miles from London, in India.

We spoke to Patrick Fitzpatrick on the telephone. He has what you might call a Radio 4 accent – educated middle class, with very precise grammar – though his sentences often tailed off into a wistful laugh, and every now and then he would drop in a hipsterish word or phrase: 'Cool!' It took us several months to trace him, largely because he has had no interest in talking about his brewing career: 'I was so devastated by what happened to the brewery – all that effort, only for everything to go so badly wrong.'

He was born in London to Irish parents in 1954. His interest in beer did not come entirely out of the blue: Fitzpatrick's family had a stake in a string of pubs – you might even call it a chain – in north and east London, as well as in Dublin.[78] The company, Murphy's, was founded by his grandfather, J.R. Murphy, in 1934, and was famous for introducing, or at least popularising, draught Guinness in the East End.

Patrick Fitzpatrick, founder of Godson's of London, in 1980.

Fitzpatrick attended Downside, a Catholic private school in the West Country. In the mid-1970s he had long, dark, curly hair[79] and was, in his own words, 'kind of a hippy'. On reaching adulthood, like many of his generation, he went East, as they say, 'to find himself'.

> I lived in India for a year when I was twenty. I hadn't decided what to do with myself and was travelling to kill some time. A friend had some trouble with a passport and we went to Bombay to get it sorted out. While I was hanging around, I went to the British Council's reading room and started looking through, I think, *The Illustrated London News*,[80] where I found an article about old family breweries like Young's and it struck me as interesting. I decided that's what I wanted to do.

He was motivated, in part, by the same instinct that lay behind the Campaign for Real Ale: 'There was a sense that brewing was an art in danger of being lost . . . The British Isles have this unique beer, and it seemed it was going to disappear.' So, on his return to England, Fitzpatrick started looking for a 'pupillage'.

> I wrote to a hundred or so small brewers. I got various books and looked up their addresses . . . Fred Martin at King and Barnes took me on. Without doubt the best way to learn brewing is actually to work . . . at one of these family breweries.

After six months at the Sussex brewery, he felt ready to take what he has called 'a great leap into the unknown'.

> My family weren't all that sure it was a good idea . . . They used to ask: 'What happens if you poison people?' Back then, if you told people you wanted to open a brewery, they pictured these great factories with towers and fifty or sixty dray trucks. People would say: 'Are you mad?' I faced quite a lot of ridicule, actually. I remember trying to explain to people that I was going to brew small batches, which is what everyone talks about now, and they just didn't understand.

He went about it with determination ('about all I learned at school') and managed to find support from various sources. His initial stake of £2,000 came from the sale of an antique desk at Sotheby's – not a huge amount of money with which to set up a business, even in 1977. He supplemented that with income from what proved to be a very clever move: a complementary 'real ale' distribution business (Godson's Ales), bringing beer from regional brewers such as Adnams' and Everard's into central London at the height of the 'real ale craze'. 'We must have supplied most of the free trade in London,' he recalled. 'There were perhaps fifty or sixty free houses, and we were in 95 per cent of them.' This side of the business was successful from the off:

> I was very conscious that I looked about sixteen, so I grew a beard to look older. I was a bit of a hippy so I also put on a suit. My first sale was at The Anglesea Arms in Chelsea, which was a very important free house. I was terribly nervous, and just went: 'Um . . . Er . . . Um . . . would you like to buy some beer?' And the landlord replied: 'What took you so long?'

He was also fortunate in being offered cheap premises in Atherton Road, Clapton, east London – a former factory due to be turned into a car park in the next five to ten years – and in managing to convince £500-a-day brewery consultant John Wilmot, formerly of Whitbread, to help him set up the brewery without upfront payment. 'He had contacts at Whitbread – he'd been on their executive board,' said Fitzpatrick, 'but had really been inspired by E.F. Schumacher's *Small is Beautiful*.' Schumacher's book argued that smaller, decentralised businesses were not only more sustainable in the long run, but also more 'humanising'. Big, centralised businesses (such as Watney's, though Schumacher doesn't use that example) were, on the other hand, dehumanising, environmentally damaging, unsustainable *and* produced terrible products. 'Small is beautiful' therefore became a mantra for those who sought to square hippy ideals with entrepreneurial instinct.

When the time came to christen his brewery, Fitzpatrick eschewed his own unmistakably Irish moniker. 'I wanted an English-style name,' Fitzpatrick told us. 'Godson came from our hop merchant, Mike Godson, in Hereford.' The full name of the company, however, was a kind of homage and joke all in one: 'All London breweries had three names – Mann Crossman and Paulin, Fuller Smith and Turner, Truman Hanbury and Buxton.' So he borrowed the names of his transport manager, Hugo Freeman, and John Wilmot, to come up with Godson Freeman and Wilmot, which sounded every inch the Victorian family brewery and gave the tiny firm a degree of credibility.

Announcing the opening of the brewery in October 1977, Fitzpatrick used language which echoed Michael Hardman's *Beer Naturally* and the 'wholefood' trend: 'We'll be using good-quality malt and hops with no sugar or other additives.'[81] He explained the thinking behind this in our conversation.

> The beer was all malt, no additives, because people were talking about breweries being 'chemical factories', as a result of big companies cutting costs and brewing time. They were using industrial enzymes and stuff like that. At Tolly Cobbold in Suffolk, the head brewer was saving money every year using 25 per cent rice and other things that don't really belong in English beer. For small breweries, that was immaterial, and I just thought it wasn't on in English brewing – that it wasn't what people should be doing.

The *What's Brewing* correspondent who visited the Clapton brewery in January 1978[82] was amused by its eccentricity.

> On the first floor of . . . a ramshackle converted sweet factory . . . head brewer Rob Adams takes what looks like a large flat sea shell from a sideboard drawer . . . It is the dried bladder of a sturgeon fish, the traditional fining material that makes beer drop bright . . . Mr Adams makes his own finings from sturgeon

bladders, bought at £7 a pound and mixed with water in a large
plastic dustbin . . . If most breweries are either made to measure
or, at the least, off-the-peg places, Godson's is distinctly Women's
Institute jumble sale.

The brewery kit was built from cast-off equipment from various
breweries that had been taken over and closed, including Fremlin's
and Hancock's. Some items also came from Whitbread, through John
Wilmot's connections with his former employers.

Adams, a recent university graduate, handled brewing, working
long days to meet demand, while Fitzpatrick managed delivery and
distribution, whizzing about London in the delivery van. It was hard
work – 'seven-day weeks, which they don't tell you' – but it was also
enormously profitable: 'We had a turnover of a million pounds a year
and there was sufficient profit to pay myself £25k a year, and the same
again to my then wife.'

By 1980, Godson's was even available on the Continent, at the
Café Gollem in Amsterdam, where its arrival was heralded by Dutch
importer Nico van Dyjk dressed in a bowler hat and waving a Union-
flag-festooned banner.

The success of Godson's revivified London brewing, but the
excitement was not to last. Before long, everything that could go
wrong for Fitzpatrick did.

Meanwhile, another sign that the 'real ale revolution' was seriously
under way appeared with the arrival, also in 1977, of Britain's first
celebrity brewery. It was foreshadowed by the revelation, in the
previous year, that two of Britain's best-known entertainers, even then
on the path to becoming 'national treasures', were real-ale devotees:

> Two men who think that real ale is Something Completely
> Different are stalwart Monty Python writers and actors Terry
> Jones and Michael Palin . . . The busy pair . . . are lovers of tradi-
> tional beer and always carry the *Good Beer Guide* with them . . .

It is a much-thumbed document, for location shooting takes the
team to some obscure parts of the country.[83]

This should not have come as a surprise to anyone who had seen
Palin in the famous 1974 'travel agent' sketch in *Monty Python's Flying
Circus*, in which Eric Idle delivers a ranting monologue with repeated
disparaging references to Watney's Red Barrel. Of the two, Terry
Jones was the more enthusiastic about beer. When his accountant,
Michael Henshaw, introduced him to another of his clients, Richard
Boston, they entered into partnership on two projects.[84] First, an
'alternative' magazine, *The Vole*, to be edited by Boston; and second,
a brewery, which they initially intended to open in Berkshire. Boston
announced the project in *What's Brewing* in January 1977:

> There are a number of free houses in the area that might take
> our beer. We have found a farmhouse with sheds that could be
> converted into a brewery ... We have got the capital and the
> place – all we need is a dissatisfied brewer working for some
> anonymous combine who would like to run and plan his own
> business, explore retail outlets and work with us to see if the
> scheme is viable.

Peter Austin was born in north London in 1920, and had planned
a career at sea until he was invalided out of the Royal Navy in the
Second World War. He drifted into brewing by accident:

> My father was a director of Pontifex and Sons, who were big in
> producing steel fittings for breweries ... Going into brewing
> wasn't my idea – it was through my father's connections. He
> got me a pupillage with Roland Storey at the Friary Brewery in
> Guildford in Surrey.

From there, he went to the Hull Brewery as third brewer,
becoming head brewer as the decades passed. He retired from
brewing for the first time in 1975, at the age of fifty-five, when Hull
Brewery was taken over by Northern Foods, and at the urging of his

second wife. 'The lady in question lived in Bournemouth,' he told us rather ruefully, 'and she kidded me that I would be able to retire and spend my time fishing, and so on, which was not quite right.' He saw Boston's cry for help and abandoned a failing sea-angling business in Hampshire to design and build a brewery. By this time, Terry Jones had become acquainted with businessman Martin Griffiths, who in 1972 had bought a ramshackle medieval farmhouse, Penrhos Court in Herefordshire, for £5,000 and turned it into a successful restaurant. The plan to brew in Berkshire was abandoned, and Austin was set to work in the farm buildings at the back of the property.

> I remember the first brew very well. It was five o'clock one morning with bats flying about as we got up. It was the last possible day for brewing because the grand opening had to be before Terry Jones went to America ... We got the mash in at six. The plumbers were ahead of us connecting up the next vessel. By 8 a.m. we were in the copper – it took hours to get it to boil ... It was a twenty-hour marathon in all, but we did it.[85]

The brewery was officially opened on Saturday, 16 July 1977, with Michael Palin, a compulsive diarist with an eye for detail, in attendance.

> At Hereford Station by one. A minibus drives us to Penrhos Court ... The beer is tasted and found to be good. Jones' First Ale it's called – and at a specific gravity of 1050 it's about as devastating as Abbot Ale. But the weather has decided to be kind to us and the collection of buildings that is Penrhos Court – basically a fine, but run-down sixteenth-century manor house with outbuildings housing the brewery, restaurant and Martin Griffiths' office and living accommodation – look well in the sunshine and provide a very amenable background to the serious beer-drinking.[86]

Jones's primary contribution seems to have been publicity. He opened the 1977 CAMRA Great British Beer Festival at Alexandra

Palace. In his opening address, he said that beer shouldn't be tasted, like wine, before dumping six pints of beer over his own head. This 'showing off' won coverage in several newspapers and a front-page photo in *What's Brewing*. Jones, a globally renowned film director and comedian, was by far the 'hippest' celebrity to lend his name to the Campaign: subsequent festivals were opened, with rather less glamour, by Labour minister Roy Hattersley and TV naturalist David Bellamy.

Jones seems to have spent much of this period wearing a Penrhos Ale branded sweatshirt, and, by 1978, it had paid off, and he declared

Terry Jones of Monty Python fame, and co-founder of Penrhos Brewery, pours beer over his head at the opening of the 1977 Great British Beer Festival.

the brewery a success: 'It can't be all that bad . . . After all, we've only been going for six months and already fourteen pubs are buying the stuff from us. And selling it.'[87]

Penrhos wasn't just a bit of celebrity dabbling, though. For one thing, it gave Peter Austin the opportunity to test himself before building not only his own brewery, Ringwood, in 1978, but also many more in Britain and around the world. For another, it was the first brewery to revive a type of beer which had last been brewed in 1973 – porter, the dark beer upon which British brewing dynasties had been established in the eighteenth century and from which stout was descended.[88] Being extinct gave porter a certain mystique, and its very name evoked a romantic image of the nineteenth century at a time when books such as Kellow Chesney's *The Victorian Underworld* were bestsellers.

Porter also offered something *different* – it was black and robust when, back then, most 'real ale' was brown bitter. Penrhos's 'dark, pleasant' example was the surprise hit of the 1978 Great British Beer Festival, and was soon followed by a much sweeter version by Timothy Taylor of Keighley in Yorkshire, based on an 1873 recipe. When a cask of that went on sale at the Eagle, the CAMRA Real Ale Investments pub in Leeds, it sold out in less than three days.[89] The excitement with which these unusual beers were greeted signalled a long, slow return to diversity in British brewing.

In just over a decade 'microbrewing' had spread from isolated obscurity in Scotland all the way to London, and had become, literally, a cause célèbre. In the next decade, some of these new breweries, and others who came after them, would coalesce into a movement and begin to influence both public taste and government policy. In the meantime, they brought some much-needed excitement to the growing subculture of beer appreciation, and fuelled the constant demand for novelty that drove a new kind of outlet: the 'beer exhibition'.

FIVE

MORE AN EXHIBITION THAN A PUB

> I cannot get near the bar for earnest, bespectacled men
> with hairy sports jackets, spending an hour over half
> a pint, and exchanging jargon-words such as 'body',
> 'bright', 'casky' and 'nose', like undergraduates who
> have just tasted their second bottle of claret.
>
> Letter to the *Guardian*, 1975[1]

In the 1970s, the Big Six not only dominated beer, they also owned
very nearly every pub in the country. If you did not like, say, Watney's
bitter, you did not go to a Watney's pub – but what if Watney's had
taken over your town? Tough luck! And if you wanted to drink the
products of one of the handful of new breweries that were opening
around the country, you were obliged to find their own 'tied houses',
hunt for a rare 'free house', student bar or social club, or perhaps turn
up at the brewery and hope for the best. As CAMRA banged their
drum, however, a new type of pub emerged to meet the demand it
stimulated.

Of course, there were plenty of pubs selling cask-conditioned
beer, albeit usually only bitter, mild if you were lucky; nor were pubs
offering a wide range of beer, cask or otherwise, entirely new. From the

1950s onward, there were a couple of London pubs known to offer a large selection of hard-to-find, out-of-town beer. Ye Olde Mitre on St Martin's Lane near Trafalgar Square, demolished during the aborted redevelopment of the Covent Garden area in the early 1970s,[2] was famous for its bottled-beer selection and a larger than usual, carefully chosen line-up of draught beers from around the country. The first really famous example, though, which Richard Boston described as a 'living gallery of beer', was Becky's Dive Bar in Southwark, just across the Thames from the City of London.

The eponymous Becky was born Rebecca Mary Dunne in 1907.[3] Her exact origins are mysterious – a woman of that name was born in Dublin in the same year; some knew her as coming from 'a family of Manchester coopers';[4] while others recall her as 'solidly south London'.[5] There are even mentions of the nickname California Becky,[6] though it seems entirely unlikely that she was American. In 1943 she married William Willeter, a sixty-five-year-old widower and veteran of the First World War, who ran the Golden Lion in Caterham, Surrey with his son, Robert. Robert resented Becky 'taking over', and there was some family strife.[7] Eventually, in 1954, Becky and William moved, without Robert, to less conventional premises at 24 Southwark Street, in the basement of the grandly Victorian Hop Exchange building. Then, in April, not long after their arrival, William died, leaving Becky a widow at forty-seven.

Recollections of Becky herself suggest a woman who, having reached her prime in the 1930s and 1940s, decided that that was where she would stay. Her hair was always dyed deep black, she wore lipstick 'half an inch round her mouth'[8] and tended to wear clothes recalling the fashions of those decades. The bar had a gramophone-style record player, which would blast out songs on old seventy-eights by George Formby, Flanagan and Allen and even the speeches of Winston Churchill, evoking the Blitz spirit in her underground 'shelter'.[9] Those who frequented The Dive recall that she drank constantly and heavily, rarely making much sense by the end of a typical night. Not to overdo the air of tragedy, though: she was also a friendly, talkative and warm personality – likeably eccentric[10] – and seems to have found something approaching a family in her colleagues and customers. There was a drunken pianist called Norman, two barmen-cum-cellarmen called Harry and Alf, as well as various heavy-drinking regulars. In a 1974 column for the *Guardian*, Richard Boston recalled a bus trip with Becky, Harry and Alf, along with about twenty-five Dive Bar regulars, around Rutland and Norfolk in search of real ale, accompanied by singing and the wheezing of harmonicas.[11]

But what of the beer? Something inspired Becky to make a virtue of the rarity and range of the brews on offer at The Dive. Perhaps she was a smart businesswoman who spotted a gap in the market and a promotional angle, or maybe she was picking up on the reputation of Ye Olde Mitre. At any rate, by the 1960s Becky's Dive Bar was renowned for being a pub specialising in rarely seen ales dispensed from casks mounted on the bar, as well as a huge range of bottled beers – more than 250 of them from all over the world – a positive freak show of beer. The Dive was most famous for its Ruddles, brought by train into Liverpool Street station, but, at one time or another, it also offered beer from Thwaites, Adnams, Dutton's and Shepherd Neame when those were rare in London. She also boasted 'Dublin-brewed Guinness', and claimed to be 'the only one here that sells it', though that was spin on her part.[12]

In fact, Becky had a knack for PR, and probably invented some of the colourful tales that sprang up around the pub. Before long, despite the building being only a hundred years old, Becky's Dive Bar had somehow come to be known as 'the oldest free house in London'.[13] Stories of its great age and character were supplemented by false rumours that its cellars were once dungeon-like cells in the grim and long-demolished Marshalsea debtors' prison.[14] If Becky did not start these rumours, she certainly sustained them. Brian Schwartz, a young American journalist writing for a magazine aimed at US servicemen in Europe, visited in 1975 and was treated to the sight of Becky rattling a set of manacles which she claimed to have found in the basement and from which she had washed blood.[15] At a reception hosted by the South Korean Ambassador at Claridge's hotel in 1969, she cornered Prince Michael of Kent and gave him the hard sell on her vast range of bottled beer.[16] The following year, she appeared as the star of an article in *The Times* about formidable female publicans where, once again, she levered in the well-worn spiel about her beer menu, describing The Dive as a 'pub crawl in one house'.[17]

Becky was not, however, a proud housekeeper: 'I could spend my time cleaning the ashtrays and polishing the bar, but then I would have no time to spend with my customers or give them a proper welcome. And what sort of pub would that be?'[18] Author Andrew Keogh[19] recalled a deathtrap of a staircase leading down into a scruffy, malodorous pit with barely functional toilets. Paul Bailey, who visited in 1974, described the aroma of 'dampness and tomcats'.[20] Another veteran London pub-goer, who wishes to remain anonymous, told us:

> The furniture was mostly beaten-up sofas, which had probably been found on a rubbish dump. A visit to the toilets was extremely hazardous as it was down the cellar steps, which were very steep and had no handrails. From memory, one could have a piss and look at the casks at the same time.

It was carpeted with leftovers, scraps and 'ends of rolls' and stank of urine, stale beer, cooking fat, human bodies and cellar damp. But its foulness, decrepitude and air of eccentricity, along with the 'exotic' beer, seem to have contributed to a certain cult appeal and an air of naughtiness. The following passage reveals why our anonymous correspondent is so coy:

> In the early 1970s, I was courting a girl who worked in the same building as me in Finsbury Square. We used to trot over London Bridge regularly to Becky's . . . as it was a place where we were confident none of our respective work colleagues would find us . . . The attraction for us, other than privacy, was that it sold my favourite beer of the time, Ruddles County, and my girlfriend just loved the bottled Ruddles Barley Wine.

It was a non-stop party, and Friday and Saturday nights, according to Andrew Keogh, were particularly exciting. Things only got busier after 1974 when The Dive was a finalist in the *Evening Standard* pub of the year award and also gained a listing in a locally published CAMRA guide to London pubs. Unfortunately, as The Dive went mainstream, its borderline-dangerous architectural features and unsanitary facilities came to the attention of the authorities. The lease had always been precarious, prompting petitions and protests to 'save the Dive' when it came up for renewal,[21] partly because the Hop Exchange's owners, J. Lyons and Co., wanted to restore and redevelop the building, leaving no room for a grotty basement bar. What probably tipped the balance were the sausage sandwiches Becky prepared in the filthy kitchen which, according to Chris Partridge, 'must have caused most of the custom at Guy's A&E on Saturday nights'. Despite a final effort by regulars to clean the place up, in 1975 it was forcibly closed down and Becky, it seems, retired. Fortunately, not long after, others picked up where she had left off, and not least among them was CAMRA itself.

Christopher Hutt, who had always championed pubs, wasted very little time as chair of CAMRA from 1973 in steering policy in that direction. In October 1974, a new company was incorporated, with Hutt as director on a salary of £4,500 per year, with the intention of buying and running a chain of pubs. Demonstrating how hard it can be to pin down CAMRA's politics, the company's chair was to be Conservative MP Nicholas Winterton, a champion of small local businesses. As CAMRA historian Tony Millns put it in 1991:

> The motive for establishing CAMRA (Real Ale) Investments (CAMRAIL) was essentially defeatist, or at least defensive: in 1974, most members of the campaign in their sober moments expected to lose in the long run, and to be faced (by 1980 or so) with keg beer in virtually all pubs.[22]

Christopher Hutt saw it another way, saying in 1982: 'I think without CAMRA Investments real ale would be dead by now because . . . it was our setting up of a commercial concern that made the breweries sit up."[23] To some extent, it was a propaganda exercise – an attempt to show that there was demand for real ale and that pubs selling it could make money. John Green, CAMRA administrator in the mid-1970s, said: 'It was supposed to be a demonstration of the CAMRA idea of how a pub should be run – not for profit, primarily, but setting an example.'

Floating at £1 a share, by Christmas 1974 CAMRAIL had raised £170,000 from keen CAMRA members, and had secured a loan from Barclay's bank. The first two pubs they bought were the Old Fox in Bristol and the White Gates in Hyde, Manchester, followed fairly shortly afterwards by the Nag's Head in Hampstead, all of which opened for business in 1975. The Salisbury Hotel in Cambridge (CAMRAIL's home city) and the Eagle in Leeds were purchased in 1976. All were immediately successful, at least in terms of their popularity with CAMRA members. New breweries, such as Pollard's of Reddish Vale near Manchester, which opened in 1975 and supplied the White Gates, certainly felt the benefit.[24]

The pubs tended to be in suburban rather than city-centre locations, and rather run-down. Though CAMRAIL refurbished them, it was always with the intention of preserving what Christopher Hutt called their 'old-fashioned and simple appeal'.[25] They were intended to be the antidote to the then popular plastic 'theme pubs' which focused on wacky decor rather than decent beer. The Nag's Head in Hampstead had been just such a pub until CAMRAIL took it on, nautically themed and labouring under a new name, The Cruel Sea. In practice, members complained that CAMRAIL pubs, stripped back to the bare bones, sometimes lacked character and atmosphere.

Politically, CAMRAIL was also a source of friction from the beginning, exposing tensions in the organisation between, broadly speaking, left-wingers with no interest in commerce on the one hand, and market capitalists on the other. Some thought CAMRA had no business running pubs at all; others that they should be run on a rather hippyish, non-commercial basis; while Christopher Hutt and his supporters saw them as a practical way to influence the market, and also wanted them to make a profit.

Nearly forty years on, Terry Pattinson, a lifelong Labour supporter, still gets angry talking about it.

> I was never in favour of CAMRA Real Ale Investments. I warned people from the moment Christopher Hutt proposed it that it was a bad idea, and that it would make some people very rich while causing problems for CAMRA . . . Hutt was very persuasive, though – watching him speak was like seeing Lenin whipping up the crowd. He won the vote and CAMRAIL went ahead.

Hutt, for his part, looked pained when the subject came up and was unwilling to discuss ancient arguments, though he did say, choosing his words carefully: 'It became apparent that there were stresses and strains because of the sharing of the CAMRA name.' Terry Pattinson went further:

> I like Chris, personally, and we always have a nice time when we meet at reunions, and so on, but what annoyed me then, and still annoys me, is that the pub chain used the CAMRA name but wouldn't do anything to help the Campaign – I couldn't get them to take membership forms, copies of the *Good Beer Guide*, T-shirts . . . nowt. I was furious.

Perhaps for political reasons, regardless of his opposition Pattinson was given a key role: 'I was on the board of CAMRAIL as a token "radical" to appease the membership.' Rightly so, as many members did have concerns, as expressed by Mark W. Martin in a letter to *What's Brewing* in March 1976:

> Our own pubs (or CAMRA Investments' pubs?) are all very welcome in some places. However, why open one in London, positively flowing with real ale compared with some regions, and quite incomprehensible in trendy Hampstead where the

Nag's Head is sited right opposite a Young's house and within walking distance of several other 'real' outlets.

Members who had invested wondered why CAMRAIL wasn't pushing into the 'beer deserts' dominated by the Big Six and taking the fight to the enemy.[26] Roger Protz, CAMRA's in-house editor from 1976, and before then better known as a radical socialist activist and journalist, was among those who questioned CAMRAIL's targeting of 'middle-class trendies'[27] in Hampstead. Finally, there was the question of CAMRAIL's business practices, as summarised in the *Financial Times*:

> Ironically . . . [CAMRAIL] has so far had to follow some policies exactly like those of the major brewers. Thus it has bought pubs in highly populated centres . . . And, although CAMRA insists that tenanted pubs are more congenial than those run by a brewer's manager, its investment company uses managers simply because it could find no other sensible way of operating.[28]

Tensions over CAMRAIL continued to simmer for the rest of the decade, and would see Hutt and Pattinson, both key figures, drift away from the Campaign.

Most important, arguably, were the handful of pubs not sponsored by CAMRA which reinvented themselves in this period. When we asked veteran drinkers to name the first 'destination pubs' to appear in the wake of the founding of CAMRA, most mentioned two in particular. First, the Hole in the Wall at Waterloo, once a rough cider joint filled with 'tramps' and popular with slumming rock stars[29] until it was refurbished in 1975 and reinvented as a bolt-hole for those with an interest in beer. (Terry Pattinson, who used to drink there while commuting home from Fleet Street, takes credit for persuading the landlord to take the plunge and serve Young's Special.) Its offer, though, exciting as it might have seemed at the time, was nothing compared to another pub: the Barley Mow at Tyttenhanger, outside St Albans, Hertfordshire, north of London.

The Barley Mow had been known as a 'beer shop'[30] or 'beer house'[31] – a drinking den rather than a country inn – since the nineteenth century, but by the 1970s was not doing good business.[32] As John Green, a St Albans native, recalled: "The Barley Mow used to be a small McMullen's pub used mostly by gypsies – there's a gypsy camp just up the road." It was out of the way and also a possible victim of anti-drunk-driving laws introduced at the end of the 1960s. Its owners, regional brewers McMullen and Sons, were excited by the coming of the motorway and wanted to build a big new pub with more parking nearby. So they did something quite unusual: in 1976, they turned the pub over to a private owner as a free house. Even today, brewers or pub companies usually prefer to let their pubs rot, be demolished or turned into houses rather than see them become a source of local competition, sometimes going as far as to put them under 'protective covenants' which forbid subsequent owners to sell beer. McMullen did not do this, thankfully for the burgeoning beer scene.

The new owner, Tom Simpson, was looking for a roof over his head more than anything else. He had worked in the electrical trade and had no experience in pubs and, frankly, was not that interested. In 1976, Hertfordshire had an active CAMRA branch, and St Albans itself was home to CAMRA's head office, so Simpson was soon buttonholed by the local chair, Steve Warnes, who convinced him to try out some beer from Fuller's of London. London Pride and Extra Special Bitter (ESB), then rarely seen outside west London, turned the Barley Mow into a beer-geek destination and put paid to Simpson's dream of quietly drifting into retirement. After experimenting with other real ales – no doubt under the influence of the local CAMRA branch – Simpson and his wife found running a knockout success of a pub too much like hard work and, less than a year after they'd arrived, moved on.

Real-ale-loving regulars at the pub held their breath, among them Steve Bury, then in his early twenties. He vividly remembers John and Betty Blackwell, the new owners. She was slim and not terribly interested in pubs, preferring to spend her time riding horses; her husband was a shorter, stocky Mancunian with a tendency to abruptness. The pub was his baby and, though neither he nor his wife had any experience, Blackwell set about learning the trade with methodical care and turned the Barley Mow into the most famous specialist real-ale pub in the country.

First, though, he had to deal with a problem Derek Cooper describes in his 1970 book, *The Beverage Report*:

> I remember the tenant of a large house in London who reckoned that for every night either he or his wife weren't in the bar the takings would be down by about £50. 'You must be very popular,' I said. 'Popular, my arse, it's these buggers on the fiddle.' He may have been exaggerating but he claimed that the last time he took his wife to a 'Masonic', he fired three of the staff the following morning.[33]

'They were very nearly bankrupted by staff giving away stock and doing fiddles on the tills,' Steve Bury told us. Blackwell cracked down on that, and then set about tidying up the rather tatty old building and readying it to sell not two real ales, or four, but an unheard of *eighteen*. Like Becky Willeter, John Blackwell realised that the keenest marketing advantage was to be found in offering an outstanding range of real ales. It worked.

'The Barley Mow was always heaving,' Michael Hardman told us. 'You could spend ten minutes getting to the bar.' CAMRA's *Good Beer Guide* for 1978 described it as 'more a beer exhibition than a pub', and Steve Bury described a cellar managed with absolute precision, plastic pipes 'like a heap of spaghetti', carefully colour coded. Before the phrase 'binge drinking' was invented, the Barley Mow even offered a 'Man vs Food'-style challenge: drink one pint of every real ale on offer and the guv'nor would pick up the tab. No one ever did, not even the Americans in their big, imported gas-guzzling cars who used to visit from nearby airbases.

The Blackwells had a close relationship with the local CAMRA branch: they gave over their back room for meetings, sold copies of the *Good Beer Guide* in the pub and subsidised the local CAMRA newsletter with an advertisement in every issue. For their part, CAMRA loved the Barley Mow, and it appeared in the *Good Beer Guide* for years.[34] This pub, more so even than those run by CAMRA Investments, represented a vision of what could be: variety and choice, not only of types of beer but of breweries from all over the country, with every beer on offer righteous and *real*. It became a mecca for beer enthusiasts in the know, as Steve Bury recalled:

> I don't think most of the customers thought about the pub in a national sense. There was a totally different attitude to drink-driving, and we would travel long distances to drink in good, real-ale pubs. What John had done was to put all the beers that we used to travel miles to drink on our doorstep. Customers would happily drive from Oxford and beyond for a night out.

The concept of the 'beer exhibition' hit the North of England at about the same time, with the opening of the Brahms and Liszt in Leeds in December 1975. Its owners were local businessman Chris Tipping, Turkish nightclub owner Tunj Osbey and Leeds United football player Johnny Giles, who was from Dublin.[35] The latter was a sleeping partner, but it is nevertheless his involvement, and the fact that Osbey was married to Peter Lorimer's sister-in-law, that is behind the common belief that its ownership was 'shared between some Leeds United players'.[36]

Once again, it owed much to the influence of a local CAMRA activist – in this case, Barrie Pepper, who was serving on the Campaign's National Executive at the time. Instead of 'freeing' a brewery-owned pub from 'the tie', a new premises was repurposed, giving Pepper the opportunity to help fashion the ideal CAMRA pub from scratch:

> I acted as a consultant when the licence was applied for before the Leeds magistrates and helped with the bar's design and selection of beers ... I gave evidence in court about the lack

of cask-conditioned ale in the city, and more importantly the absence of choice.

Local publicans did not welcome the additional competition, however:

> We were fiercely opposed by the Licensed Victuallers [the body representing local publicans], but because the application restricted sales of draught beer to cask-conditioned beer, the magistrates accepted our application and granted a licence with the following condition: 'To sell bottled beer of all descriptions and draught beer that is brewed from the traditional materials and allowed to mature in the barrel after leaving the brewery, and served to the customer without the introduction of extraneous gas.'

The grand opening was announced with a half-page advertising feature in the *Yorkshire Evening Post*[37] headlined: INTRODUCING ... A PUB WITH NO KEG FOR REAL BEER DRINKERS. It boasted of the presence on the management team of a 'beer expert', and suggested that there would soon be a bound 'beer list' describing each brew's 'special qualities'. 'Soon the walls will carry posters and pictures of Austria,' it said, 'to link with the composers theme.'

It occupied the cellar of the now demolished Devereux Building on East Parade, the upper floors of which were occupied by Osbey's nightclub, a chicken-in-a-basket discotheque with the fabulously period name 'The Nouveau'. The Brahms and Liszt was apparently modelled after a German beer hall, and Chris Martin, who worked there as a teenage barman, remembered fifteen-foot benches and tables at which people were packed every lunchtime and, especially, on weekend nights. As for the beer, Martin sums it up neatly: 'There were other pubs in Leeds that sold real ales, but this was the first time I had seen a long bar filled with so many strange ones.' As well as a full roster of Yorkshire beers, there were also rotating 'guest ales' – then a new concept. The Brahms and Liszt, just like the Barley

Mow, was a product of the real-ale 'craze' –
a type of business targeting a market
that hadn't existed five years earlier.

The pubs with the most taps
and the hardest-to-find beers
gained cult followings, and
the phrases 'real ale pub' and
'CAMRA pub' began to creep
into journalese, meaning not
merely a pub with *some* real ale
but one affiliated with the Campaign,
formally or otherwise, popular with
its members and with real ale at its
heart. At the same time, however,
they began to attract snide criticism:

Brahms and Liszt pale ale,
brewed specially for the pub
in Leeds by Martyn Sykes'
Selby Brewery.

they were pretentious 'beeraramas', to paraphrase one contemporary journalist,[38] while even 'real ale' enthusiasts questioned the
price premium on out-of-town beers, and whether a pub with many
handpumps could really keep all that beer in good condition.[39]

There was also the accusation that the kind of pub haunted by the
'CAMRA fellow traveller' was no longer a 'true local'.[40] A stereotype of
the obnoxious CAMRA member began to emerge: capable of 'boring
for hours',[41] conceited and perhaps a little odd. Though the majority
of members were ordinary people who attracted little attention,
there were some who could not resist showing off their knowledge,
lecturing fellow drinkers and berating publicans. The Campaign
acknowledged the problem:

> A number of incidents involving CAMRA members over the past
> few weeks underlines the need for the Campaign to maintain a
> good public image at all times . . . A Yorkshire newspaper recently
> featured a letter from a landlord who had a group of CAMRA
> members in his pub noisily expressing their approbation of the
> 'real stuff' . . . About the same time, a member of CAMRA's

National Executive no less was getting himself thrown out of a
pub in County Durham ... [after] he complained about [keg]
beer and began to tell a number of customers they were drinking
'sweet, alcoholic lemonade'.[42]

In Dorset in 1977, a small splinter group was founded under the
name The Real Ale Liberation Front (RALF), and they engaged in
acts of 'civil disobedience', annoying publicans by ordering keg beer
and refusing to pay for it.[43] Steve Bury, an early CAMRA member
based in St Albans, looked back regretfully on his own behaviour
during this period: 'I upset a lot of people including, on occasion,
other CAMRA members. We were all very passionate, but sometimes
had the bull-in-a-china-shop approach.'

After several years of uninterrupted success, however, CAMRA
were about to encounter bigger problems than their public image.
Internal tensions would begin to compromise the united front, and
the big breweries would retaliate in the sneakiest way imaginable: by
doing just what CAMRA had asked.

THE EMPIRE
STRIKES BACK

**CAMRA is in the same business as we are – promoting
beer. Certainly it has created a much greater interest in
beer among certain sections of the public.**

Watney's chairman, 1975[1]

In the 1960s and 1970s, before CAMRA gained momentum, the Big
Six had free reign to promote keg beer, sure in the belief that they
were responding to consumer demand. Watney's would test markets
carefully before removing locally produced beers from sale and
replacing them with 'chilled and filtered beers' brewed in London.[2]
But decisions weren't always made with the consumer so firmly in
mind: throughout the late 1960s, Watney's continually chipped away
at the strength of their keg bitters purely in response to financial
pressures, with each step down saving them a fortune in taxes.[3]

People noticed, but, when there were occasional grumbles about
the flavour and strength of the new products, about the disappearance
of local brands and the erosion of choice, marketing 'spin' was used
to head them off. From 1961, Watney's were talking up the ingredients in Red Barrel – 'It is brewed from Norfolk malts and Golding
hops, naturally matured for weeks' – and insisting that it possessed
'all the traditional characteristics of the best English bitters'.[4] Having
been brewed since the 1930s, it had heritage, they insisted, and

certainly wasn't the space-age, sterile product its critics liked to imply. Similarly, in 1967 full-page newspaper advertisements from Whitbread countered insinuations that the drive towards monopoly was reducing choice:

> Outside pubs all over the place you can see our new cherry-red sign sticking up . . . Sticking up for a really decent choice of beer . . . That's not just a slogan. We recently totted up the average number of beers you can expect to find behind our sign . . . It came to no less than twenty different beers, four draught and sixteen bottled.[5]

Then, from the start of the next decade, even before CAMRA had turned up the pressure, things began to get tricky. First, the Big Six had the government on their backs with the Monopolies Commission report of 1969 laying bare the intricate details of the running of their businesses. That was followed by tabloid newspaper reports detailing the strength (or, rather, weakness) of their keg beers as compared to the 'traditional draught' products of smaller regional brewers, of which this front-page story, from 1971,[6] is just one example.

> BEER: WE REVEAL THE BITTER TRUTH . . .
> Ask any pub man. He will tell you that draught beer isn't what it used to be. Definitely.
> Of course, he couldn't PROVE it. So today the *Sunday Mirror* proves it for him. We find that British beer is generally weaker and dearer than ever before . . .
> KEG beer is considerably weaker than many ordinary bitters;
> CHEMICALS and modern production techniques HAVE made a big difference;
> SOME brews are virtually near-beer;
> and NORTHERN beer is not stronger than that of the South.

Which? magazine joined in, too, carrying out a consumer test of keg bitters and reaching a damning conclusion.

Our tasters thought none smelt very strongly in the glass – none was either unpleasant or very pleasant . . . As far as taste went, the overwhelming impression of our tasters was that none of the keg beers had any very characteristic taste . . . Keg beer is a bright, chilled, fairly fizzy, moderately expensive, bland-tasting beer of average strength . . . We can see little reason for preferring one keg bitter to another, and even less for preferring them to their brewers' own alternative bitters, which are cheaper and in some cases stronger.[7]

From 1971 onward, Watney's rebranded and relaunched their flagship Red Barrel with the simpler name 'Red'. They promoted it relentlessly, with a campaign that used lookalikes of Communist dictators and referred to a 'Red revolution'. They also used an April 1973 advertisement to rebuff criticism, making the point that Red was stronger than 'the average pint of beer brewed twenty years ago' (that is, in 1953). 'It's set the brewing industry back twenty years,' it said, implying, with all the marketing man's customary slipperiness, that it was 'new and improved', while at the same time being a good old-fashioned pint. Within the company, however, there were grumblings of discontent.

Mike Cowbourne was a 'production brewer' who worked at Watney's in the early 1970s. He told us that neither he nor any of his colleagues could bear to drink Red which, contrary to the wholesomeness implied by the marketing, was brewed using a quantity of cheap, unmalted 'raw' barley broken down with 'added enzymes'.[8]

One of the Communist-themed advertisements from Watney's 1971 campaign for Red, the successor to Red Barrel.

Gerald Milward-Oliver joined Truman's of east London as a young public relations executive in 1973, at a turbulent time. In 1971, Truman's had been unexpectedly taken over by industry outsider Maxwell Joseph's Grand Metropolitan, which ran hotels and pubs including the famous Berni Inn chain. In 1972, Joseph also took over Watney's, and then, in October 1973, merged the two, creating Watney Mann and Truman Holdings. Milward-Oliver:

> After the merger, Grand Met decided that Watney's marketing and PR just wasn't working, so they replaced the previous team with the marketing and PR people from Truman's. Heading the marketing team was Anthony Tennant (who went on to become chairman of Guinness), with Paul Walmsley heading up the PR side. There were cuts everywhere in the company, huge cuts.

At first, Ted Handel, who had argued so bitterly with CAMRA's Christopher Hutt in the pages of the *Financial Times*, remained in charge, as Milward-Oliver recalled:

> He was the most charming man you could ever hope to meet, and didn't have a bad bone in his body. But he was from a more gentle style of PR than was needed, if the reputation of Watney's was going to be salvaged.

When Ted Handel retired, Paul Walmsley, a charismatic Australian in his early thirties,[9] took his place and adopted a very different approach to handling CAMRA. Where Handel had been defensive, Walmsley practised what would now be called 'engagement', and began to meet Hardman and other CAMRA high-ups both formally and socially, even accompanying Michael Hardman to a rugby game in Wigan.[10] In March 1975, this détente bore fruit for both parties when Watney's announced that it was to reintroduce cask-conditioned beer to London, having given it up in the 1960s. Milward-Oliver:

> It resulted in the reintroduction of a broad range of cask beers, produced in the traditional manner and, it has to be said, with

CAMRA lighting the way for us! The brewers were generally only too happy to go back to brewing cask.

They pitched it as a 'pilot', putting their new Fined Bitter into six London pubs, with a premium price befitting a niche product aimed at enthusiasts.[11] Customers and landlords were delighted and, after a week, Watney's declared that the pilot had been a success and that it was to be expanded into 150 pubs across London and the South East.[12] Watney's new chairman, Stanley Grinstead, issued a carefully worded written statement to *What's Brewing*, which included the following:

> Now that CAMRA is established, one would hope to see it become a more genuinely informative organisation. It would continue as a watchdog of consumer interests as it sees them – and brewers would need to accept this.[13]

Other breweries soon followed suit, not only reviving 'real beer' but also looking at other aspects of their business practice, including their approach to PR.

✺

Richard Harvey grew up in Whitbread pubs run by his father, John, who was President of the National Federation of Licensed Victuallers. After a career in journalism, he joined Allied Breweries as a PR man in the mid-1970s, and described to us the feeling in the industry at the time.

> I joined Allied when CAMRA were at their absolute peak. At that time, they were seen by the big brewers, including Allied, as a very noisy, very vocal, very media-savvy irritant ... CAMRA ran the most effective PR campaign I've ever seen. It was classic David and Goliath stuff – these little lads standing there against the might of the big brewers.

Throughout 1974, those independent regional breweries, such as Shepherd Neame in Kent and Fuller's and Young's in London, which had resisted being taken over by bigger national breweries, announced huge bumps in sales of, and profit from, cask-conditioned ale.[14] In 1976, Gaskell and Chambers, who then produced almost all of the handmade pump handles used in British pubs, announced that they couldn't meet the surge in demand for their products, having sunk to a low of four a week at the height of 'kegmania'. A market the Big Six had written off was turning out to be not only fashionable but lucrative. Richard Harvey recalled the turnaround:

> The view from the boardroom at Allied, as at other Big Six breweries, was 'CAMRA shall not cross this threshold' ... My view was that CAMRA had the ear of the press, they weren't going away and they had this huge membership, and so we should engage with them – the senior guys from CAMRA in particular.

When Allied launched a new 'premium' cask ale in 1976, Harvey made sure CAMRA's National Executive were with them every step of the way.

> We organised tastings across the South, inviting the mayor, local dignitaries, press and CAMRA branches. It was a hot summer, which meant some of the landlords struggled to present it at its best, but we pulled it off – it was a huge success ... I also organised a trip to Burton upon Trent for members of the CAMRA National Executive and a bunch of journalists ... There was always a risk that CAMRA wouldn't behave themselves and would disdain what we were trying to do, but it went off like a dream. They travelled up on the train and were whisked to the brewery in a luxury coach. I think they appreciated being asked along – it felt like a breakthrough to us, and to them.

Thereafter a full-page advertisement for Draught Burton Ale became a regular fixture in *What's Brewing*, even as the editorial continued to criticise the 'frightening stranglehold' of the big brewers.[15]

Douglas Strachan, head of Allied's beer division in 1978, said at the time: 'The whole industry was too slow to react to CAMRA ... We missed the point that CAMRA made beer news again.' He set about making Allied look less monopolistic by decentralising and reviving twenty or so old brewery brands across the country, many of which began, once again, to produce their own regional cask ales.[16]

By giving up some ground, Allied and the other Big Six companies had done something very clever: though neither Milward-Oliver nor Harvey believe that this was a cynical strategy on the part of the Big Six brewers, it left them poised to divide CAMRA and conquer it.

                                     🍺

At the National Consumer Congress in September 1976, chairman Michael Young (later Baron Young of Dartington) held CAMRA up as an example and, chatting with the then chair, Chris Holmes, declared it 'the most successful consumer campaign in Western Europe'.[17] This became part of CAMRA's official legend, and was repeated often. Meanwhile, in 1977 John Young, chairman of Young's in Wandsworth, south London, said: 'Thanks to CAMRA, the clock has been turned back . . . We simply cannot meet the demand.'[18]

It was true that, in only a few years, CAMRA had taken a vague catchphrase – 'real ale' – and given it sufficient meaning and weight such that huge companies dared not apply it incorrectly to their products. They had turned 30,000 disparate grumblers into a more or less organised army of volunteers and campaigners. The rot had been stopped, and breweries such as Young's and Fuller's were no longer simply under threat but were booming. It was possible to find cask-conditioned beer in every corner of the country without too much trouble, when only a few years earlier it had required the sharing of intelligence between enthusiasts.

It is hardly surprising that some CAMRA members began to suggest, tentatively, that the battle had been won. This kind of talk signalled the beginning of CAMRA's first crisis.

As early as 1975, Michael Hardman was declaring the future rosy for real ale and suggesting that it was time for CAMRA to push on and begin to repurpose itself as a more generalist beer consumer group, lobbying government for clearer labelling.[19] Having been united around one well-defined aim, there was suddenly room to breathe and talk and, at that point, for divisions to emerge. *What's Brewing*, which, in its early days, had recounted one scandal or triumph after another, began to fill up with bickering point-counterpoint letters and articles on the minutiae of policy. This is a typical exchange from 1976:

> Fanatics of all kinds always annoy me and I must therefore comment on your correspondent . . . who wrote of his CAMRA colleagues drinking 'pressurised muck' at their local as if they are on a level with Judas Iscariot. [D.C. Hall, in the March issue.]

> I didn't think I'd ever see the day when I would read a spirited defence of fizz from a CAMRA member . . . I despair at the idea of any CAMRA member regularly drinking fizz because it is sometimes inconvenient to drink real ale . . . It is the very fanaticism (purism would be a better word) of many CAMRA members that has held back the tide and retained real ale for us. [Brian M. Desmond, responding in April.]

Other debates centred around whether the Campaign should or shouldn't focus on social issues such as class, race and sexuality, and on pub decor and the banning of Northern-style 'sparklers', a device that puts creamy heads on pints as they are pulled. People even began to debate whether Watney's were all that bad. The running of the Campaign itself, slowly growing into a sizeable bureaucracy with an office and more than ten employees, and the membership fees of 30,000 members in its coffers, also became a hot topic, and its democratic processes and spending habits were called into question by members. Finally, in 1977 a row broke out which was both bitter and utterly boring to anyone not engaged in it. The subject was an obscure technical issue – the use of 'air pressure' to dispense beer.

This particular debate prompted Richard Boston, once an important supporter of CAMRA, to say, with some impatience: 'When someone gets round to writing the history of fatuous arguments, their discussion will surely deserve a prominent place alongside those of the most pedantic of medieval theologians.' He too thought the Campaign had achieved its aims, and that this bickering represented the Campaign's death throes: 'In the past, CAMRA have done a magnificent job. That is the trouble. They have done the job. On the major issues the polemical battles with the brewers have been fought. In so far as it ever will be, the information has been put across to the public.'[20]

While the more involved members bickered with each other, those who had joined with less serious intent, perhaps also feeling that the job was done, quietly let their memberships expire. John Green, the Campaign's first employee and chief administrator, recalled that rising membership fees, propping up the newspaper, head office and secretariat, were also a problem:

> By the time I left, membership was at 30,000, but it took a dip
> when the membership fee went up. When it was a pound, it was
> quite easy to recruit new members. You'd give them a nudge
> and say, 'Oi, give us a quid,' and they'd join on the spot. It got
> harder when the fee went up to two quid, then four, then eight.
> No one wanted to hand over eight pounds on the spot. Also, a
> lot of those casual members wouldn't bother renewing without
> anyone to remind them.

From a high of 30,000 members in 1976, CAMRA's numbers slowly dwindled until, in 1978, it had slipped as far as 22,000[21] and high-profile National Executive and founder members began to drift away. With tensions over CAMRA Real Ale Investments continuing, Terry Pattinson resigned from the board of CAMRAIL in 1976. At the same time, Christopher Hutt was under constant fire from those within the Campaign, as this December 1976 article from *What's Brewing* made clear.

> If a journalist hostile to CAMRA had wandered into the
> Campaign's southern regional conference last month, he could

> have sold a story to the *Morning Advertiser* headlined with some
> justification: 'Big row over CAMRA pubs – members say close
> them down' . . . For when CAMRA Investments . . . came up on
> the agenda, the quiet Sunday-morning session at Bournemouth
> suddenly became heated and there were few good words to be
> said for the company.

Members barracked Hutt, complaining about the siting of the
pubs, the quality of the service, their support for CAMRA's ideals and
the 'lavish' expenditure of members' money on refurbishments.

From June 1977, the satirical political gossip magazine *Private
Eye* turned its gaze on CAMRA, beginning with a short report
exposing what its editors evidently saw as the hypocrisy represented by the installation of fruit machines in CAMRAIL pubs.[22]
A letter in the following issue, from one 'Virgil Skunt', aired the
Campaign's dirty laundry less subtly. He rebuffed *Private Eye*'s
suggestion that CAMRAIL was 'ailing' before suggesting that, for
real dirt, the magazine should look at the supposedly wasteful,
self-serving National Executive.[23] For months afterwards, *Private
Eye*'s 'real ale correspondents' (notably 'Grotney Spewman') would
continue to needle the Campaign's 'drastically emotional'[24] National
Executive by providing detailed accounts of their behaviour, often
accompanied by unflattering pen portraits. Michael Hardman,
they alleged, was a drunk, unpopular within the Campaign and
prone to pinching women's bottoms; 'odious and barrel-shaped',[25]
hypocritical and flatulent. The *Eye* also reported that he and Roger
Protz had grappled with each other at a meeting.[26] This last dig
finally prompted a breezily good-natured letter, signed by both
men, suggesting that *Private Eye* might have 'gone too far' and
denying outright everything except the flatulence.[27] Despite these
denials, the stories were damaging and bred paranoia at CAMRA's
head office.

By the end of the decade, Hutt, who had once been CAMRA's
intellectual powerhouse, came to have his detractors. Speaking to

us recently, one long-serving activist growled: 'He should write a sequel to his book – *The Death of the English Pub: My Contribution*.' CAMRAIL became Midsummer Inns in 1983, when the final ties to CAMRA were broken off, and Hutt himself left to found Unicorn Inns in 1984.

Michael Hardman resigned from CAMRA in 1977, after three years as a permanent employee: 'I got pissed off with people taking it too seriously – taking themselves seriously. By then, the bearded hippy stereotype had taken hold, and there were a lot of these over-earnest people about, suddenly.'[28] Graham Lees also drifted away, resigning from the National Executive during the 'air pressure' debate,[29] cropping up occasionally in *What's Brewing* with articles about German beer (he moved to Munich) or bad-tempered, grandfatherly polemics demanding that members pull themselves together and *do* something.

Sales of the CAMRA *Good Beer Guide* also began to drop off. In the first few years of its life, it sold many more copies than there were members and continued to be printed in runs of 100,000 copies until the 1980 edition. In that year, 20,000 copies went unsold, causing the Campaign serious financial difficulty.[30] With real ale much more widely available and easier to find, there was perhaps no longer the same need for it and, in 1981, only 60,000 copies were printed.[31] 'We worked bloody hard to keep it afloat,' said Barrie Pepper, resentful of suggestions that anyone was profiting from serving on the National Executive. 'There was a lad who was in charge of expenses, and if you went to him with receipts for thirty quid, he'd give you six copies of the *Good Beer Guide*, ten T-shirts and say, here you are, sell those, that's your expenses.'

CAMRA's new generation of leaders weren't happy with the lack of direction. Joe Goodwin, a perpetually beaming, bearded young man, was chair from 1979 to 1980 and a close friend of Barrie Pepper's:

> Joe was a lovely bloke. He had a permanent grin and there were always three darts sticking out of his top pocket. He was

Lancastrian ... and had this mission to visit every football ground in the country. He'd turn up in pubs all over the place, like the time he arrived in my local on a Friday night on his way from a game in Stockport ... [and say] 'Have you got a bed, Barrie?' Then he'd look round and find someone to play darts with.

In his official capacity, Goodwin often sounded like an officer calling for retreating troops to return to the front line, as he did in a piece that ran under the headline DANGER OF THINKING BATTLES ARE OVER:

Superficially it might be argued that the Campaign has now achieved most of its aims and could be wound up without harm ... Nothing could be further from the truth. If CAMRA ceased to project a loud and effective consumer voice, the improvements in the availability of real ale in most of Britain could – and would – be wiped out in much less than the eight years it has taken to achieve them. The early and mid-1970s could still be written off as a small hiccup in the relentless march of bright and keg bitters and phoney lagers towards uniformity.[32]

Despite Goodwin's efforts, membership kept falling and several branches, such as the one in North Devon, popped out of existence.[33]

But Goodwin was right. Perhaps a little too late, one reason for the big brewers' willingness to appease CAMRA by reducing their promotion of keg bitter became clear: they were slowly shifting their attention to lager. In 1976, a spokesman for Allied Breweries indicated which way the wind was blowing: 'Forget kegs and real ale. They're all peanuts compared to lager.'[34]

Lager had been drunk and brewed in Britain since the nineteenth century, but had remained rather a niche product. In 1960 it had just a one per cent share of the UK beer market[35] – a seemingly tiny amount, but enough to excite the attention of the money men. If colder, fizzier keg bitter had been seen as a way to attract younger drinkers and women, then lager was all that and more: not brown like Grandma's dining table but gleaming gold; not evocative of the shires or grimy terraces but of continental holidays, sophistication and wealth.

By 1975, lager represented almost 20 per cent of the market;[36] by 1980 it had taken nearly a third, and showed no sign of slowing down.[37] It achieved this success despite the fact that much of what passed for lager in Britain was either of the 'bastard' variant (brewed like ale but lighter in colour and chilled, and often given an ersatz-German name, such as 'Grünhalle' from Greenall's), or a foreign brand applied to a beer brewed in the UK 'under licence'. These beers were also much more costly, in most cases, although generally relatively weak, the inflated prices perhaps adding to the air of exclusivity and sophistication. They were, as, much later, the Stella Artois slogan would put it, 'reassuringly expensive'. Lager appealed especially to the Big Six, who could afford to invest in state-of-the-art lager-brewing plants, leaving their regional competitors in the dust.

There was no single trigger for the sudden upward lurch in lager sales from the late 1960s onward. People sometimes put it down to hot weather; to the rise in foreign holidays; or to relentless hard selling by the breweries. We have not been able to find a convincing correlation with climate or overseas travel, however, and as for marketing, though the curve mirrors lager sales, it *follows* the increase rather than leading the way.[38] Where we have found a possible connection is in the coming of age of the post-war baby boom, which led to an increase from the early 1960s onward in the proportion of the population aged between eighteen and twenty-four.[39]

This generation were better educated and more socially mobile than their predecessors. Some (like the founders of CAMRA, perhaps) reacted to social mobility by embracing the signifiers of working-class cultures – mild and bitter, games of darts – all the more closely. Most, though, were happy to leave behind pits, factories and terraced houses. Lager was a modern drink, which went with Danish furniture, fondue sets and holidays in the sun. It was simply, somehow, *cleaner*.

People *liked* lager, and the fact that CAMRA did not made the organisation seem rather parochial and backward-looking. They'd been able to offer a clear alternative to keg bitter – something similar yet better, purer and more authentic – but could not provide the same for lager. Some of their figureheads, such as Roger Protz and Graham Lees, acknowledged that there was such a thing as good lager, but it was only to be found in Prague or Bavaria.[40] This opened the door to a new category of beer which would combine the arcane lore of 'real ale' with the sophisticated appeal of Continental lager: it would be known as 'world beer'.

Foreign beer took its time arriving in the UK. Though travellers had enjoyed exotic European oddities for centuries,[41] xenophobia continued to inform British attitudes to foreign beer. Belgian beer was considered dangerously strong – 'loopy juice' – and was blamed for the rampaging hooliganism of English football fans in Ostend in 1964.[42] American beer was viewed as uniformly and downright awful.[43] German beer was admirably pure, if rather cold and fizzy. There were cheap flights and ferry trips to German and Belgian beer festivals[44] but, on the whole, the point of those was to get drunk with 'the lads' rather than to appreciate the ale.

In 1974, an event called the World Beer Show took place at Olympia in west London, but did little to challenge the prevailing view that foreign beer was colder, blander and more homogeneous than British ale: there were Japanese lagers, Spanish lagers, German lagers, Scandinavian lagers, Czech lagers . . .[45] It was a demonstration of the complete global dominance of the pilsner style. From the point of view of the British press, the most interesting feature of the festival seems, in fact, to have been a sex shop selling inflatable dolls and 'marital aids' which, at one point, was raided by police.[46]

However, the same year Belgian Trappist beer appeared for the first time on the shelves of British shops when Arthur Rackham, a company named after its founder, began to import Chimay and sell it in its chain of off-licences.[47] Made by the monks of the Abbey of

Scourmont, it had immediate cult appeal, albeit founded in part on its potency, and was also 'CAMRA approved' because it was neither pasteurised nor filtered and was 'refermented in the bottle'.

Though Chimay and a handful of other interesting beers, such as the intensely bitter Czech Pilsner Urquell, were fairly readily available, it wasn't until 1977 and the publication of a book written by a Yorkshireman that the floodgates really opened.

Michael Jackson was born in Leeds, West Yorkshire, in 1942, to a Lithuanian-Jewish father, Jack Jackson (born Isaac Jakowitz[48]), and an English mother. Jackson grew up in Huddersfield and, in an autobiographical short story written in 2003, he described an upbringing that featured both British cod 'n' chips and Jewish 'gefilte' fish.[49] Though his parents were teetotal, he drank from an early age, working out a way for him and his friends to get a pint at the pub while they were supposed to be running cross-country.[50] He went to work as a journalist straight from school, at the age of sixteen, and quickly became a confirmed beer drinker: 'Newspapermen talked beer, drank beer and wrote about wine.'[51] In 1958, his first year working on a local paper, he proposed a column about pubs, although he was still too young legally to visit them. Given the go-ahead even so, he collaborated with an older colleague on a series of fifty or so articles under the heading 'This is Your Pub'.[52] As his career in journalism progressed, he ceased to be a 'pale-faced kid' with 'gloomy Slavic features' and 'bubbly curls'[53] and became someone 'medium-sized, solid, with a tendency to bulge in the middle'.[54]

After years working as a journalist, dabbling in writing about beer when he could, he finally found an opportunity to discuss the topic at length when, in 1976, a fellow writer failed to deliver a manuscript for a large-format illustrated book called *The English Pub* to Quarto Publishing. Jackson was drafted in as a replacement by 'an anglophile American' at the publishing house. The resulting book was understandably rushed and rather superficial, padded out with large photographs and collages, with rather too much attention paid, for example, to pub signs. Though entertaining, its real value was as a calling card for his next, much more personal project: *The World Guide to Beer*.

The *World Guide* was a hefty, luxurious volume designed to look very much at home next to the potpourri and the *Reader's Digest* on the middle-class coffee table. It was published by Mitchell Beazley, whose stable also included *The World Atlas of Wine* by Hugh Johnson, and was an attempt to 'elevate beer to wine status', whatever that means.[55] Jackson explained the thinking behind it in a later interview:

> I thought, it's very good that CAMRA is fighting for British tradition, but what about the tradition of these other countries? ... I think the motivation was almost like ... those musicologists like Alan Lomax who went down to the Mississippi Delta in the 1950s and recorded old bluesmen before they died. I wanted to kind of record Belgian beer before those breweries didn't exist any more.[56]

Unlike Richard Boston, who would often say he preferred gin to beer and whose book *Beer and Skittles* was cobbled together from weekly newspaper columns, Jackson approached his subject with the zeal of a serious investigative journalist. He visited breweries, telephoned brewers and devoured technical and historical texts, and so became a true expert – *the* authority on beer. As a result, *The World Guide to Beer* seemed revelatory, exposing many readers to fascinating and previously unsuspected beer cultures all over the world.

Jackson broke the news that there was much more to German beer than lager, and that even that broad category contained numerous subtleties and sub-varieties. He shot down the theory that all American beer was atrocious, finding something positive to say about light lager, identifying regional oddities and highlighting the 'idiosyncratic' beers of the then recently revived Anchor Steam Brewing Company in San Francisco. He likewise reminded his readers of the full variety of British beer beyond the usual bitter and mild, kegged or otherwise. Like a latter-day William Herschel, peering into a pint glass rather than up at the stars, Jackson tracked down, tasted and classified hundreds of brews, single-handedly inventing a now pervasive framework of beer 'styles', from 'Russian Stout' to 'Süddeutsche Weizenbier'.

Jackson was rightly proud of his achievement and the book's success. Brian Eno is supposed to have said: 'The first Velvet Underground album only sold 10,000 copies, but everyone who bought it formed a band', and Jackson's work occupies a similar place in the development of an alternative beer culture in both Britain and America, mentioned time and again by brewers, bar owners and later generations of writers.

Jackson's book debuted, ahead of its official publication date, at the 1977 national CAMRA beer festival.[57] Many of the Campaign's members and officials were beer enthusiasts first and foremost, and found his vision of 'world beer' inspiring. There had been imported Schumacher Alt beer from Düsseldorf at the Cambridge Beer Festival as far back as 1974, but the pace picked up after 1977 when articles on interesting foreign beer began to appear in *What's Brewing*, starting with a piece by Frank Baillie, author of *The Beer Drinker's Companion*, which acknowledged its debt to Jackson's *World Guide*.[58]

In August 1979, the Salisbury Arms, CAMRA Investments' Cambridge pub, began to sell Hannen Alt, also from Düsseldorf, and rebranded, perhaps predictably, as 'Real German Ale'. Then, in September, the Great British Beer Festival included, for the first time, an international beer stand. 'I suspect some purists will say we should have nothing to do with this,' said Roger Protz at the time. 'But rubbish is being foisted upon the British drinking public. We should have this quality in British pubs.'[59] But, commencing a debate which still bubbles away today, some baulked at the prices of these exclusive imports: Anchor Steam Beer, an early American 'craft beer', was £1.65 a bottle, compared to an average price of 38p for a pint of real ale.[60]

There soon followed a small boom in independent beer importers, many of which are still operating today, such as Cave Direct founded in Welling, near Bexley, Kent, in 1979. When Brian Gillespie was offered an early redundancy package with an index-linked pension, he decided to invest in his passion, which was wine. His son, Colin, who now runs the company, told us how beer came into the picture:

> The idea was to tour around Europe – France and Germany, mainly – to bring back wine for restaurants and wine clubs. They often used to go to Belgium, his wife being Belgian. On one occasion in a Belgian supermarket, they happened to bump into the Riva brewery people, offering their speciality beers.[61]

At first, they moved slowly, bringing in a few cases of bottled beer and selling them alongside wine. Eventually, in 1983, they opened a shop with 'a small range of Belgian beers tucked in a corner'. There proved to be a large and increasing demand for such beer, with customers asking for particular brands, until there were more than 200 varieties of beer on offer.

Meanwhile, a handful of 'real ale pubs' such as the Mason's Arms near Windermere, Cumbria – 'a whitewashed house with slate floors, a leaded fireplace and, on the walls, five originals by Alfred Wainwright, the guru of fell walking', according to Michael Jackson[62] – also began to broaden their horizons. It was run by Nigel Stevenson, who was something of a 'beer freak':

> I started with a Kölsch beer in the early 1980s. This came from a composite wholesaler called Lakes Wine, and was the only 'unusual' beer they had. Sometime after that, I started to increase the number of beers we stocked to maybe ten. Then Allied Breweries and Grand Metropolitan [Watney's] began to run import companies of their own. I went to depots on the outskirts of London to collect cases of beer including Tusker, Henry Weinhard's Private Reserve, Lutèce Bière de Garde and Grimbergen Dubbel. Then I came across a chap based in Manchester who used to live in Brussels and he stocked Belgian beer. The scales were lifted from my eyes! I got draught Liefmans Kriek in the late 1980s via this route.

The company in question was Interale, run by David and Ann Sherry of Macclesfield, whose advertisements in CAMRA's *What's Brewing* boasted the 'biggest directly imported range of Belgian beers ... more than thirty at present', and screamed 'WE'LL GET ANY AVAILABLE BELGIAN BEER – PROMISE!'[63] Nigel Stevenson:

> I eventually* bought [Interale] and supplied people around the
> country wholesale. Before long, I was selling two hundred beers
> at the pub.

With an infrastructure in place,[64] strong, strange and distinctive imported beers began to make their way towards the mainstream. In 1985, the CAMRA *Good Beer Guide* included a long feature by various authors on beer around the world. Its tone was part tongue-in-cheek xenophobia, part serious analysis, with an emphasis on products which, in one way or another, fit the Campaign's idea of 'real', i.e. unpasteurised, with live yeast in the container.[65] Founder member of CAMRA Graham Lees, long a fan of German beer, contributed a section on West Germany, following in the footsteps of Michael Jackson. Charlie Papazian, best known for his contribution to American home-brewing culture, provided an update on an American 'microbrewery' scene which had begun to blossom in the few years since the publication of *The World Guide to Beer*. Meanwhile, Michael Jackson's distilled version of the *World Guide*, 1982's *Pocket Guide to Beer*, found its way into the baggage of more than one young traveller.

※

Battered, confused and maligned as CAMRA might have been by the early 1980s, it had achieved a great deal. Cask-conditioned ale was never again to be the everyday drink of 'the people', but CAMRA could claim to have 'saved it' as a niche product. Something, surely, to be proud of. It had proved that a market existed for beers other than the fairly bland products of the biggest manufacturers, and it had

---

* by 1986

played its part in bringing into existence a great many new pubs and breweries willing to serve them. It had also put in place a framework for the appreciation of all kinds of beer, not just real ale, with a calendar of festivals, multiple publications and a 'social network'.

SEVEN

BREWERIES, BREWERIES, EVERYWHERE

By 1988, when we sold up, we were spending £100,000 a year on pub pianists.

David Bruce[1]

The first time he saw what became the Goose and Firkin, he didn't just look at it – he actually broke in. He pushed the door very hard and walked straight in and wandered around.

Louise Bruce[2]

As the 1980s began, CAMRA was struggling with falling membership and public image; big-brewery lager was seizing a huge slice of the beer market, and Britain was entering a recession that would last for fifteen months. Even so, the microbrewery movement continued to blossom. By one estimate, sixteen new breweries opened in 1979, eighteen in 1980 and thirty-six in 1981. New openings slowed down to a still remarkable thirty-two in 1982, many of them, after a sluggish start, in London.[3]

Most of these new breweries were, frankly, very similar in approach. They tended to be conservative, brewing bitters and best bitters to meet a nostalgic demand for the defunct products of larger local breweries taken over and closed down by the Big Six in the preceding decades. A handful also brewed mild, and some had stronger 'old' or 'winter' ales. In general, they traded on their connection to a particular town, city or region, often with an eye on tourist markets.[4]

Many were set up by former big-brewery men: Simon Whitmore, who founded Butcombe, had worked for both Guinness and Courage; Aston Manor of Birmingham was run by a group of Ansell's brewers who had been made redundant; and Old Mill of Goole in Humberside was founded by Bryan Wilson, who began his brewing career in 1954 but was made redundant by Watney's in 1982. Stories like these abound.

Redundancy, whether in the brewing industry or elsewhere, is something of a common thread. There were 187,000 redundancies nationwide in 1979 but, as the recession bit early in 1980, that number more than doubled to 494,000.[5] With few jobs available, and their redundancy cheques in their pockets, many chose to indulge their interest in 'real ale' and set up breweries. Goacher of Kent is one example of a brewery which began life in this way.

Others were simply caught up in the excitement – keen home brewers or CAMRA members, or both, who dreamed of escaping office or factory jobs in favour of something with a little more glamour.

What many new breweries of the period had in common was advice from Peter Austin of Ringwood. His brewery installation and consultancy company, which had grown out of his work with Penrhos in 1977, was by 1986 responsible for some twenty-seven breweries, and he came to be known as 'the father of the new brewery revolution'.[6] Many similar firms sprang up around the same time, such as Inn Brewing, run by former Whitbread men Robin Richards and Peter Shardlow, which installed nineteen breweries between 1982 and 1986.[7]

Many were very small indeed, and a considerable number operated out of, and brewed for, single pubs. Richard Hall of the Globe Inn,

Dyfed, told Brian Glover that his small brewery was a way of offering cheaper beer in the wake of the 1981 Budget, which put 5p extra duty on the price of a pint:

> Thus committed, I then had to find equipment and learn how to brew. Fortunately, I met Peter Shotton of maltsters Munton and Fison, and he gave me a two-hour lesson on brewing in my car, parked outside an office in London.[8]

This in itself was a noteworthy revival of an older tradition – that of the 'home-brew house'. Where once most towns and villages had more than one pub or inn brewing on site (there were almost 50,000 breweries in 1750[9]), by 1973 when Frank Baillie conducted his survey, only five remained, with several having blinked out of life in the preceding few years. Baillie listed the All Nations Inn in Telford, Shropshire; the Blue Anchor in Helston, Cornwall; Mrs Pardoe's Old Swan Brewery, near Wolverhampton; the Three Tuns at Bishop's Castle in Shropshire; and Traquair House in Peeblesshire. The All Nations was typical:

> Mrs Lewis does all the brewing and has done so for the last thirty-eight years . . . Once a week, when most good citizens are in the depths of their slumber, Mrs Lewis rises in the small hours and commences operations at 3 a.m. . . . The vats hold about 260 gallons, and Mrs Lewis used to move the liquor from one vat to the next by means of a hand ladle.

Throughout the late 1970s, these odd survivors were joined by a handful of new 'home-brew' pubs, but there were still a paltry nine by 1979.[10] Just a few years later, in 1985, there were to be more than seventy pubs brewing their own beer on site. The roots of this sudden boom can be traced to the arrival on the scene, and instant success, of the Firkin chain of brewpubs, whose story showed that 'alternative' beer did not *need* CAMRA to succeed, and, in many ways, prefigured that of the more modern 'craft breweries'.

David Bruce is a more complex character than his constant smile and tendency to 'work the room' might suggest. 'He is incredibly energetic, but the funny thing is, he gives so much in his work that sometimes, at home, he just collapses. He can be almost morose,' said Louise, his wife and business partner of forty years, with a mix of affection and exasperation. 'I think all entrepreneurs have baggage,' said Bruce himself, 'and here's mine.'"

Bruce was born in India in July 1948. His father was an officer in the Army Intelligence Corps but, stricken with polio, became headmaster of a boarding school in Shimla. Bruce's mother was a twenty-six-year-old widow who went to India from Britain with her baby daughter and took a job as matron at the school. Almost inevitably, the two fell in love and married, and later, once David was born, the family moved back to England, where his father became headmaster of the Queen Elizabeth College for Disabled Children. When Bruce's father died in his forties, the family were left in genteel poverty: 'I'm certain that the fact that I didn't have a rich daddy, or any daddy, is what made me so determined to succeed.'

Unable to pass maths O-level at the age of seventeen, while his friends were going on to university Bruce took a place on a management trainee scheme at Courage Barclay and Simonds in Reading. He had no particular interest in beer: 'It was just a job.' As an eighteen-year-old in 1966, he moved into 'digs' and began his working life as a white-coated, 6 a.m. shift brewer, brewing 'beautiful, yummy beers' such as Courage Best Bitter and Imperial Russian Stout: '[It] was real "craft brewing" . . . I was a wooden-spoon brewer. I'd never get a job as a 'proper' brewer . . . but I could certainly brew.'

As a trainee, he was also given a solid grounding in pub management, sales, wine and spirit importing and even whisky blending. In an organisation mostly run by former military men ('Brigadier This, Colonel That'), Bruce's tendency to walk around with his hands in his pockets earned one formal reprimand; another warning was triggered by a piece of crude graffiti about his manager.

Nevertheless, at the end of his training, they offered him a job, but not, as he had hoped, as a regional pub manager:

> Instead, they sent me to Bristol, to George's Brewery, and stuck me in this office with brown and cream walls and green radiators. This was just at the time when they'd got a computer to run the payroll, but they didn't trust it and still wanted everything copying into this huge Dickensian ledger, so that's what I did.

Before long, a better opportunity presented itself through a family connection. Bruce's uncle by marriage, Dick Theakston, was a doctor living and working in Yorkshire, and distantly related to the Theakston brewing family of Masham. His uncle mentioned to him that Paul Theakston's father had died, and his uncle had retired, leaving Paul, who had little experience, to run the brewery alone. Bruce and Paul Theakston hit it off immediately and so, at the age of twenty-three, Bruce became his new head brewer. The two young men shared a cottage on Masham's market square and were sufficiently close that, when Christopher Hutt visited while researching his book, he assumed the two men were related.[12]

This perfect arrangement collapsed when Paul Theakston invited a cousin who had recently been made redundant to step in as company chairman. Bruce was aware that CAMRA were beginning to create some interest in real ale. 'Do you think I could ever have shares in your brewery?' he asked Michael Theakston, who bluntly rejected the idea. 'At that point I thought, fine, fuck you – I'll go off and start my own brewery,' said Bruce.

When he married Louise in February 1973, he was unemployed, and, out of desperation, took a job as a catering manager with a Northern nightclub impresario, who was then bought out by Mecca. He summarises this experience with one of his favourite words: 'Nightmare!'

By now firmly on the 'nasty side of leisure,'[13] Bruce took a role with nightclub and pub company Charram, on the recommendation of a Masham drinking pal, TV presenter Richard Whiteley.

Charram was owned partly by Bass Charrington and partly by a group called Rambutan. Responsible for twenty-eight establishments from Scunthorpe to Newport, Bruce, who had by this time moved to London, found the role exhausting. The time had come, he thought, to start his own business, and so, borrowing £5,000 from an acquaintance, he bought a 20 per cent share of a company called Leisure Sales Development (LSD). It didn't work out, though, and he once again said 'fuck you' and moved on. His next job was with the Star Group, which owned pubs and nightclubs across the North, and meant Bruce was hardly ever at home. He was sometimes reduced to tears by the pressure. On the phone to Louise from a hotel one night, almost at breaking point, he told her that he had worked out the problem: he simply couldn't bear working for other people. 'Then quit,' she replied.

Some more baggage: Bruce had started running when he was nine years old, desperate to shake a nickname he had picked up at school – 'Jumbo'. Years later, while unemployed, he filled his days by putting on a tracksuit and going for long-distance runs from his home in Battersea to every corner of London, trying to work out what to do next. He considered cafés, sandwich bars and restaurants; several years before they took off, he even thought about a wine bar. Then, one day, he was stopped in his tracks.

> I ran to the labour exchange in Battersea to sign on and collect my dole money, and then along the Embankment as far as Southwark Bridge. I was on my way home when I saw this pub, completely derelict, with weeds growing out of the roof, boarded up.

The Duke of York, a grand Victorian corner pub on Borough Road, which had been run for many years by Truman's, was decorated with green carvings of grimacing, pagan green men, and curling ivy, but its stained-glass windows were covered with boards and it was in a state of near collapse, with rotten floors, vermin, no mains water and a leaking roof from which the lead had been stripped.[14] Standing on the pavement, panting, in the shadow of a railway bridge with trains thundering overhead, Bruce saw the potential. According to Louise Bruce, with his usual impatience and determination he tested the door and broke in to look around, before running all the way home in a state of great excitement. 'I've just seen this fantastic corner site where I'm going to start a brewery!' he announced. At a viewing with the City of London Corporation's head surveyor, Bruce shook hands on the deal, agreeing an annual rent of less than £10,000 – 'peanuts'.

Although Louise had a good job and was able to keep them both, they estimated that they needed £23,000 to refurbish the pub and build a brewery. With no private fortune to fall back on, they would have to borrow. Louise took David's half-thought-out ideas and turned them into something like a business plan. After approaching several banks, whose managers thought the idea a non-starter, they secured a £10,000 loan from Lloyds, sourcing the rest by borrowing from breweries Bass Charrington and Shepherd Neame under so-called 'free trade' terms. Existing in an ethical grey area, the 'free trade loan' was a cunning way for bigger breweries to assert control over pubs outside their own empires, obliging them to sell a certain amount of the lending brewery's beer each year.

More money was saved with a kind of non-renovation: 'I decided to gut the place and make it into a boozer,' Bruce recalled in 1981, 'with lots of wood, brass and glass. I cannot stand droopy red lampshades and green Dralon button-backed banquettes.' But he was also inspired by a particular Watney's pub – the Clarence, in Whitehall – which had just been decorated in a similar style, and even hired the builder responsible. We're now familiar with a 'shabby chic' approach, but at the time not only was it something new, but it also expressed the essence of 'pubbiness'.

With advice from Peter Austin, who he called on spec, Bruce built a five-barrel plant in a space at the bottom of the stairs. He also renamed the pub, as part of its fresh start: 'Goose and Firkin came from the Theakston's archive, which listed a pub of that name which was closed down and delicensed years ago.' Finally, having been told that it was bad luck to paint pubs green, Bruce followed his contrary streak by doing exactly that.

The night before the pub opened in July 1979, he and Louise were still cleaning and hanging curtains. One City of London expert who had reviewed their business plan had dismissed it as hopeless. Just in case he was right, they had kept back enough cash to pay for a one-way flight to Australia.

🌺

The next morning, David Bruce left the pub to collect some change and, when he returned shortly before opening time, he was astounded by what he saw: 'There were queues at both doors . . . We took as much on our first night as we'd expected to take in the entire week, and it never let up.' The mob was made up of medical students, 'gorgeous nurses . . . smart boys from the City in suits', and south London locals. Bruce insisted when we spoke to him that much of what made the Firkin brand came from these customers. Though by his own admission he had always had a puerile sense of humour, and is not shy of cuss words, it had never occurred to him that 'Firkin' might have a double meaning until customers began to joke about having 'another Firkin pint', or saying it was 'Firkin good beer'. It was

David Bruce, founder of the Firkin chain of brewpubs, pictured in 1986.

also a customer, Jimmy, the nightwatchman at the nearby London College of Printing, who first lifted the lid on the old piano and introduced music to the Goose and Firkin.

Brewing at the pub could be a challenge, not least because the gent's toilet was directly above the brewery.

> When they were peeing, blokes would shove their cigarette ends
> into the vents and they'd fall down into the brewery, so I had
> to make sure to keep the lids on everything. Once, I remember
> the urinals got so clogged with cigarette butts that they started
> overflowing and coming through the ceiling. I had to run around
> dragging tarpaulins over my open fermenting vessels or else I
> wouldn't have any beer to sell in a week's time.

Despite the rather chaotic and improvisatory nature of the operation, Bruce remained furiously ambitious – he wanted to be a millionaire by the age of forty – and, by the beginning of 1980, was already making plans to expand.[15] In February of that year, Bruce's Brewery placed an advertisement in the trade press, seeking managers for a new pub, in characteristic style.

IF YOU ARE:
1. CAPABLE of maximising profit from £¼ million turnover.
2. IMAGINATIVE in your catering ideas and confident of developing food sales to at least £1,500 p.w. (boring pub grub not allowed!)
3. EXPERIENCED in handling and enthusiastic about real ale.
4. SEEKING a five-figure remuneration package.
5. KEEN to develop traditional boozers rather than droopy, red-lampshaded saloon bars.
6. PROUD of at least three trade references which will be taken up prior to appointment.

THEN: Write today in confidence and convince me that you must be on my shortlist.[16]

The premises he had his eye on was in Lewisham. If potential investors had thought Borough Road a poor location, then Lewisham, deep in south-east London where it begins to feel more like Kent, was an even less likely prospect. The property was a 'scruffy old disco pub', in the words of Roger Protz, which Bruce transformed into a 'rollicking boozer'. With its brewing kit on show, occupying the space where strippers had once danced, and a resident pianist, a stuffed fox and an old pulpit for decoration,[17] it was soon filled with customers every night of the week. In 1986, reflecting on the popularity of his pubs, Bruce said:

> I madden my accountants ... every time we go and spend £250,000 on a pub, they ask me where are the customers coming from? I always say I don't know, but they'll be there . . . Wherever we open up, we seem to get the same sort of punters. The best description is that they appear totally classless and informal.[18]

Roger Protz disagreed with this assessment, however:

> [Most] of the people who pack the Firkins day after day are young and T-shirted, unconventional and sporting risqué badges. They are members of what has been loosely dubbed the 'lager generation'. But they are not drinking lager.[19]

Like many of the trendy breweries that would follow over the next thirty years, the Firkin pubs thrived partly because they charged a premium. Despite the fact that he had few transportation costs, and had cut the middleman out of the process, in 1979 a pint of Bruce's Borough Bitter at the Goose and Firkin cost 48p, which the *Financial Times* correspondent reckoned was about 3p more than a comparable beer at any other London pub.[20] The decision to charge this much was made at the very last minute before the Goose and Firkin opened.

> Someone said, 'What are we going to charge for a pint?' and I sent people out to check on a few pubs that were known to be expensive, including the Clarence, and then made our beer 10p

more per pint than the most expensive. I just thought we might
as well be the most expensive pub in London, and see if we could
make a bit more money. It wasn't a strategy, as such – just a sort
of whim.

But what were customers paying for? Was the beer of a particularly high quality? Michael Jackson found that, in general, Firkin
brews 'lacked complexity',[21] a gentle criticism that Bruce shrugged
off when we reminded him of it: 'I was just brewing pretty basic
beers for people to drink lots of, really.' At a time when people were
obsessing over the purity of their beer, Bruce was using malt extract
at the Goose and Firkin because the cellar was big but not big enough
to mash grains – a turn-off for the purists, but of no concern to
most drinkers. Similarly, he was not brewing 'real ale' according to
CAMRA's technical definition, and, in an article for *What's Brewing* in
1985, Roger Protz grappled with the issue of what he called 'a rather
itchy relationship' between Bruce and London CAMRA members,
concluding that the technical issues were not really the problem:

> [He has] built a small chain of riotously successful pubs that
> owes little to the Campaign ... the Firkins have carved out a
> loyal band of supporters who like hand-pumped beer, but who
> probably consider CAMRA members to be over-serious and
> pernickety about their ale.[22]

The money those affluent customers spent in the pubs was
invested back into the business, most obviously in purchasing new
pubs and fitting them with breweries. By 1987 there were eleven
brewpubs in the chain, as well as two without their own breweries.[23]
The Phoenix and Firkin in particular (1984) was a substantial
investment, and had Bruce working with the Camberwell Society
and the Southwark Environment Trust to renovate an old British
Rail ticket hall that had been destroyed in an arson attack in 1980.[24]
In yet another example of the active network in the 'alternative beer'
world, the suggestion for this venture came from Monty Python

member Terry Jones, who used to drink in the Goose and Firkin on his way home to Denmark Hill.

Bruce also invested, perhaps counter-intuitively, in a spin-off business which created competition for the Firkins by building and installing complete pub microbreweries under the name Bruwell. One notable customer was Allied Breweries, who opened a string of Firkin-like brewpubs.

They weren't the only ones: a decent-sized industry had developed around the design and fitting of small breweries. Sensing in the Firkins either a threat, an opportunity or both, Watney's began to employ other companies, such as Peter Austin and Partners, to install breweries in their 'Firkin-alike' Clifton Inns chain of brewpubs. Whitbread also jumped on the bandwagon. By 1986, CAMRA's *Good Beer Guide* was reporting a boom in brewpubs – almost extinct in the 1970s – with a total of seventy-six in operation around the country, a third of which were owned by Watney, Whitbread or Allied.

Bruce claimed not to be anxious. For one thing, he was confident in the value of his personal brand to the point of arrogance: 'The big brewers might be able to dress a pub like a Firkin,' he explained, 'but they don't have that loony element. I don't use architects or designers. I just stand there and wave my arms about: a chandelier here, a fan there.'[25] And anyway, easily bored – 'I'm like Mr Toad' – Bruce seems to have relished the competition, even joking, at one point, that he might set up his own rival chain – 'Kangaroo and Kilderkin, Parrot and Polypin, Heron and Hogshead' – just to keep things interesting.[26]

With the Firkin chain, David Bruce established an important principle: that younger, trendier consumers would buy relatively expensive beer as long as it was strong on brand and had a story behind it. Dogbolter wasn't so different to Theakston's Old Peculier, and Goose Bitter was hardly an exciting beer, but people loved the beaming Bruce, the opportunity to see him in his brewing overalls on the premises and the yarns and gags that came with every beer.

EIGHT

TASTE THE DIFFERENCE

> I think every beer should have a sensory flavour hook
> with which customers can identify. To me, it's part of
> brand identity. It moves beer into the sensory category.
> You can take that further by including balance,
> complexity, intensity and length of flavour. Suddenly
> you're talking about esoteric flavours that compete
> happily with wine.
>
> Sean Franklin[1]

For better or worse, in the early 1980s there came about one of the few genuine innovations in the recent history of British beer: the application of an approach to 'tasting' from the world of wine. After a decade or more of fretting over how to retain beer's essentially 'simple, honest' character in the face of an onslaught of interest from the moneyed middle class, some British beer enthusiasts began to expand their vocabulary. With a more 'sophisticated' language came rules, rituals and yes, a certain pretentiousness.

It is not that beer drinkers had not always been discerning. From 1938 to 1942, researchers from the social study group Mass Observation haunted pubs in Bolton, where they found that most people chose what to drink based on its price:

> There are, however, drinkers who do care for the quality of their beer, and who will congregate at pubs whose landlords keep the beer in good condition . . . And some will go out of their way to try a brew that is new to them.[2]

Andrew Campbell, in his 1956 *Book of Beer*, says of the various brands of strong ale that 'they are as different as clarets or burgundies from different vineyards'.[3] In passing, Campbell sets out an argument for tasting beer in the same way as wine, 'two or three brews at a time, sipping just a little and then washing off the tongue with distilled water'.[4] But attempts to put this into action were ridiculed, as when Egon Ronay hosted a beer-tasting event prior to the launch of his pub guide in 1969 and the *Financial Times* sent its anonymous diarist 'Observer' along. Under the headline BURP!, he wrote a dismissive piece which concluded: 'A wine man would have called the whole affair precocious.'[5] Later, the *Daily Mirror* accompanied a piece on CAMRA and 'beer snobbery' with a cartoon of a 'pseud' dipping his enormous nose into the froth on his pint, eyes closed, to appreciate its aroma.[6]

Perhaps out of self-consciousness, the conversation about beer did not generally run deep for many years to come. Des de Moor, in his 2011 essay 'The Language of Beer: a long journey',[7] noted that the beer writers of the 1970s rarely discussed flavour. Richard Boston, Frank Baillie, the editors of the CAMRA *Good Beer Guide* and even Michael Jackson tended to restrict themselves to general observations about the 'pleasantness' or otherwise of a given beer. This passage from Boston is typical:

> [Worthington] White Shield is quite strong . . . but not so strong as to have the sweetness that spoils many barley wines and other strong beers. It has a distinctive, dry flavour that is often described as nutty, and it's one of the world's great beers.[8]

'Nutty' is the only truly specific descriptor, and even that is reported second-hand. There is an appealing straightforwardness about such an attitude, but some of those championing beer felt that, as long as it was seen as 'just beer', it wouldn't get the respect it deserved. In their view, it needed 'elevating'.

Ian Nairn, no stranger to subtlety of expression or deep analysis when it came to architecture, was one of the first writers to adopt the new tone that came to characterise the appreciation of beer with these lines from his important 1974 *Sunday Times* article:

> [Draught beer] with luck has first a bouquet, like Adnams – the wine parallels are apt – then an immediate flavour and explosion at the back of the mouth as though the odd system of palate and uvula had suddenly become a sounding-board. To switch similes, it is something like the difference between Danish Blue and a ripe old Roquefort.

If he had written more about beer, perhaps at book length, he might have stolen a march on Michael Jackson. As it is, this essay was his longest work on the subject, and even he stopped short of describing the details of the aroma or flavours he experienced, though he went further than many others.

The change finally arrived with a shift in perspective when it came to thinking about hops. Hops are the green flowers of a plant called *Humulus lupulus,* part of the same family as cannabis, and are one of the key ingredients of beer as we know it today. In 1980, few beer drinkers, even 'serious' ones, knew a great deal about hops. Scientists had only just begun the work of understanding the hundreds of chemical compounds (e.g. linalool, myrcene) that make up the hop aroma,[*] and their research had yet to become common knowledge, so the flood of beer books from the late 1970s onward tended to repeat the same basic facts: hops have a preservative effect, make beer bitter and give it aroma. They might also mention one or two specific, 'classic' English varieties: Fuggles and Goldings. Even Michael Jackson, who explored the subject further than any other contemporary writer (outside the technical brewing journals) in his 1977 *World Guide to Beer*, added little more.

John Keeling, head brewer and board member at Fuller's of London, had trained in brewing at Heriot-Watt University in Edinburgh in the late 1970s, and confirmed that the same was true even within the world of brewing:

> Interesting flavours were seen as negative because more people would dislike them than like them . . . So, in terms of hops, they were there to produce the correct measured bitterness as cheaply as possible, and not much else . . . All hops were viewed as either alpha hop or aroma hop. Alpha had to deliver the cheapest bitterness, and aroma the cheapest Golding- or Fuggle-like hop character.[10]

It was in this businesslike context, however, that the names of new varieties of hop which offered high levels of 'alpha acids', responsible for the bitterness in beer, began to appear in technical journals:

> CASCADE: This is a new bitter variety, planted commercially in 1972. Its alpha acid content varies according to where it is grown (Washington, Oregon or Idaho) between 5 and 7 per cent. It is bred from 3/8 English Fuggles, 1/8 is a Russian variety and the other half is unknown . . . Its aroma is mild 'American'.[11]

'American' was not considered a complimentary term when applied to hops, but a few original thinkers began to question whether that wasn't simply a cultural prejudice. Among them was Sean Franklin, a young brewer who was to pioneer the use of 'new world' hops in British beer:

> Until the early 1970s, American hops had a poor reputation. There were maybe half a dozen of them available and they were all said to have a 'cat's pee' quality. It's a derogatory term – if you said it of a wine, it would be a serious criticism – but actually, if instead of cat's pee you say 'gooseberry leaves', or 'blackcurrant leaves', it doesn't sound so bad. It doesn't colour your perception of the taste and aroma the same way.[12]

Franklin is an almost reclusive man who squirms at the idea that he is considered a trailblazer by brewers and beer enthusiasts: 'I find talking about myself as some kind of expert or special person faintly embarrassing.' Born in a nursing home in Leeds, West Yorkshire, he went to school in Harrogate. He has vivid early memories of walking past the Harlow Hill Working Men's Club in Harrogate, where he first smelt 'old beer' in the air. After leaving school in the late 1960s, he took a job in the wine industry, moving to London to work as a labourer in the vaults of wine and spirit merchants George Idle Chapman.

The subterranean cellars of London's docks were known in the nineteenth century for their intoxicating fumes and pungent odour of wine and 'rot',[13] but the aromas that really interested Franklin were on the walk from the Tube station at Wapping: 'The warehouses, now expensive flats, smelt of hops and spices. Wonderful.' After two years in the cellars, he was promoted to head office, and then became a quality controller in the sample room. There, he undertook 'simple lab work' and joined tasting sessions under the leadership of 'the small, bright, bespectacled'[14] Bill Warre, a grandson of the founder of Dow Warre. He was an expert in his field, and Franklin remembers him fondly.

Eventually, Franklin began to travel to France on business as often as possible, before working for several years, under his own steam, at the wine communes in Aloxe-Corton, Burgundy, in the east of the country. Finally, in 1974, at the age of twenty-five, he enrolled at the Institut d'Oenologie at the University of Bordeaux, taking a degree in Oenology – that is, all aspects of winemaking except the cultivation of grapes. 'One of the profs was a guy called Émile Peynaud,' he recalled. 'World famous, and a great taster. He changed the face of Bordeaux wine quality in a generation.' Franklin absorbed Peynaud's key principles – that grapes must arrive at the winery in the peak of condition; that they should be treated with care to extract only the best flavours; and that fermentation should be carefully controlled – a factor which would later come to inform his own approach to beer:

> I was a pretty good wine taster by the time I left the wine trade,
> but Émile Peynaud and the course gave me the framework that
> allowed me to look at each of the facets of taste sequentially. It
> made more sense of the tasting experience.

Franklin learned to appreciate the look of a wine, to take time to consider its aroma and then to identify the components of its flavour – acid, bitter, sweet – as well as deconstructing how it felt in the mouth.

On returning to Britain, despite his Diplôme Universitaire d'Aptitude à la Dégustation, Franklin found quality-control work in the wine industry hard to come by, as much of it had reverted to the exporting countries after Britain joined the European Economic Community (EEC). Eventually, after a period working as a labourer, he took a job as a taxi driver – a rather unsatisfactory conclusion to a decade's worth of study and hard work.

In 2001, Michael Jackson wrote a piece recalling how he first came to speak to Sean Franklin, and how the latter 'encountered the light on the road to Damascus' with regard to beer.[15] Franklin scoffed at Jackson's suggestion of an epiphany, but does remember the key moment with complete clarity. In the spring of 1979, he happened to visit the Turkey Inn at Goose Eye, near Keighley in West Yorkshire. The pub – the entire village – is built of grey stone and sits at the side of a river, opposite the remains of a once-great paper mill where, in September 1978, a small brewery had been set up by the Turkey Inn's landlord, Brian Eastell.

> I went to check it out at 'early doors' one bright, cold, spring
> Sunday morning. The pub was filling up, and I was looking
> around, smelling the beer . . . I thought to myself, if he could do
> this, perhaps so could I.

Franklin cannot recall whether it was this event which took place first, or an eye-opening visit to the United States, though the purpose of that trip was to research Pinot Noir, rather than beer:

I had contacted Michael Jackson to ask about breweries as an
additional attraction. He sent me a closely typed two-page list
of breweries and their addresses. He also put me in touch with
a friend of his out there, Vince Cottone, who kindly put me up
for a week or so.

Cottone was a local beer enthusiast and home brewer, and a
disciple of Michael Jackson. He would later go on to write the first
book about the beer and breweries of the Pacific Northwest and, in
1979, was the best guide Franklin could hope to have. Franklin was
especially interested in the Willamette and Yakima Valleys in Oregon
and Washington State respectively. Wine writer Alexis Bespaloff
described the Yakima Valley for *New York Magazine* in June 1982:

> This area, protected from the Pacific rains by the Cascade
> mountain range, was a semi-arid desert before extensive
> irrigation was introduced . . . The area is now one of the nation's
> principal agricultural regions . . . The days are longer there than
> they are in California . . . and the cold desert nights enable the
> grapes to retain their natural acidity.[16]

Yakima, and the Pacific Northwest region as a whole, presented a
distinct contrast to grey, rainy Yorkshire and, as luck would have it, was
also an important centre for US hop growing. In 1975, the 'fertile but
gaspingly dry'[17] Yakima Valley produced $30 million worth of hops,
and, along with the nearby Moxee Valley, was responsible for more than
65 per cent of total US output.[18] The Willamette Valley in Oregon gave
its name to a particularly potent variety of hops, as did the Cascade
Mountains mentioned by Bespaloff. Franklin found the landscape
lovely, with 'rolling hills, fertile plains, rivers to die for', but realised he
could not afford to buy a vineyard and came home disappointed but
happy: 'The sun shone enough to make it a memorable trip.'

Having visited America and drunk at the Turkey Inn – in
whichever order – his urge to brew grew irresistible and, in 1980,
Franklin's Brewery opened for business:

An old barn at the Gardeners Arms in Bilton, Harrogate was the spot I eventually found. With the help of friends, I got planning permission and refurbished the place to Environmental Heath requirements. Drains across the car park. Tanks and pumps I begged or borrowed ... I found a brewing research chemist called Jeff Ellison who ran the Leeds branch of Phillips Yeast, who made fish food out of 'spent' yeast.

There, Franklin set about attempting to recreate in his beer the complexity of aroma and flavour he had learned to appreciate in wine, and turned to hops to provide the kind of variation that different varieties of grape give to the wines that bear their names. He began by dissecting the characteristics of beers brewed with English hops:

I remember very clearly going to Burton upon Trent, picking up some brewing gear, or something. When all was done, I had a spectacular pint of Marston's Bitter at the Plough. The hops, whatever they were, had a powerful aroma of oranges ... Theakston's bitter was very pale and smelt like rice pudding ... Then there was ... Timothy Taylor's Landlord, at the Junction Inn, Otley. This was more than thirty years ago, but the moment is frozen in time. I remember who I was with, the light, the aroma of the beer – tangerines and grapefruit.

Franklin once suggested, in an article setting out his philosophy of taste and tasting, that it is important to open the mind to the idea that 'beers can taste of anything'.[19] That is now widely accepted, but, when he first began to brew, noting flavours of fruit or 'rice pudding' would have seemed downright eccentric. At first, Franklin's Bitter was made with Goldings and Fuggles, but soon he sought to turn up the volume and make it really distinctive.

I was reading everything I could. I read in the *Journal of the Institute of Brewers*, in about 1978, that Cascade was the most aromatic hop in the world. That was the starting point for my use of US hops. Although I think it was later that I tried it in Sierra Nevada [pale ale], there's no denying the influence of the early American craft brewer on the developing UK beer scene.

Though Cascades were at first intended to mimic European hops to save American brewers the cost of importing them, and then considered a failure because of their 'catty' aroma, Franklin recognised that they weren't necessarily flawed: they had a distinctive character of their own. What Franklin had identified was that Cascade, as a kind of 'super-Fuggle', had the orange, tangerine and grapefruit qualities he had found in those particularly transcendent pints of Marston's and Landlord, only more so:

> When I decided to switch from Fuggles and Golding to Cascade, I rang up my hop merchant. It was as simple as that. I must have been one of the first people to ask for them, but they had them in stock, so someone else was using them. Maybe an American beer being brewed under licence over here.

Outspoken veteran beer enthusiast Gazza Prescott, now a brewer himself, and one of the stars of the documentary *Beer Tickers* (directed by Phil Parkin in 2009), recalled the results and how it was received by drinkers:

> I'd tried the fabled Franklin's Bitter, which everyone said tasted 'weird' . . . well, it did, and I wasn't sure what to make of its bizarre flavours at the time, although looking back now, I can see it was Sean Franklin's Cascades at work and I was simply too young to appreciate it.[20]

Though the 1983 CAMRA *Good Beer Guide* described Franklin's Bitter in three words – 'bitter and fruity' – the 1984 edition included an essay called 'A Matter of Taste'. In a few hundred words, it set out all of the anxieties prompted by 'pretentious' tasting habits:

> Take a mouthful of beer. Roll it round your mouth. Swallow it (it's too expensive to spit out). How would you describe its

taste? The chances are that if you ventured more than a couple
of words you'll feel an uncomfortable sense of embarrassment
crawling over you . . . The language of taste tends to be associated
with snobbery, pretentiousness and writing worthy of 'Pseuds'
Corner'.[21]

It went on to argue that there are good practical reasons why beer
enthusiasts should get over their embarrassment. First, because taste
was why they were choosing one beer over another; and second,
because they needed to be able to persuade fellow consumers and
brewers of the merits of those beers. The piece also suggested a few
words that beer drinkers might find useful in describing the taste of
their beer – a snapshot of an emerging 'higher' vocabulary of beer
which is now commonplace:

There are hundreds of words that describe tastes, some of them
unusual and surprising, like 'cardboardy' and 'cabbagey', some
well known, like 'rubbery' or 'rancid', and some specialised, like
'aldehydic' and 'ribes' (curranty, hence 'Ribena').

This new ideology of taste had taken years to filter through, having
been proposed within CAMRA as early as 1975.[22] But many members
of the Campaign, even though they were predisposed to take beer
seriously, railed against it. As recounted by Des de Moor, members at
the 1990 AGM protested that it was Southern, middle-class beer snob
behaviour. 'We'll be laughed out of the public bar,' said one.[23] Barrie
Pepper recalled the opposition among the ranks: 'There were a few
people who said, this is bloody nonsense – it's for the Belgians; they
put cherries in their beer!' Founder member Michael Hardman was
among the critics of 'irritating . . . pretentious descriptions'.[24] And so
was born the beginning of a row over the 'winification' of beer which
is still going on today. It might even be called a schism – the point at
which 'drinkers' and 'tasters' parted company.

Mark Dorber was studying for a PhD when he took a holiday job
working at the White Horse on Parson's Green, west London in 1981.

Applying an earnest, academic approach to managing a pub cellar, he gained the pub a reputation for serving perfectly conditioned Bass pale ale, and, from the early 1980s onward, was running festivals to highlight the 'endangered' styles of beer that Michael Jackson had written about in his *World Guide*. Dorber, who is as expert in wine as he is in beer, was an eager proponent of serious beer tasting from the beginning, and has no time for those who dismiss it:

> I've always hated it when people say beer is a working-man's drink, and that tasting is pretentious: that's a moronic, Luddite point of view. We need to celebrate what's in the glass. That kind of attitude is about them, not the flavour of the beer. It's about their own personality and prejudices, not about appreciating the endeavour, skill and pleasure embodied in beer, whether it's from a bottle, cask or keg.[25]

Sean Franklin, meanwhile, even as parts of the beer world were beginning to come round to his way of thinking, was running out of energy. His 'weird' beers were not finding a market, and he was not enjoying himself making the same product, over and over, batch after batch. In 1985 he sold Franklin's Brewery and left the industry. Just when he ought to have been pushing the boundaries of British beer yet further, and riding high on the adulation of enthusiasts, he found himself once again driving a cab, all the time brooding on his decision:

> The minute I'd finished with my first brewery, I knew I'd made a mistake, and that I should have stuck at it. I had a family, though, and I needed a steady income. I spent three years in the taxi saving up and thinking about a business plan, marketing and designing a new brewery called Rooster's.

When he returned to the industry seven years later, he would find that British beer had finally caught up with him, with drinkers more receptive to his pioneering use of 'new world' hops, and critical tasting, if still a niche practice, no longer a joke.

NINE

SMALL BEER

It was a great day when the Beer Orders were passed. OK, it was a botched job, and I'm not justifying Punch and Enterprise and pub companies of that sort, but does the consumer now have a better choice? I think so.

Christopher Hutt, 2013[1]

In the late 1980s, SIBA, an organisation founded in 1980, finally found its feet and began to exert a powerful influence over British beer.[2] Just as the Campaign for Real Ale had represented a new subculture of drinkers, so SIBA spoke for a group of brewers which emerged as a similar 'supply side' reaction to the dominance of the Big Six. Since 1980, it has been an increasingly persuasive lobby, claiming credit (probably with justification) for several influential government interventions in the industry. Though a very serious organisation today, as with many of the other groups described in these pages, it began as something much less formal.

David Bruce recalled that, in 1979, he and the handful of other London brewers were on friendly terms (his affectionate nickname for the founder of Godson's, Patrick Fitzpatrick, was 'Pricktrack Pissfucktrick') and, in the spirit of collaboration and mutual support, formed a group called the Small London Brewers' Association, which just happened to abbreviate to a puerile Bruceian pun:

> SLOBA used to meet at the Boot and Flogger in Southwark on
> the last Friday of every month. There would be all these little

pick-ups parked outside with firkins rolling around in the back, and the rule was that we'd start at lunchtime and couldn't leave until it was dark, which was fine in winter.[3]

David Bruce claims some credit for the initial impetus to bring weight to the unofficial, boozy SLOBA network, and suggested that, as with many of his ideas, it began with an 'incident':

> When I got my first brewing licence for the Goose and Firkin in 1979, I immediately applied to join the Brewers' Society. I got a sniffy letter back: 'No, you can't become a member, because you're too new and too small.' I wrote back: 'That's not fair. John Courage and Samuel Whitbread started out brewing in one room and they were new once, too.' Basically, it was a club for family brewers, and so, once again, I said, 'Fuck you!'[4]

Other brewers had had similar experiences, including Peter Austin.[5] Being some thirty years older than many of the other small brewers, and an industry veteran, Austin fell into a leadership role, and suggested that all the country's new small brewers should take part in a kind of summit. The venue was to be the Cross Keys pub in Wootton Bassett, Wiltshire.

James Lynch, CAMRA chairman from 1977 to 1978, had founded his own brewery, Bourne Valley, in November 1978,[6] and took on the role of secretary to the nascent organisation. He sent a letter, dated 21 January, that established a businesslike tone quite different to SLOBA's booze-ups:

> We are all extremely busy people, so meetings are likely to be few and far between ... and it is very important that we derive maximum benefit from the meeting. A convivial gathering of kindred spirits would be enjoyable but not very productive. Therefore an element of formality has been introduced in the form of an agenda.[7]

On 26 January 1980, brewers including David Bruce, Patrick Fitzpatrick, Simon Whitmore (Butcombe) and James Lynch braved midwinter conditions to descend on the pub. The meeting commenced at 11 a.m. with a presentation by Ron Matthews of the Brewers' Society, there to make a last-ditch effort to stop the breakaway group in its tracks by offering a concession: associate membership for small brewers at a cost of £50 per year, which would entitle them to very little other than access to the technical journal, and certainly no voting rights.

As Christopher Hutt suggested, brewers had tended to present a united front, with the Big Six and certain larger regional breweries keeping smaller ones in check and 'on message'. Since CAMRA had come along and driven a wedge between the Big Six and the regionals, the last thing the Brewers' Society wanted was yet another faction and more bickering within the industry.

After adjourning for a few pints – the meeting was not an entirely sober affair – the small brewers rejected the offer as 'an insult'. The fact was that the interests of the smaller brewers were entirely at odds with those of the more established firms. The former were, on the whole, struggling to get their beer into pubs, as Simon Hosking of Tower Bridge Brewery, present at the Wootton Bassett meeting, later recalled in his advice for people considering a career in brewing:

> Because of the tie and brewery loans, the amount of genuine free trade is restricted. This small sector is very, very competitive. What makes you think you can win against Fuller's, Sam Smith's and Marston's, to say nothing of your fellow small brewers?[8]

More established brewing companies, even smaller regional ones, having built up estates of pubs obliged to take their beer, would never be in favour of opening those pubs up to the free market. The man from the Brewers' Society was told where to go, and the Small Independent Brewers' Association, SIBA, came into existence, with Austin as chairman and Lynch as secretary.

Though they planned to meet every three months, that was not to be and, to some extent, as CAMRA had been in its first year, SIBA was rather dormant. Eventually, policies began to take shape: their primary campaign issues would be a reduction in customs duty (tax) for small brewers, an end to the brewery tie, and – ironically, given that David Bruce's business had been built on them – the banning or regulation of brewery loans to publicans.

In January 1981, SIBA wrote to Sally Oppenheim, Minister for Consumer Affairs, about cheap brewery loans, kicking off an Office of Fair Trading investigation.[9] In November 1982, Austin and David Bruce met government officials to plead their case on small brewers' duty allowances and other issues, but were given the brush-off. How, ministers and officials asked, could any of this be managed without a great deal of bureaucracy and expense? Just as the individual brewers in its ranks had been locked out of the Brewers' Society, so SIBA was locked out of consultation with government.

Membership of SIBA remained disappointingly low (it peaked at 100[10] in 1982), with many newer small brewers deciding against paying £15 a year to join. Then, as soon as it had come, the boom – such as it was – ended, and membership of SIBA sank as low as thirty[11] as first-generation 'microbreweries' such as Godson's began to flicker out. Many small brewers struggled to get their beer into pubs, which were in large part owned by the Big Six, and were reliant on unsustainable borrowing to stay afloat.

Bill Urquhart sold his Litchborough Brewery to John Heaverman in 1980, and, after a move to Daventry, it continued under his management until 1983 when Liddington's, a wholesale drinks company, bought it and brewing ceased in 1986.[12] In the same year, Terry Jones and Martin Griffiths closed down Penrhos: 'It was delayed payments that really killed it,' said Griffiths. 'You can work like mad, but if you have not got the cash flow you constantly run into problems.'[13] CAMRA's Brian Glover reckoned that, altogether, fourteen breweries closed in 1983, and declared: 'The small-brewery boom – as far as the free trade brewers are concerned – looks to be over.'[14] By November 1984, he was reporting a further eight closures: 'The squeeze is beginning. The worry is that the shake-out will land a number of new breweries in the gentle lap of the Big Six.'[15]

Many breweries from this period did survive, however, and are still in existence today, such as Banks and Taylor, and Chiltern (both of which Bill Urquhart had a hand in setting up), Essex's Crouch Vale, Woodfordes of Norfolk and Peter Austin's own Ringwood.

❀

Throughout the mid-1980s, the personnel at the top of SIBA changed constantly. Though SIBA's official history skirts delicately around the issue, Austin himself told us he was 'relieved' of the chairmanship because he had been too busy installing breweries all over the world, from Africa to Siberia, to give the role his full attention. He stood down at the AGM in August 1985 and was replaced by the more forceful and determined Paul Soden, owner of the Jolly Roger Brewery in Worcester, who also ran a brewery installation company, Total Brewing Services.

It was on Soden's watch in 1986 that SIBA convinced David Trippier, a junior minister at the Department of Trade and Industry, to visit Aston Manor Brewery. Trippier is a plain-speaking Lancastrian who has described himself as 'content to enjoy an occasional pint of wallop' and 'munch the pork scratchings'.[16] He is also a close friend of CAMRA-supporting Conservative heavyweight Kenneth Clarke. He was evidently sympathetic to the small brewers' cause and, as Minister for Small Firms, influenced the decision to invite SIBA to the table when the Monopolies and Mergers Commission (MMC) issued a call for evidence for an investigation into the brewing industry.

Successive governments of every persuasion had from the 1960s onward seemed convinced that there was something intrinsically wrong with the monopolistic set-up of the brewing industry, and there had been numerous enquiries and attempts to regulate, each of which had left 'unfinished business'. This was to be the latest round.[17] Determined to influence its outcome, SIBA prepared a twelve-page submission arguing that large breweries held the market in a 'stranglehold'. It is not a dry document but a passionate, rather melodramatic polemic reminiscent of the tone of Christopher Hutt:

Concomitant with the process of concentration has been an equivalent loss of the crafts and skilled traditions that brewing created: skills which offered a choice and value to all, employment for many and a product to be proud of the world over. In its place is left an amorphous ruling oligarchy of financial consortia battling it out for final control in the beer wars, the theatres of which have extended far beyond national frontiers.[18]

The solutions to this problem, SIBA argued, were:

- to remove the requirement for those who wanted to open new pubs to win over magistrates, thus subjecting big-brewery 'tied houses' to real competition on the high street;

- to allow publicans the right to stock beers from breweries other than their pub's owner;

- to make it illegal to describe a pub as a 'free house' if it wasn't truly 'free'; and

- to find a way to prevent large brewers aggressively discounting.

In November of 1986, Peter Austin, Paul Soden and three other SIBA executive members were called to give evidence in person. SIBA had been forced to cancel their annual general meeting because of low attendance, and their VIP status in the consultation apparently caused some irritation at the Brewers' Society, which published statistics emphasising that SIBA's members brewed less than 1 per cent of the UK's beer.[19]

In December 1987, the MMC announced findings that broadly coincided with SIBA's view – a monopoly did exist, and something ought to be done. It commenced what would prove to be a year-long review. 'The beer-bores' brewers', as a journalist in the *Economist* described SIBA's members,[20] had struck a blow. When the MMC's final report was published in March 1989, it was clear that the small brewers – a somewhat disorganised band of what might fairly be called oddballs – had achieved an incredible victory. The MMC's recommendations to the government might almost have been drafted by Paul Soden himself:

> We ... recommend that no company or person with brewing interests should be permitted to own or lease or have any other interest whatsoever in more than 2,000 on-licensed outlets in the United Kingdom ...
>
> We recommend ... that the Secretary of State take such steps as may be necessary to effect the changes in the present arrangements ... that will result in the ending of the granting of loans by brewers in return for secured business ...
>
> It has been represented to us that small brewers in the United Kingdom, unlike their counterparts in much of Europe and the USA, pay the same rate of duty on beer as the very large brewers. We consider that it would encourage the growth of such brewers, and hence improve competition and consumer choice, if a sliding scale were to be introduced that would allow small brewers to pay a lower rate of duty on some part of their beer output.

This was a crisis point: would the government politely ignore the MMC's recommendations, and side with the Big Six brewers? The big brewers were traditionally Conservative, and had been for centuries. Or would they disregard traditional loyalties and accept the paper wholesale? Prime Minister Margaret Thatcher believed fervently in the power of competition and was thus opposed to monopolies on principle. The Brewers' Society, SIBA and various other parties commenced furious lobbying, each setting out just how much was at stake from their perspective. Paul Soden gave strident interviews to anyone who wanted them, as in this article from *The Times*:[21]

> The world will be our oyster, so long as the Government stops the big brewers exploiting loopholes in the new system ... None of the changes that have been suggested can mean anything but good for the customer.

In the same article, a spokesman for the Brewers' Society responded:

> If the large breweries are forced to reduce the number of their
> outlets, as the report proposes, they are likely to keep the largest,
> and seek to maximise their turnover . . . The largest houses tend
> to be managed pubs, and so tenancy will decline. The places
> which will suffer are those at the rural end of the scale.

If the brewery tie was abolished, the big brewers argued, they
would have no choice but to sell off thousands of their least profitable
pubs, which would either be bought up by foreign investors (and, by
implication, ruined) or simply go out of business. 'You would think
we had stolen them from somebody,' one 'brewery insider' was quoted
as saying. 'They are our property, built up through hard work,'[22] they
argued, as those operating monopolies tend to do when faced with
government interference. Their opponents might have pointed out
that the big brewers' 'hard work' had included the aggressive takeover
and closure of many small breweries with the aim of seizing control
of their local pub estates – if not theft, then at the very least a form of
cultural vandalism.

For much of the 1980s, CAMRA struggled to recruit members
and seemed rather aimless, riven as it was with internal conflict.
Even so, it had become a national institution, and as such it was the
government's favourite means of being seen to consult 'the man in
the pub', and therefore the third prominent voice in the debate. More
than one SIBA brewer spoke to us in disdainful terms about CAMRA
and, though it might be assumed their interests were aligned, in fact
CAMRA had always balanced a supportive interest in new breweries
with loyalty to established ones, especially regional family concerns.
In the early days of the Campaign, before microbreweries began to
open, CAMRA had explicitly allied itself with Theakston's, Fuller's
and Young's, who, in turn, had given them both moral and practical
support. (Fuller's had arranged a licence for the 1975 Covent Garden
Beer Festival.) In truth, many CAMRA members were more interested in solid, respectable beers such as Adnams bitter and Young's

Ordinary than in the products of untried, amateurish, one-man-band breweries. Having supported the retention of 'the tie' in their evidence to the MMC, CAMRA eventually lobbied for a watered-down set of reforms,[23] concerned that the market would be sent into shock if the big breweries had to dump too many pubs at once. They also argued that regional brewers should be exempt from any changes.[24]

Of the three points of view, CAMRA's was probably the most balanced and least partisan. SIBA's position was either hopelessly optimistic – based on a belief that the big brewers were bluffing – or born from a downright anarchistic desire to destroy the system and then rebuild it in their own image. The Brewers' Society were, of course, equally self-serving, and seemed determined to put off the inevitable collapse of the vast brewing and pub-owning empires.

As campaigns and counter-campaigns played out, and the government ruminated, the industry held its breath.

❦

Uncertainty over the outcome of the report had a destabilising effect on one important brewing concern: David and Louise Bruce's Firkin chain of pubs. In 1981,[25] the Bruces had been hit with the realisation that, phenomenon though it was, Bruce's Brewery hadn't actually been making any money. Having 'muddled through' the finances for some years, when they showed their paperwork to tax advisers Touche Ross (now Deloitte), they were astounded to hear that they were dangerously close to 'running out of funds'. As a stop gap, they sold a 10 per cent stake to the government's Industrial Commerce and Finance Corporation (founded in the 1940s to stimulate small-business growth) but, after that scare, the thought was always on Bruce's mind: 'Flog it or float it.'

At first, he gave serious thought to selling shares and, twenty years before another brewery would come along with an extremely similar idea, talked about a scheme in which particularly loyal customers – fans, of which the Firkins had many – could buy a stake in their favourite company. Despite his excitement at the prospect of a new type of equity arrangement, with prospectuses dropped onto bar tops and pub tables, it did not prove practical. He spent, in his own words, 'an agonising winter in 1987 dithering over what to do', indecisive for perhaps the first time in his life. He had become a father, for one thing, and also sensed that 'the market seemed to be cooling down'. Lager was then reaching a peak of popularity, and consumption of wine, already becoming trendy, was soaring after a drop in duty prompted by the EEC.

He was also fed up with being mobbed by 'beer bores', and even took to wearing thick-rimmed glasses, a deerstalker and a ripped Barbour jacket in the hope of throwing them off the scent.

But it was nagging anxiety about the Monopolies and Mergers Commission report – something he himself had lobbied for while active in SIBA – that pushed him over the edge:

> We didn't know what it was going to say, but my suspicion was that it would flood the market with free houses and our 'unique selling point' would be lost. At any rate, I knew it was going to create turmoil in the industry.

Finally, in 1988, he decided to sell up:

> I spoke to Barry Gillham at Fleurets who said, 'I'll get you £6.5 million – trust me.' So I put it on the front of all the trade press, the *Publican* and the *Morning Advertiser*: FIRKINS FOR SALE. We got an offer of £6.6 million from Midsummer Inns, who had just bought CAMRA Investments. By the time we'd paid taxes, debts and commission on the sale, we were left with about £2 million net – better than a poke in the eye with a sharp stick, I suppose.

After being sold on again, the Firkin brewpubs finally ended up in the hands of one of the Big Six, Allied, who proceeded to open more than 170 new Firkins[26] all around the UK and abroad, around sixty with in-house breweries. Though they attempted to keep the spirit of the company alive, Bruce was appalled by their clumsy, rather desperate efforts, which replicated the superficial but failed to capture what really mattered:

They put 'Firkin' on everything – Firkin ashtray, Firkin toilet, Firkin barmaid, Firkin table. A real low point was seeing a billboard on the Fleece and Firkin in Bristol advertising female mud-wrestling.

CAMRA, which had just about tolerated the Firkins under Bruce's leadership, became vocal critics as the chain went national, and they coined the phrase 'to Firkinise', meaning to buy up a perfectly good local pub and give it an identikit 'crass, fake Edwardian interior'.[27] They became 'naff' hangouts for students, drawn by the promise of strong beer and loud music.

In the meantime, Bruce, who considered the idea of retiring at forty 'immoral', invested in or consulted on the roll-out of several more pub or brewery chains, including the Slug and Lettuce, founded by a friend of his, Hugh Corbett, as a 'female-friendly' Firkin-alike, and the Frog chain of English-style pubs in France. Brewing ceased in the Firkin pubs on 8 October 1999,[28] at which point Bruce's most enduring legacy – an army of trained brewers and a multitude of small but perfectly formed brewing kits – would become apparent.

As for the MMC recommendations, Lord Young, Secretary of State for Trade and Industry, decided to sit on the fence after months of lobbying from interested parties, and suggested a 'balanced package' – a compromise, which prompted the *Daily Express* to declare HIS LORDSHIP POPS IN AT THE HALFWAY HOUSE.[29] In the House of Commons, Opposition members took the opportunity to accuse Lord Young of performing a U-turn, and of casting aside consumer-friendly proposals from the MMC as a result of pressure from the Conservative Party's friends in the Brewers' Society. No opportunity for populist gestures was missed, from broad statements of support for 'rural pubs' to spirited praise for microbreweries and their wares.[30]

Nonetheless, in December 1989 what came to be known as the 'Beer Orders' passed into law, requiring any brewery owning more than 2,000 pubs to dispose of half of the excess, and also making it compulsory for those with more than 2,000 pubs to allow a 'guest ale' to be bought by pub tenants from a third party. The new guest beer law also specified that the beer in question had to be a 'real ale', as per CAMRA's definition – and thanks to their lobbying. 'We regret this decision,' said a spokesman for Whitbread, 'but it is better than the original report.'[31]

As the dust settled and the first effects of the Beer Orders began to be seen, Jeff Evans, editor of CAMRA's *Good Beer Guide*, gave this summary in his Foreword to the 1991 edition:

> We enjoyed the flavour of the new guest beer law, despite the underlying bitterness surrounding its introduction, and savoured the cheerful effervescence of the smaller brewers which has ensued. However, the sediment of big brewers' evasiveness has soured the taste and left us wondering just how the next mouthful will prove.[32]

In a more detailed analysis, his colleague, Steve Cox, outlined the 'dirty tricks' big brewers were using to keep 'guest beers' under control. They were, he claimed, using negotiations over rent increases to put pressure on landlords not to 'step out of line'; they were putting obstacles in landlords' way over the use of brewery-owned equipment to dispense guest beers; and, in line with their 1970s tactic of giving a little to derail protest, they were supplying limited ranges of 'safe' guest beers themselves, thus discouraging tenants from shopping around:

> The original intention of the guest beer, a hassle-free choice by tenants from all possible suppliers, is being gradually subverted, so that tenants will meekly stock from a shortlist of three provided by their brewery.[33]

What supporters of the Beer Orders had hoped for was the opening up of the market and the creation of hundreds of new 'free houses', as brewers sold pubs to their tenants in order to come under the 2,000 pub threshold set by the government. Instead, what happened over the course of the next decade was a catastrophic rending asunder of the symbiotic relationship between the pub and brewing industries.

Companies such as Whitbread and Bass, founded in 1742 and 1777 respectively, were thought to be more sentimentally attached to brewing than proved to be the case. In an act of pure pragmatism, they began to withdraw from brewing, selling their beer brands and breweries to international concerns, and turning their attention to hotels, coffee shops and chain restaurants. Over the course of the next decade, several hundred years of history withered to a dead halt.

Elsewhere in the industry, Scottish and Newcastle stayed in brewing but chose to dump pubs rather than run them on a non-tied basis. As a result, some 6,000[34] 'surplus' pubs were sold, not to their enterprising tenants, but to hard-nosed pub companies with no history in brewing and less paternalistic attitudes towards their tenants.[35]

For publicans and ordinary pub-goers, little advantage was gained. The only real beneficiaries were some smaller breweries, and drinkers for whom price was a less important consideration than flavour, provenance and novelty – that is, beer geeks. Even though brewers and pub companies ensured that 'guest beers' sold at a premium, they sold well enough that the number of small, new breweries began to increase, as Jeff Evans noted in the CAMRA *Good Beer Guide* of 1995:

> The present boom in new microbreweries has been little short of staggering . . . [Last year] we triumphantly proclaimed the birth of some fifty new breweries in the previous two years. That number now stands at eighty-five in three years, and we know plenty more are in the pipeline.[36]

Although SIBA was small and dwindling, and CAMRA's attitude more conservative, it does seem that, between them, they provided civil servants and politicians with the ammunition they needed to counter an argument the Big Six had been repeating for decades to scupper government intervention in the industry: that consumers were satisfied with the quality and choice of beer provided by the big brewers.[37] And though the much-hoped-for flood of new free houses did not materialise, the idea of the 'guest beer' took hold, ushering in a new, crowded and competitive market that triggered a wave of astonishing creativity among brewers.

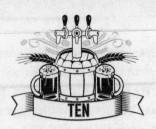

TEN

SPICING UP THE RELATIONSHIP

Britain now has a beer for all seasons. The once staid world of mild and bitter, with winter warmers for the Christmas period, has been embellished and enlivened by a flood of new beers. Brewers are dusting off ancient recipes and generating new ones in a rush to produce a plethora of brews that are seasonal or occasional.

Roger Protz, 1994[1]

As the 1990s approached, 'real ale' was a well-established part of British culture. Membership of the Campaign for Real Ale, having sunk as low as 18,000 in 1981,[2] began to climb again, reaching over 20,000 by 1986.[3] Many regional family breweries reaffirmed their commitment to brewing cask ale. And, despite the closure of a number of the first generation of 1970s microbreweries, a core group toughed it out and survived, many of which are still trading today, such as Butcombe of Bristol. New breweries continued to open, too, until there were 144 in operation by 1987, according to Brian Glover[4] (though he also pointed out that another 143 had come and gone).

Up to this point, most 'real ale' breweries produced at least one bitter, often a slightly stronger best bitter and perhaps a strong ale, usually dark in colour. After the revival of porter in 1977, a handful also brewed porters or stouts, though the market was dominated by

Guinness. With more competition among many small breweries, and exotic imports providing inspiration, real-ale brewers began not only to produce wider ranges of historic 'styles' from the framework established by Michael Jackson, but also to introduce some genuine innovation. We use that word with caution: these days, it has become an annoying buzzword, often paired with 'passion' in brewery mission statements and manifestos. But in the late 1980s, it was still possible to come up with ideas that seemed substantially new to all but the most adventurous and studious drinkers.

Among the first new developments in British brewing of the period was the invention of the 'golden ale', as light in colour as lager. As beer writer and historian Martyn Cornell has pointed out in his book *Amber, Gold and Black*, there were beers calling themselves 'golden' and some that were very pale in colour long before the 1980s (e.g. Boddington's Bitter), but they had either disappeared, become darker in line with fashion or were extremely obscure.[5] When the first new golden ales began to appear on a market awash with deep-brown beers, they had immediate appeal.

The vast majority of British beers, even the darkest in colour, are made using mostly pale malted barley, kilned under dry heat until the grains are very lightly coloured. The darker amber, brown and black colours of the majority of beers is a result of the addition of a small amount of more highly kilned malt, which also adds a more or less caramel, toasted or roasted flavour. In particular, British bitters have, in the latter half of the twentieth century, tended to include among their ingredients a dose of 'crystal malt' to impart sweetness, fullness of body and, to varying degrees, a defining 'brownness'. The (re) invention of the golden ale in the 1980s only required the omission of such darker malts – the simplification or stripping back of recipes to a minimalist core.

In the late 1980s, independently of each other, and surely influenced by the new dominance of lager, brewers began to experiment. In 1986, Exmoor Ales of Devon, then known as Golden Hill, began to produce a beer under the name Exmoor Gold, which is still brewed today and bears the slogan 'The Original Golden Ale'. But as Martyn Cornell observes, it cannot claim to have triggered a trend for such beers, and it was not until 1989 that a beer appeared on the market that could genuinely claim to have opened the floodgates: Summer Lightning.[6]

In the 1970s, John Gilbert had worked as a brewer at Watney's vast Mortlake complex in south London. In the early 1980s, he was involved in running two new related breweries, the Battersea Brewing Company, founded in 1982 and known as BBC1, and the Brixton Brewing Company (1983, BBC2). In 1986, he and his wife, Julie, left the capital for Salisbury, Wiltshire, where they bought a large suburban corner pub called the Wyndham Arms and, in 1987, closed it for three weeks to install a brewery. Inspired by a carved detail on the pub's exterior, Gilbert made the brewery's logo the lascivious, gurning face of the Roman god of wine, Bacchus, and called it after an item of traditional British brewing equipment – Hop Back.[7]

At first, he and his colleague, Roger McBride, produced four barrels of beer every week, bitter and best bitter, but Gilbert soon announced his plans to brew both a stout and a lager.[8] It was this latter idea which, though it did come to fruition, led him to brew Summer Lightning, named after a P.G. Wodehouse novel and as yellow as any pilsner, though brewed with English malt and hops and fermented just like a bitter.

What really established Summer Lightning was winning the gold award in the 'New Brewery Class' in the Champion Beer of Britain competition at CAMRA's 1989 Great British Beer Festival.[9] It went on to win a silver award as 'Best Strong Bitter' in 1991, and gold in the same category in 1992.

After a disastrous period in the mid-1980s, when it had begun to look as if the Great British Beer Festival would be abolished in the wake of financial difficulties and bickering over its location, it came back better organised and more professional, with something of the atmosphere of the trade fair rather than a piss-up. Even so, judging for best beer was far less clinical than it is today, as Michael Jackson recalled:

> Colin Dexter, the author and creator of Inspector Morse, was
> fond of Hop Back Summer Lightning, from Salisbury, which was
> chosen as the best strong ale. 'My only qualification for judging
> is that I drink a lot of beer,' he sighed. 'I can't think of a better
> qualification,' suggested [the cartoonist] Mr [Bill] Tidy, who
> conceded that he was getting confused by the time the barley
> wine arrived.[10]

Exactly how much credit Summer Lightning deserves for
kick-starting the 'golden ale' trend is debatable. There were plenty of
beers *described* as 'golden', 'straw coloured' and 'very pale' in the late
1980s – perhaps as a response to the increasing popularity of lager,
or merely reflective of the broadening vocabulary of beer enthusiasts
as 'tasting notes' became fashionable. Certainly, after Summer Lightning's string of victories, more beers were being *marketed* as 'summer'
or 'golden' ales. A count of those beers with 'summer', 'gold', 'golden'
or 'sun' in their names listed in the *Good Beer Guide* shows that there
were four in 1989, eleven by 1992 and eighteen by 1993. Many more
were described as summer ales in the notes even if their names did
not reflect it – almost fifty, in fact. Whitbread, too, got in on the act,
with their nationally distributed 'Summer Ale', launched in 1993.[11]

Hop Back had to expand production of Summer Lightning to meet
demand, quickly outgrowing its back-room brewpub facilities. It is
still trading today, and Summer Lightning remains its flagship brand.

Meanwhile, many British brewers began to retread the path of
early pioneer Sean Franklin in experimenting with new varieties
of hops, unusual approaches to their use or both. Perhaps surprisingly, among these were Whitbread, who released a series of 'single
hop' beers in 1994.[12] Though these employed traditional, more subtle
varieties – Fuggles and Goldings from England and Saaz from the
Czech Republic – the very idea of using only a single 'premium' hop
and advertising the fact signalled a recognition that beer enthusiasts
wanted to engage with beer on a level beyond brand recognition.

Moreover, in a post-CAMRA, post-Michael Jackson world, many had the knowledge and vocabulary to do so.

Northern Irish brewer Brendan Dobbin was another early 'experimenter' whose beers gained a cult following and, even today, are spoken about with awe by veteran beer geeks. That Dobbin himself is a complicated character, who, in the late 1990s became, in his own words, 'a hermit', only contributes to the retrospective hype. In the months it took us to make contact with Dobbin, we spoke to many people who had worked with or knew him, and heard conflicting reports. Some told us he was 'lovely', a 'great guy', with a famous sense of humour; others warned, 'Be careful!' The oft-repeated story was that he had retired to Cork in the south of the Republic of Ireland, where he was growing bananas, which sounded entirely unlikely.

When we did finally get hold of him, through a former colleague, we were given instructions to call a Manchester number, which we were told would reroute our call to Ireland. He answered, began to talk in a Belfast accent and barely stopped for several hours. Dobbin, it turned out, was all of the things we had been told to expect: friendly, charming and funny, with an endless supply of anecdotes, complete with impressions and accents; but who also, every now and then, remembering some slight or irritation, had a tendency to snarl. That hard side is surely a product of his upbringing: 'Here's the way I tell it: I was born in Belfast, christened a Catholic, but it didn't work', and a youth spent in a tough city 'with a name like Brendan at the time the Shankill Butchers were dragging Catholics off the street and killing them by slitting their throats'. With shades of the self-mythologising bravado of Muhammad Ali, he also occasionally referred to himself in the third person as 'one B. Dobbin'.

Born in 1958, he showed an early talent for science, and won a scholarship to a Catholic boarding school, where he did well enough in his A-levels to gain a place studying chemical engineering at Queen's University in Belfast. He was due to commence his degree in 1976 but, weeks before, was involved in a motorbike crash, breaking his leg in nine places. He turned up at university six weeks late, only to be told he couldn't hope to catch up. He refused to leave, and the authorities relented. Not long after that, his fascination with brewing began:

> I went to the Chemistry Society (the Crucible Club) Christmas party. Some of the postgraduates had made home brew, and put it into these big two-and-a-half-litre Winchester bottles. That was it: I knew then that brewing was what I was interested in. It was science, chemistry, engineering, and it was to do with beer! Before the end of my first year, I'd made a resolute decision.

But he knew that he was studying the wrong subject in the wrong city. After consulting a book called *Brewing as a Career*, he contacted Heriot-Watt, and was advised to finish his degree in Belfast and then study as a postgraduate student in Edinburgh. Reluctant to waste any time, while he continued to study at Queen's he began to educate himself through home brewing:

> I spent every penny of my grant money on equipment. I even had a wardrobe, insulated, with a light in it. I started brewing to the classical descriptions of beer at first, using these extract kits, giving myself awful headaches. Then I got a copy of Dave Line's *Brewing Beers Like Those You Buy* and started brewing with grains. I bought my kit at a hardware store that was famous for its home-brewing supplies – they had everything, all from Young's, I think.

When he went to Edinburgh in 1980, he gained a reputation as serious, hard-working and perhaps a little arrogant, as a contemporary, John Keeling, now head brewer at Fuller's, recalled:

> Brendan was certainly a star pupil ... [and] always seemed a man apart who would bend things to his will. He would have to do things his way. Everything he did he had to become an expert at ... I kind of liked him ... Others did not like him at all, but he would not have worried or noticed.[13]

Dobbin's research won the Brewers' Society of Scotland Prize – a 'poxy ten quid', which he spent on beer, of course. He then went on to carry out further research with a scholarship. At this point, as a skilled technical brewer, he could have gone to work for one of the Big Six breweries, as did many of his peers. He got as far as an interview at Guinness:

> I got down to the last five out of 20,000 applicants. I was sat in front of this Church of Ireland Protestant who said, 'So, where do you see yourself in twenty years' time?' and I'm a boat-rocking Belfast man, so I said, 'In your seat, but doing a better job.' He was a stiff. I didn't get the job, funnily enough. Thank God I got turned down, because I'd have died of boredom. Don't get me wrong – the training they give you is second to none, brilliant training, but working in a beer factory making keg beer, watching the kegs go by on a conveyor . . . No thanks. Where's the creativity?

Pioneering UK brewer Brendan Dobbin with Ann Scullion, the founder of Northern Ireland's Hilden Brewery, in 1982.

Instead, while he finished his research, he undertook a 'sort of pupillage, six weeks long' with Peter Austin, founder of real-ale micro-brewery Ringwood: 'We were like two headbangers, working through the night, driving all over the country, brewing and delivering beer, visiting breweries.' It was Austin's recommendation that sent Dobbin to Lisburn, County Antrim, to construct and run Northern Ireland's first 'new generation' brewery, Hilden, in 1982:

> I will say it: I was a pioneer. Contrary to what some little Meantime men claim for themselves, I think I'm right in saying I was the first of the British microbrewers to make lager . . . And that system, with the carefully selected yeast, you'll now find all over the world, stamped 'B. DOBBIN'.

It was while he was at Hilden that he first began to think differently about hops.

> [We] were brewing Hilden Ale with a lot of East Kent Goldings for dry hopping in the cask, and it tasted totally different from one pub to the next. I looked into this and found that, for example, at Queen's University Staff bar, they were keeping the casks in a warm corridor for three weeks, where it was devel-oping this *huge* floral hop character, which affected not only the aroma, but the mouthfeel too.

Once he had got Hilden up and running and had submitted his research paper for evaluation, Dobbin headed for America, as Sean Franklin had done four years before.

In parallel with developments in the UK, the US was also rapidly developing its own 'alternative' beer culture in the face of the complete dominance of big-brand 'light lager'. First, there was Anchor Brewing of San Francisco. A much older company, it was taken over by Fritz Maytag, a young member of a wealthy industrial dynasty, in 1965. He revived 'Steam Beer', which had become much degraded, and turned it into a cult product for discerning drinkers. The US trailed behind Britain but, in 1978, home brewing was legalised by President Jimmy

Carter, which led to a flurry of small start-up breweries. Among the earliest was Sierra Nevada of Chico, California, founded by Ken Grossman and Paul Camusi in 1979, whose beers were bolder and stronger than many British examples, and certainly more characterful than home-grown 'domestic' lagers. By 1984,[14] America – a nation of 230 million people – had fourteen new breweries and brewpubs.

Dobbin hoped to find work at one of those new breweries – River City in Sacramento, California, founded in 1980 by twenty-six-year-old Jim Schlueter, a 'bearded and barrel-shaped' former employee of national giant Schlitz. While other new American breweries were rejecting lager and brewing British-style pale ales and porters, Schlueter chose to produce a 4.8 per cent lager – something mainstream, but with more character. But, as he recalled, Dobbin arrived a little too late:

> Brendan showed up on my doorstep about three days before we closed River City Brewing. Obviously, I couldn't offer him a job, but did agree to help him get a green card and let him move in with my family while we tried to start another brewery. Nothing came of those efforts, but Brendan became a very good friend of myself and my family... He bought an old Suzuki motorcycle and took a job with Campbell's soup... He is hardworking, loyal to a fault, and one of the few people I have ever met who is a bigger risk taker (some might call it crazy) than I am. He was an extremely talented brewer, and genius level smart. [15]

While working in Sacramento, Dobbin took the opportunity to enjoy the local beer, and liked what he found. He described the experience, thirty years on, with evident excitement in his voice:

> I got to drink things like Sierra Nevada Pale Ale, which was very much up-and-coming, highly esteemed, fifty bitterness units, with this loooong aftertaste: you could still taste it on the bus home. It came with a quarter of an inch of thick white yeast sediment in the bottle. Another one was Henry Weinhard's

> Private Reserve lager from Blitz-Weinhard – very widely
> distributed and with the absolutely unmistakable flavour finger-
> print of Cascade hops.

He would hold onto that thought, and dwell on the wonder of
Sierra Nevada Pale Ale, in the years to follow. 'I think Sean Franklin
probably used Cascades before me,' he conceded, but, even so, in 1984
he and Franklin were among a very small number of people who had
ever tasted the citrusy, fruity, perfumed pale ales of the American
variety, let alone conceived of brewing them.

When Dobbin returned to Britain in 1985 to continue working
with Peter Austin, it was as technical adviser to Austin's brewery-
building firm. Dobbin was soon on the road again, gaining yet more
experience of unusual flavours and techniques, building breweries
in Nigeria and China. Throughout, he continued to experiment with
local hops – it turned out that almost every corner of the world had its
own unique-tasting varieties – and to ponder what could be done to
get the best from them. In 1987, having established his own office and
workshop in Stockport, Cheshire, he built himself a small brewery
in which he could experiment freely, and set about recreating Sierra
Nevada Pale Ale and playing with hops from the New World:

> I made Oatmeal Stout, which was fantastic, and three lagers,
> using an old converted freezer . . . I used three different hops,
> one in each: Green Bullet, Super Alpha and Sticklebract. I got
> into those New Zealand hops, installing a brewery in Auckland
> for Peter Austin, and I even had a little brewery of my own set
> up out there.

These hops were all much more potent than the English varieties,
providing, variously, pungent lemon, tropical fruit, pine and (an
acquired taste, but desirable) 'catty' flavours and aroma from a
compound not found in hops grown in the UK.[16] If anyone else in
Britain at this time was using hops from New Zealand, they certainly
weren't shouting about it.

Finally, in 1989 Dobbin set about finding suitable premises for a full-blown brewery, to be called West Coast Brewing, and a pub in which to sell its beer. He settled on the Kings Arms Hotel in Chorlton-on-Medlock, south of Manchester's city centre, bordering on the notorious Moss Side. South Manchester, in the early 1990s, had serious problems with drugs and gangs, and tabloid newspapers gave Moss Side such overblown nicknames as 'Britain's Bronx' or 'Gunchester'.[17] When we spoke to various beer enthusiasts about visiting the Kings Arms, they all said much the same thing: that it was terrifying. Beer obsessive and now brewer Gazza Prescott has compared the estate on which the pub was located to 'a post-nuclear wasteland littered with abandoned prams and cars with feral groups of locals prowling around, intent on mischief', observing that most of them 'seemed to have Stanley knives in their back pockets'.[18] By the time the pub opened on 2 April 1990, Dobbin – used to tough types from his early days in Belfast – had taken steps to establish order:

> This was in the middle of an estate where maybe 50 per cent of the residents had been in prison. We'd virtually rebuilt the pub throughout, totally refurbished it and I had an ex-Army chef in a white coat behind the hot food counter, basically intimidating them into behaving. We treated them with respect, and we expected them to treat us with respect, and it worked. For a while.

Nervous though they might have been, beer geeks and CAMRA members couldn't resist what was on offer: on day one there were nine beers, five of them lagers made with various exotic hop varieties, along with a 'clone' of Tetley's Bitter to appeal to the conservative regulars. After six months or so, 'guest beers' began to appear on the bar – Dobbin's own loving recreations of beers he had enjoyed around the world, such as Sierra Nevada Pale Ale and Henry Weinhard's Special Reserve, with no attempt made to disguise their inspiration. Drinkers were astounded by the enormous hop flavour and, ten years on from Sean Franklin's 'weird' bitter, were now ready to appreciate Cascades. Gazza Prescott recalled the experience:

I raised the glass to my mouth – there was no point in sniffing beer back then as all it smelt of was caramel – but here, rising from the glass in sticky green tendrils, was a bouquet of something very different, something I'd not experienced before, and I was intrigued. I took a long sniff and was astonished by aromas I'd never imagined a beer could possibly possess prior to this moment, aromas suggestive of pineapple, lemon, grapefruit and a hundred things my still-young taste buds hadn't experienced and therefore couldn't match a name to as yet. [19]

Word of this truly remarkable beer spread and the Kings Arms became a place of pilgrimage, as Dobbin remembered:

We used to get busloads of people from the University of Manchester, and groups from CAMRA, and so on, but their cars and buses would get broken into by the local yobbos while they were in the pub.

When Dobbin's Sierra Nevada Pale Ale began to win prizes – it took silver in the 'New Brewery Class' at the 1989 Great British Beer Festival[20] – it came to the attention of the Sierra Nevada Brewing Company in California, who were not impressed. Dobbin reacted with characteristic chutzpah:

I said to them, look, calm down – it was my beer that won the prize, not your brand name. I told them they could make one of my beers under licence, a reciprocal agreement, but they weren't happy with that, so I changed the name, and it became Yakima Grande Pale Ale.

Though it was his hoppy beers that brought the greatest acclaim, and on which his lingering cult reputation is built, Dobbin resisted the temptation to indulge only that market, and is rather scornful of 'hopheads':

> Hops aren't the only flavour in beer . . . My Yakima Grande
> Porter – that had some flowery hops, but it also had almost
> every other flavour you could want . . . There was a ginger beer
> – 6 per cent ABV, low bitterness, two types of ginger, and it
> was *huge*. A student bar, Robinski's, in Manchester, used to buy
> hogsheads of the stuff. So, no, hops aren't everything.

Unfortunately, acclaim and enthusiasm did not pay the bills, and
Dobbin began to feel like a 'glorified tax collector'. After a honeymoon
period, handling the locals also became hard work:

> Do you know what affray is? It's one step down from a riot. We
> had that at the pub. Our staff were attacked, it was madness . . . It
> just got too much – heroin needles on the floor outside the pub,
> break-ins . . .

In 1995, leaving his fans wanting more, Dobbin shut down West
Coast Brewing and entered the final phase of his brewing career,
installing customised brewing kit for the many new Firkin brewpubs
being opened across the country and globally by the chain's new
owners. He also established a raft of new microbreweries in Ireland,
and brewpubs for the Porterhouse chain, the latter producing lager
and nitrogenated 'smooth' stouts using equipment of Dobbin's own
design.

Dobbin's influence can be felt in many breweries still operating
today, from Rochdale's Pictish, which uses kit he designed for the
Freelance and Firkin in Dundee, to Manchester's highly regarded
Marble Brewery, which he built, and whose initial recipes, in Gazza
Prescott's words, 'had that unmistakable "Dobbin's" taste to them'.[21]

And it turns out that the rumours were true: in recent years, he
has directed his engineering skills to 'rewriting the rules of the glass-
house', successfully growing thirty-nine varieties of banana, as well as
mangoes, peppers and Italian pomodoro tomatoes, not far from the
windswept Atlantic Coast.

At about the same time as Dobbin's Manchester brewing concern was in full flow, in September 1992 Sean Franklin arrived back in the brewing industry after seven years spent driving a cab. His new brewery, Rooster's, would fit right into the mid-1990s scene where pale, aromatic, unusual beers were the order of the day:

> Unless you want to use the malts as your 'flavour hook', hops are best shown off against a plain background – just pale malt, without any crystal at all ... Hop Back Summer Lightning ... was a great inspiration, a lovely beer ... The plainer the background, the better it allows the varietal character of the hops to show.

He had unfinished business with Cascade hops, which he had first used in the early 1980s, and now, with a new philosophy, was ready to exploit to the full for their exotic effect. His 'straw-coloured'[22] Yankee clearly proclaimed its American roots. This time round, while some were still put off by the intense 'perfume' character ('washing-up liquid'[23]), Franklin's beers were widely admired, and championed by Michael Jackson at every opportunity.[24]

Writing in the *Sunday Times* in 1997, Andrew Barr summarised the appeal of pale-coloured beers which emphasised hop aroma:

> Many real-ale lobbyists fail to understand what real people want from a pint of beer ... The level of bitterness, as well as much of the flavour, depends on the type of hops that are added to the beer. By using a more aromatic type of hop, it is possible to produce a more flavoursome yet less bitter beer. Above all, a beer needs to be refreshing.[25]

At a time when lager had around 50 per cent of the beer market[26] and was especially popular with young people,[27] golden or 'summer' beers gave real ale a chance to compete, at least superficially. Barr also observed that hops were not the only variable with which brewers were beginning to experiment:

Some have made the beer from wheat as well as barley, in order
to soften it and give it a spicy flavour. Others have actually added
spices to their beer, such as ginger and coriander. They have
made real ale more interesting, as well as more accessible.

Sussex brewers King and Barnes, a family brewery founded in a
merger in 1906, represent an interesting case study. In 1990, they had
just launched a new best bitter, augmenting an already conservative
line-up of beers. By 1997, however, they had gone into overdrive
producing specials, many of them experiments with speciality malts:
Crystal Malt Ale, Rye Beer, Amber Malt Ale, Oatmeal Stout, Summer
Ale, Corn Beer and Wheat Mash were just some of the seasonal beers
they announced,[28] to acclaim from Michael Jackson, among others.
There was a sense that, at last, British breweries were beginning to
spread their wings and explore their potential. Ruth Nicholas, writing
for CAMRA, noted where this trend led: away from seasonal towards
novelty and then into a full-blown and rather desperate pursuit of the
bizarre:

Microbreweries and majors alike are pouring their efforts into
creating a diverse ... range of speciality beer, brewed from
almost anything you can think of. Flora, fauna and fruit figure,
as do shellfish, spices and smoked malts ... There is red, white,
green and ginger beer, oyster stout containing real oysters ...
and ale brewed with flowering heather, treacle, banana, lemon,
pepper and coriander. Novelty beers are the latest phase of the
brewers' long-running campaign to combat declining volume.[29]

Amid the silliness (food colouring and artificial flavourings), some
brewers took a more thoughtful approach. Once again inspired by
European beers, especially those from Belgium, as well as British
brewing history, they began to play with herbs, spices, fruit and even
the complexities of yeast.

Right at the beginning of the 'real ale craze', Mike Cannon at the
Studley Brewery in Warwickshire was adding herbs and spices to his

beer, between 1978 and 1982,[30] but it wasn't until the 1990s that the practice became relatively commonplace. In 1990 Nigel Stevenson, landlord of 'world beer' mecca the Mason's Arms, went from selling Belgian fruit beer to producing his own on the premises, commencing with a brew made using damsons from the nearby Winster Valley.[31] In Suffolk, brewer Ian Hornsey, inspired by a recipe from the 1750s, brewed a beer for Nethergate which contained coriander seeds, as do most Belgian wheat beers.

Perhaps the most extreme end of this tendency was to be found at Liverpool's Passageway Brewing. It was founded in 1994 by Phil Burke and Steve Dugmore, both of whom worked at a secondary school in the city, the former as a chemistry teacher, the latter as a lab assistant. From the outset, their intention was to indulge an obsession of Burke's and produce Belgian-style beers. Whereas others might have looked to Dave Line's home-brewing manuals and produced a mere cosmetic approximation using whichever ingredients were at hand, Burke went to the source.

The key to an authentically Belgian flavour, he knew, was the yeast. While malt and hops provide beer with its body, sweetness and much of its aroma, yeast also plays a vital part. Most Bavarian wheat beers, such as those from Erdinger or Weihenstephan, which have a character usually described as reminiscent of cloves, bananas and bubblegum, demonstrate vividly the impact of yeast on the flavour and aroma of a beer. This is a result of the production by yeast during fermentation of tiny amounts of chemicals called 'esters', which are also given off by ripening fruit.[32] To a less obvious extent, many Belgian breweries are just as dependent on their own 'house strains' of yeast to provide the distinctive spicy fruitiness which distinguishes their beers.

For a decade or so, a favourite trick of British home brewers had been to buy 'bottle-conditioned' beers with yeast sediment in the bottom and to cultivate a larger batch from that small amount, feeding it until it multiplied, in laboratory-like conditions. On this front, Burke, as a chemistry teacher, had a clear advantage, and set about gathering yeast from bottles of Belgian beer, but was unable to achieve satisfactory results. Refusing to give up, he wrote to an eighty-six-year-old 'Father Theodore', the head brewer at a Belgian abbey, for advice. To his surprise, the reply was more than helpful: it was an invitation to visit. Burke got in his car and took a ferry to the Continent.

Burke has never publicly named the Belgian brewery which supplied him with the yeast, but the most famous Father Theodore in Belgian brewing was the genius behind the beers brewed by Chimay, at Scourmont Abbey in Hainaut. Founded in 1862, Chimay's beers, which had been imported into Britain since the 1970s, had a cult following worldwide, not least because they were championed by Michael Jackson. In his 1990 television documentary series '*The Beer Hunter*, Jackson visited Scourmount and interviewed Father Theodore, who was dressed in white robes with a brown cowl, was white-haired and appeared somewhat pop-eyed, reminiscent of Herbert Lom.'[3] He described to Jackson how, in the years after the Second World War, with the guidance of brewing scientist Jan De Clerck, he had personally isolated yeast cells which were then cultivated to create Chimay's distinctive strain.

Whichever Father Theodore Burke met, he was astonished to be given not only a pep talk but a viable sample of the brewery's yeast, on condition that it would not be passed on to any other brewer. This extraordinary act of generosity gave Passageway a distinct edge in what was becoming a crowded marketplace. Just to be one hundred per cent sure, however, Burke also collected a few gallons of holy water from a well dedicated to St Arnold, patron saint of Belgian brewers and hop pickers, at his birthplace of Tiegem, West Flanders.

Back in Liverpool, in an industrial unit five minutes from the docks and wharves of the River Mersey, Burke and Dugmore set about producing, alongside a standard 3.6 per cent British bitter, a series of monastically themed beers, including one named after St Arnold. As well as using the Belgian yeast, each brew of St Arnold was also fortified with a half-pint or so of holy water (the amount varies with the telling of the story) as well as a prayer spoken in Flemish. None of this made any difference to the taste, but it did provide a remarkably effective marketing angle, with even the *Catholic Herald* covering the story.[34] HOLY ORDERS was the headline in the *Guardian*, where Burke, referring to the supposed powers of the well in Tiegem, was quoted as saying:

> We thought it would be nice to sell something which doesn't make people blind drunk. We've even got one customer with cataracts who drinks our beer in the hope that his eye problems will be cured.

Despite achieving a higher profile than their size might have warranted, and winning awards at the CAMRA Great British Beer Festival in 1996 and 1997 in the newly created 'Speciality Beers' category,[35] Burke and Dugmore were reluctant to go 'all in', keeping their day jobs and brewing only at weekends and in the evenings. They would go on to brew Franconian-style Rauchbier, using smoked malt from Bamberg, as well as stronger Belgian-style beers, for a few more years before closing the brewery in 2001.

They and others like them had opened minds. The ever more distinct group of 'beer geeks', many of them by now chatting online and hovering around the more adventurous foreign beer stand at CAMRA's Great British Beer Festival, had seen that British beer could be something more than the brown bitters which dominated 'real ale' culture. From here on, British brewing was to become ever more experimental. In the process, it would make common cause with a new generation of drinkers and entrepreneurs who had little affection for Victorian pubs and country inns so beloved of the SPBW and CAMRA. In the 1990s, the quintessential setting for British beer's continuing diversification would be the modern, minimalist bar.

ELEVEN

UNREAL

Bars and clubs are ideal spaces in which young designers can experiment. The life expectancy of a bar is often no more than three years, so the concern is not to produce a classic design, but instead, more often than not, to create a symbol of the times.

Bethan Ryder, 2002[1]

In the 1990s, the conditions were right for a new niche to emerge – 'a third way', to borrow a catchphrase from the decade, which was neither real ale nor big-brand lager. Its first steps took strange forms – restaurants with beer, and breweries with chefs, and a self-conscious elitism with price tags to match.

In the 1960s and 1970s, lager was marketed as an expensive drink for sophisticates, but British culture soon knocked it down a peg or two. By the 1980s, advertisements for big-brand beers had come to resemble comedy sketches full of cheeky cockneyisms – 'The water in Mah-jor-ka don't taste like what it oughter!', 'Follow the Bear', 'I bet he drinks Carling Black Label' – and in 1988, the term 'lager lout' was coined. Any air of Continental class had gone, replaced by an association with football hooliganism and town-centre scrapping. But those 'louts' were getting older, and the youngsters following in their wake were keen to keep their distance, as one advertising executive observed:

It is not simply that there are fewer young people but, at the moment, anything alcoholic is considered untrendy. Young people are more likely to spend Friday night at a rave with a couple of bottles of Evian water and a tub of Vick's Vapour Rub.[2]

Meanwhile, real ale was trying to rectify its own image problem, as summarised by Andrea Gillies, a 'yuppie with principles', who became editor of CAMRA's *Good Beer Guide* in 1988:

CAMRA is at a crossroads . . . We have to pull together a manifesto for the 1990s, not unlike the Labour Party. We have to convince people that there is something to be done and that the people doing it are not hippies with open-toed sandals, braces and beer bellies.

Under Gillies' leadership, the *Good Beer Guide* became a platform for 'New CAMRA' spin. There were articles about matching beer with food, and 'Women and the Pub'. In the 1990 edition, wine writer and television personality Oz Clarke made the direction of travel clear:

At this very moment, wine and good food are at least democratising themselves and becoming accepted pleasures, available to all sections of society at a none-too-daunting cost . . . I advocate the creation of an elitist attitude to beer. It is a phase which *has* to be gone through.

For their part, the large brewing companies attempted to drag beer 'upmarket' with more expensive and sophisticated advertising, until, by the 1990s, many commercials resembled art films, with gorgeous cinematography and wilful surrealism where previously there had been gags.

From 1987 onward, it was not a lager producer but Guinness who arguably led the way, with a series of offbeat 'Pure Genius' commercials starring Dutch actor Rutger Hauer. Whitbread followed with a campaign for their Belgian lager brand Stella Artois, launched in 1990, which aped the look and feel of the French films *Jean de Florette* and *Manon des Sources*. As a reporter for the *Observer* put it,

'Not, perhaps, an obvious cultural reference for the lager fraternity.'' When Guinness launched Enigma lager in 1995, the supporting TV commercial was a lavish pastiche of Salvador Dalí, concluding with the line: 'I have to go now – my giraffe is on fire.'

It worked, to an extent. The message was that these beers were expensive products for sophisticated people, but it actually made them more appealing to what one brand consultant called '*Loaded* readers, men behaving badly''. Beer, and lager in particular, was the official drink of an emerging 'lad culture'. The protagonists of sitcom *Men Behaving Badly* swigged it. Swaggering Mancunian rock group Oasis carried cans around almost as a fashion accessory, a symbol of their class identity. Lager maintained its share of the market, but there was no way to make it posh again.

CAMRA, too, hit a brick wall: for all Andrea Gillies' efforts, and those of the senior leadership, the newspapers continued to refer to beards, sandals and beer bellies, and the rank-and-file membership resisted Oz Clarke's call for elitism.

There was an approach, however, that would appeal to both aspirational young people and to those wealthy sophisticates who had come to find the wine bar utterly naff. On the one hand, this gave us the 'gastropub', which came into being circa 1991 and which was really an informal restaurant in a pub building, with very little emphasis on beer. On the other hand, it prompted the emergence of European and American-inspired venues – distinctly *not* pubs – selling beer with 'provenance' to go alongside fashionable 'free range' meat and organic vegetables.

First, there was Belgo, a chain of Belgian-themed restaurants, which opened its first branch in Chalk Farm, north London, in 1992. The founders were French-Canadian Denis Blais and 'Anglo-Belgian' André Plisnier, whose father was a 'Spitfire ace' who had settled in the UK after the Second World War. Their 1997 *Belgo Cookbook* is filled with self-mocking photographs, with the two of them rather resembling a culinary version of Gilbert and George: grey-haired

Plisnier in country tweeds and Blais, with long black hair, in retro pinstripe, a loud tie and yellow-tinted spectacles. The inspiration for Belgo was, they claimed, their disappointment on trying to buy 'a large casserole of moules with crispy frites and lashings of mayonnaise' to celebrate a Belgian football victory in 1986:

> We had to settle for a lukewarm pint of Stella Artois and a bag of soggy chips. That night we made a promise to bring the moules-frites-bières experience to London . . . Our biggest obstacle was investment. But our second one was Belgium: people simply laughed at us.[5]

They were also told repeatedly that the English 'will not eat mussels'. But they found investors, and spared no expense on an interior design intended to evoke 'a monastic refectory', 'the artistic and the political landscaping of Europe in the 1990s', the 'European brewery eating hall' and 'concrete sea barricades from Oostende to Blankenberge'. The kitchen extractor fans were, apparently, 'mechanomorphic'.[6]

When critic Jonathan Meades reviewed that first branch of Belgo for *The Times* shortly after its opening in early April 1992, he gave a dazzling description of its appearance, the work of designer Anand Zenz:

André Plisnier (left) and Denis Blais as pictured in their cookbook, preparing to enjoy a glass of Leffe Blonde.

> The street front is concrete, incised with the name in elemental sans serif. The door handle is a very heavy hunk of nautical scrap . . . Once through this door you enter a corridor designed for sensory deprivation and vertiginous imbalance. It slopes. The walls are concrete. Suddenly it all opens up. Down to the left is a chasm, the kitchen . . . The dining room is long, half a barrel vault. Waxed wood tables, chairs whose legs are shaped like axe handles.[7]

He rightly identified that it was both a little confused (Danish *akavit* instead of Belgian *genever*; the words of a French poet on the walls) and rather a caricature, but suggested that none of that mattered: 'Beyond these are the beers, which are probably the real point of the place.' There were six on draught and twenty in bottles,[8] which, as Meades also noted, was no more than many specialist off-licences then carried, despite the founders' claims that their 'unique Belgian beer selection' was 'the best in Britain.'[9]

Even so, Belgo was an enormous success, and in the years that followed was reviewed time after time by newspaper food and drink critics. It was also credited with a sudden craze for beer appearing with equal billing alongside wine in certain expensive restaurants:

> At the Greenhouse in Mayfair, where Gary Rhodes cooks for business-suited Britain in the English mode, the proprietor, David Levin, proudly pointed out to me that the restaurant's bar serves draught real ale (Arkells, in fact) ... Charles Fountain's Quality Chop House in Farringdon Road serves Greene King, Abbot Ale and White Shield Worthington, and ... a carte des bières at Stephen Bull's Bistro in St John Street has recently included Traquair House Ale and Orkney Skull-splitter, as well as bottle-conditioned Belgian, German and Australian curiosities.[10]

If some thought that 'beer tasting' was pretentious, then matching beer with food was something else. Belgo suggested specific beers to accompany dishes from the menu – part of everyday life in Belgium, they argued. In Britain, it did serve to make beer more appealing to those who might otherwise be turned off by the drink's rough-and-ready machismo.

In 1995, Belgo expanded, opening a second, much larger branch in London's Covent Garden. 'World beer' had come a long way from the days of classified ads and Transit vans on cross-Channel ferries: it looked ready to conquer every high street in the country, and make Plisnier and Blais very rich. They had proved the existence of a new market, and it was only a matter of time before others decided to join the race.

🕮

These days, Oliver Peyton is best known for his appearances on TV cookery programmes, most notably *Great British Menu*, on which he is the 'bad cop' judge, his face permanently contorted into a look of disgust and boredom. He might not thank us for revealing, then, that when we interviewed him he was rather softly spoken and pleasant, with a tendency to clear his throat and switch into his 'plain-speaking cynic' persona only when delivering what he knew was a particularly juicy sound bite. Today he is a restaurateur who specialises in turning museum and gallery cafés into destination eating places, and a family man in his fifties. In 1996, when he entered the world of brewing, he was just thirty-four years old, 'an animated Irishman of a certain style with a Tin Tin haircut and a designer jacket with all four buttons done up', and with a reputation for serious partying.[11]

Born in Sligo in the North West of Ireland, he spent some time in New York as a teenager, working in construction and then as a waiter, where he was inspired by the city's culture of informal 'eating out'. At university in England in the 1980s he became a keen clubber, which led him to open a basement club in London.

His first foray into the beer business was as an importer during the 'designer beer' boom of the late 1980s and early 1990s. This brief craze saw the first introduction to the UK of some highly rated beers from Belgium and elsewhere, which was mainly about the packaging, and Peyton was attracted to the space-age design of the cans used for Japanese lager Sapporo. At a time when Japanese culture was cool, thanks in part to computer games, comic books and cartoons, Peyton became the sole British importer for the beer.

When he graduated from basement clubs, it was to the Atlantic Bar and Grill near Piccadilly, the place to be seen in 1994 and unashamedly modish, according to a reporter for the *Independent*:

Queues form outside; people plead with Alex the doorman and grumble as those with dinner reservations breeze past. Celebrity spotters mention Rifat Ozbek, John Galliano, Ben Elton and Kate Moss . . . True, the place gets fearsomely hot and smoky, and true, some customers complain about the lengthy wait for expensive drinks at the main bar, but this does not deter the glamour babes in A-line minidresses or cheekboned men with tight T-shirts and muscular torsos; this is the place of the moment. You don't have to be a member and you can drink here until 3 a.m.[12]

Oliver Peyton photographed by Barry Marsden in 1999, with suitably futuristic-looking fermenting vessels in the background.

After the huge success of the Atlantic, and of a Mayfair restaurant, Coast, Peyton headed North to expand his empire. He chose Manchester, a city at the forefront of what Tony Blair would soon christen 'Cool Britannia'. Peyton called the new venture Mash And Air, and chose a former industrial building on the corner of Chorlton and Canal Streets, at the centre of the thriving 'gay village'. Constructed of red brick, it wouldn't look out of place in New York, which is perhaps why it caught his eye. Mash, on the lower floors, was for 'informal dining' and drinking, with Air, on the top floors, a more formal restaurant. Mash's interior, designed by Australian architect Mark Newson, was lime green and orange, with rounded edges and portholes. Banquettes were sunk into the floor with tables at ground level. It looked like something from *Star Wars* or *Space 1999*. 'It was totally a reaction to CAMRA and the Firkin pub and all that,' said Peyton:

> To be in CAMRA you had to be restoring a Triumph Bonneville; have a beard; have a rather stretched gut at the age of forty-five . . . I hated the idea that CAMRA 'owned' beer, and that you had

to go to one place for wine, another for cocktails. Why couldn't they be in one place, and you drink what you like? That's what I was doing with Mash And Air.

The centrepiece, and inspiration for the name, was a brand-new, state-of-the-art microbrewery worth £200,000, capable of producing 18,000 pints of beer a week.[13] Mash And Air opened at the beginning of December 1996, and the brewery, installed in a well, which rose through the height of the building, was visible on every floor. Writing for the *Independent* in January 1997, Caroline Stacey described it as 'a brilliantly contemporary-looking engine room – a canny tribute to a place that understands the attraction of manufacturing like no other.'[14] When Peyton posed for portrait photographer Barry Marsden, he stood in front of the fermenting vessels with their space-age numbers, reflective steel and lurid carrot-coloured paintwork. After the elitism of champagne at the Atlantic, this was a populist gesture, of sorts, as Peyton recalled:

> It seemed to me that beer was either about spit-and-sawdust, old-fashioned pubs, or it was imported or brewed under licence with a foreign name. Why does something have to be foreign to be good? Having good food, good beer, is such an important part of national identity. I wanted there to be some really good British beer, especially lager. I suppose I wanted it to be 'younger'.

Having a beautiful brewery was all well and good, but who was going to run it? Where would he find someone who would understand what he was trying to do, was creative and was also technically competent? Brendan Dobbin might have been a good choice, but instead, Peyton poached a young brewer who was already working for a similar, if less ambitious operation in London:

> Someone suggested Alastair Hook to me but, to be honest, how many 'young', different brewers were there? Who else really knew how to make lager? He'd studied in Germany, and where else do you go to learn about brewing lager?

Alastair Hook grew up in Greenwich and Blackheath and speaks with a soft but distinct nasal south London accent.[15] The first beer he ever drank was a pint of Theakston's Best Bitter in Cartmel in the Lake District when he was thirteen years old, under the supervision of his father. His education was furthered at Thomas Tallis, the comprehensive school in Kidbrooke he attended until 1982:

> A big influence was my music teacher, Keith Lark, who used to travel around the country researching and writing about beer. My friend Martin Bennett and I used to go with him on the train sometimes, to places like the Black Country, Manchester, Oxford, searching out cask ale.

He also had an eye on what was going on outside the UK. His stepmother was German, and he spent many summers visiting cousins there. After school, he travelled around Europe on an InterRail ticket, a copy of Michael Jackson's tall, slim paperback *Pocket Guide to Beer* in his rucksack. On his return, he started a degree in economic and social history at the University of York, but, while working on a paper about Arthur Guinness, it dawned on him that he was in the wrong place, studying the wrong subject: 'I realised that what I really wanted to do was brew, and so I left after a term, before I forfeited my grant, and went to Heriot-Watt to study brewing and distilling.'

In Edinburgh, he was an active student CAMRA member, founding what was, rather surprisingly, the university's first beer society. That there wasn't already such an organisation when he arrived was, with hindsight, a warning sign: 'Heriot-Watt was very much about the industrial side of things, the process – there was a lack of passion. I knew there had to be something more.' It was at this point that his gaze turned, once again, towards the Continental tradition: 'I noticed that about half the literature in the library was in German and no one was reading it, so I learned German.'

In 1989, he left the UK and headed to Munich, where he studied at 'the world's oldest brewery', Weihenstephan. Bayerische Staatsbrauerei Weihenstephan is a working brewery but also acts as the brewing school for the Technische Universität München (TUM). There, studying under the 'beer pope', Dr Ludwig Narciss – a serious scientist worshipped by technical brewers as if he were a rock star – he found what he was looking for: 'A universal reverence for beer.'

> Going to Germany was like a pilgrimage. They were maturing things for three to six weeks, wouldn't think of pasteurising anything. Local and authentic ... What I saw in Germany was that brewery-conditioned beer has many advantages over cask-conditioned beer. With cask-conditioned beer, a passionate brewer works so hard to create a beautifully crafted product, and then hands control over to untrained people in the supply chain who don't respect it.

After Weihenstephan, he was employed at another Bavarian brewery, Kaltenberg, owned and run by Prinz Luitpold of Wittelsbach, great-grandson of King Ludwig III (most of the brewery's beers are marketed under the name König Ludwig). It was in 1990, while working at Kaltenberg, that he received a long-distance telephone call that would bring him home to Kent. Clive Butler and Roger Quinn, proprietors of The Packhorse, a country-inn-cum-nightclub near Ashford, had paid a quarter of a million pounds for a very small (eight-barrel) German brewery installation and wanted a genuine German brewer who could speak English to run it. They called Dr Narciss, who put them on to Hook.

For the first time, still only in his twenties, he was head brewer, and with no obligation to brew the kinds of British 'real ale' in which he was no longer especially interested:

> We made three beers – a golden pilsner, a Viennese amber and a Munich dark lager. I used Weihenstephan yeast with local Kentish malt and hops. It was properly funded and the system was good enough to give real control over the process for brewery conditioning.

This was, as far as we have been able to tell, the first British micro-brewery producing only lager, though others had certainly tested the water. It wasn't an entirely happy experience for Hook, however: the locals did not share his 'reverence for beer' and, though they liked lager well enough, weren't particularly interested in its provenance: 'They just wanted to get drunk and pull.' After three years, the proprietors cut their losses: 'They sold the brewhouse to Uzbekistan, put in Foster's taps and that was that.'

Unfortunately, having decided that 'brewery-conditioned' beer was where his ambitions lay, Hook would need substantial capital before he could launch another brewing venture. After a period editing a magazine for SIBA and doing some consultancy work, by 1994 he was running Brewers Imports Ltd, taking advantage of his connections in Germany to source unusual brands.

One of his customers was Mark Dorber, manager of the White Horse on Parson's Green, Fulham, west London. Since gaining a cult reputation among west London CAMRA members in the early 1980s, the pub's reputation had grown hugely, thanks to Dorber's efforts in sourcing American and Belgian beer to sell alongside famously well-cared-for, cask-conditioned ale. 'Parson's Green came to be a sort of "beer central",' he told us. Together, Dorber and Hook ran a 'Bavarian Beer Hunt' in late 1994, showcasing a series of German beers with great success: they sold 2,500 pints of Schneider Weisse wheat beer in August that year, at what was then an eye-watering £2.60 each.[16] (Approaching £4.50 in today's money, and a pound more than the average price of a pint in central London at the time.[17])

The White Horse was sometimes known as 'the Sloaney Pony' (much to Dorber's annoyance), as it was the haunt of numerous wax-jacketed, public-school-educated wealthy types, as well as Michael Jackson and other 'beer freaks'. While in the orbit of the pub, Hook was approached by Ewan Eastham, a property developer and architect based in the area. Eastham had been travelling and decided that there was a gap in the UK market for 'serious lager' of the type he had enjoyed abroad and, in a mews in Fulham, established the Freedom Brewery. Hook:

> He was a Sloane Ranger. He decided that Fulham would be the perfect place for a brewery producing German-style, Continental-style beers. He struggled to get the money together but we set it up for about £100k. It wasn't quite good enough – you couldn't bottle the beer and have it stable for more than about four or five weeks.

The brewery began trading in early 1995, and Michael Jackson spoke to Eastham about its name in an interview in May the same year: 'When I asked about the name, he explained that "freedom" was the most important word in the language. I thought that response a trifle pompous, but I concede he has some good ideas.'[18]

For his part, Hook, despite his youth, was developing a confidence in his abilities which, at times, led him to sound rather arrogant. 'British brewers don't make good lager through ignorance,' he told Roger Protz. 'They don't understand the subtlety of the system. They haven't spent months in Bavaria revelling in the joys of bottom fermentation.'[19] Perhaps that swagger was justified: Freedom Lager was successful and, stylishly packaged, found its way into supermarkets and hip restaurants and bars across London.

'The best customer for Freedom,' Hook told us, 'was Oliver Peyton and his Atlantic Bar and Grill. When he wanted to set up Mash And Air in Manchester, he poached me.'

Being part of Peyton's empire – 'a proper investment' – was a vast improvement on Freedom and a million miles from the real ale of his teenage years:

> At Mash And Air, we brewed every style under the sun. It was all about 'styles', which is great because of the difference between them – the demarcation lines between one beer and another are really clear. There's a huge spectrum of different beers.

Oliver Peyton echoed that:

> We were making these great lagers, and fruit beer, very complex,
> good with food – nothing like the kind of brown, sort of
> one-dimensional British beers there were then, and no one else
> was really doing it.

This perhaps overstates the originality of the beer Hook was
making – by that time others were also producing fruit beer, lager
and American-style pale ales. But it is certainly true that Mash And
Air took the marriage of food and beer to a new level, and undeniably
achieved a high profile outside the 'beer geek bubble', as Alastair
Hook described with great pride:

> We were also into beer and food, starting all that in Britain. I was
> working with Jason Atherton and Bruno Loubet designing beer
> and food menus – things like peach beer to go with hoisin duck
> pizzas, amazing things like that. We were having brewmaster's
> lunches on Saturdays, but also making those classical styles like
> German Alt and Vienna lager.

Those lunches cost around £15 per person, and consisted of a tour
of the brewery, followed by a two-course meal and 'tutored tasting'.[20]
This kind of thing, and especially the 'high end' pricing, alienated
more traditional beer enthusiasts. In an article for the local CAMRA
newsletter, *Opening Times*, local beer guru John Clarke reflected on
that problem:

> It's difficult to see just who Mash And Air is aimed at. The
> customers you would normally expect to patronise a brewpub
> (or even a brew-restaurant) will be put off by both the 'non-real'
> beers and the ludicrously high prices. On the other hand, the
> money-is-no-object smart set which would seem to be the target
> audience are unlikely to appreciate or understand the beers
> which are being and will be produced. In fact, the inclusion of a
> microbrewery would seem to serve no purpose other than as a

fashion accessory to the eating and drinking experience on offer,
rather than be a serious attempt to enhance the city's beer and
brewing scene.[21]

When we spoke to him, Alastair Hook refused to be drawn on the
criticism he has received from real-ale devotees over the years, saying,
with a steely note: 'You're not going to get me to slag off CAMRA.'
Oliver Peyton, however, was not so reticent: 'What *is* CAMRA, now?
It reminds me of those preservation societies, and I just think, *let it
go*. I'm not saying traditional beer isn't worth preserving but *please!*'
At any rate, in the 1990s both shrugged off accusations of pretentiousness – or perhaps even welcomed them. Word got round that,
to borrow the headline of a rather reluctantly positive review in the
Manchester Evening News, PEYTON'S PLACE DOES LIVE UP TO
THE HYPE. The review in question summed up the appeal of the
bar-restaurant complex rather archly:

> The view over the Rochdale canal might not match a vista over
> the Thames, but at Mash And Air you just know where the heart
> is. No other Manchester restaurant has been so consciously
> hyped as an outpost of fashion-statement carousing than
> Oliver Peyton's concept slap-up in a brewery ... One flash
> Sunday columnist on a magazine was proclaiming Mash And
> Air THE place to go in Manchester at least three months before
> it opened.[22]

The bar-restaurant complex became popular with local celeb-
rities,[23] and Peyton had great plans for expansion along the lines of
the Belgo model, saying at the time: 'Mash is the company's vehicle
for going forward. I see it as a thing you could put anywhere – Leeds,
Bristol, Edinburgh, Oxford and Glasgow – but sites are difficult.'
He also revealed that guidance had been produced so that Mash
could be easily cloned anywhere in the country.[24] The concept was
exported to London, with Mash 2 opening on Great Portland Street,
near Oxford Circus in 1998, under Hook's supervision. It, too, was

successful in that it drew crowds of young people interested in the latest 'thing', but even so, that was as far as plans for a chain went.

First, Hook left to found Meantime Brewing: 'In 1999, I got to do what I wanted to do all along, really, move on to open my own brewery. Mash And Air were my first customers, I was brewing for them under contract.' Then, in January 2000, Air, the restaurant part of the Manchester operation, closed; Mash lingered on until August the same year. Mash 2 in London is still operating, but brewing ceased there in 2007.

Peyton hasn't been involved in brewing since but, these days, with beer once again hot property, he has considered 'maybe opening a little pub brewery'. For his part, Alastair Hook has gone on to find great commercial success with beer very much of the kind he was making for Peyton, but packaged with a greater respect for tradition. In 2001, Meantime gained a 'brewery tap' in Greenwich, which, though certainly not 'spit and sawdust', was more or less pub-like in style, with stripped-back wood and Victorian fittings and furniture.

Mash And Air and the Belgo chain, with their duck pizzas and moules-frites, actually appealed to the people the big TV campaigns for lager could only aspire to reach. Without expensive advertising campaigns, by selling products with what Hook has called 'layers and a story, and people', they drew in British drinkers who were turned off by anything that smelt of Olde England and who wouldn't have dreamed of going near a CAMRA festival.

They demonstrated, too, that beer could not only be trendy, but also exclusive. Where CAMRA had always fought against 'rip-off' prices for real ale, Hook felt no qualms about charging what he felt was a fair price for a 'premium' product. If that put off the 'beer bores' and kept the crowd young, rich and beautiful, so much the better. There would be plenty more 'overpriced craft beer' in the years that followed.

TWELVE

NEITHER ART NOR SCIENCE

> The present generation of young drinkers is the most
> credulous, malleable and undiscerning ever . . . [They]
> appear to be complete suckers for tasteless beer in
> tasteless bars. This lot would drink their granny's
> widdle if some smart-arse copywriter came up with a
> line that persuaded them into thinking it was a fresh,
> exotic and sexy kind of lager. Heaven knows what they
> will turn to next.
>
> Matthew Engel, 1999[1]

The term 'craft beer' did not appear so much as evolve, and the word 'craft' has been lurking in conversation about British beer for about as long as there has been a conversation. 'A Drinker', author of 1934's *A Book About Beer*, was groping towards the idea:

> What is brewing? Is it an art or a science? My own answer to
> this question is that it is neither an art nor a science, but a *tradi-*
> *tional procedure*. It is complicated and it is exact; but it does not
> appear to owe much to the investigations of trained research
> workers. Pasteur's examinations into the diseases to which beers
> are subjected seem distant and academic when one is standing
> on the brewing stage savouring some of the most marvellous
> perfumes of the world.[2]

These thoughts reflected a debate within the industry about whether brewing was art, craft or science, with one commentator suggesting that 'As an art, it was old. As a science, it was very new'.³ Worthington's of Burton upon Trent employed the phrase 'the craft of brewing' in advertisements during the 1930s with that thinking in mind, downplaying the industrial processes behind large-scale brewing and instead promoting a more traditional, homespun image. The same distinction was perhaps also behind the use of the term 'Craft Brothers' to refer to home brewers by Ken Shales in his 1967 book, *Brewing Better Beer*.

By the 1970s, E.F. Schumacher, in his influential book *Small is Beautiful*, was identifying 'craft' as preferable to 'mechanisation', citing philosopher Ananda Coomaraswamy's observation that a 'craftsman' can always 'draw the delicate distinction between the machine and the tool'.⁴

From the late 1970s onward, those who did not believe that all 'real ale' was good and everything else bad began to search for a catch-all term. Michael Jackson, in his 1977 *World Guide to Beer*, used the phrases 'craft brewers' and 'craft-brewed' in reference to Belgium, France and the USA, but only in passing.⁵ (This was probably a direct translation of the French *artisanal*.) Throughout the 1980s, however, he tended to talk about 'distinctive' or 'characterful' beers. Danny Blyth and others, writing for CAMRA at the same time, borrowed this approach, especially when referring to 'distinctive bottled ales'.⁶ Paul Soden of SIBA came up with this far-from-catchy description: 'Most of us produce non-chemical, non-keg, hundred per cent malt brews.'⁷ Latterly, Jackson began to prefer the term 'boutique beers',⁸ which today sounds like a relic of the 1980s. In the 1990 *Good Beer Guide*, CAMRA employed the clumsy formulation 'hand-crafted beers of character and distinction'.⁹

It was in the United States, where the consumer revolt was not over keg vs cask but small vs big, that the word 'craft' would really find a footing. Though acknowledging that he might have picked it up in conversation with CAMRA activists on visits to the UK in the mid-1980s, American brewer and beer writer Vince Cottone has staked a claim to popularising its usage in America[10] because his 1986 *Good Beer Guide: Brewers and Pubs of the Pacific Northwest* included this statement:

> I use the term Craft Brewery to describe a small brewery using traditional methods and ingredients to produce a handcrafted, uncompromised beer that is marketed locally ... The name Craft Brewery is used in lieu of several other terms which have been used recently to describe small breweries ... I chose Craft Brewery because it better describes the breweries we are discussing.[11]

Ian Garrett has served as a volunteer on the 'foreign beer bar' (now called Bières Sans Frontières) at CAMRA's Great British Beer Festival since 1988, when it consisted of 'a side table with about thirty Belgian beers'.[12] He recalled that American beers began to appear in greater numbers from the early 1990s onward and were being described as 'craft beer' by their brewers. He also suggested that perhaps 'BSF', a popular destination at the festival, especially for brewers themselves, helped to popularise the term in the UK.

When a slew of articles about exciting developments in American brewing began to appear in Britain in the early 1990s, it became clear that 'craft' had won the writers' vote: Ed Vulliamy wrote for the *Observer* about US 'craft ale' in 1994.[13] Roger Protz, also by this time a frequent visitor to the US, followed him in 1995 by applying the term to British brewing in a round-up of Manchester's 'independent craft breweries'.[14]

So far, so good, but confusion arose as the term was co-opted by different interest groups. When a new national society for home brewers launched in 1995, it was called the Craft Brewing Association, as founder James McCrorie recalled:

> I wanted something that didn't include the term 'home brewing' – it had come to mean, in Britain, 'a can of crap and a kilo of sugar'. I'd never heard the term 'craft beer' ... Since then, it's

taken off thanks to sloppy journalism, and because people like Roger Protz started using it.[15]

At the same time, when Frank Baillie, CAMRA stalwart and author of *The Beer Drinkers' Companion* (1973), used the term 'craft breweries' in an article for short-lived magazine *The Taste* in 1998, he was referring specifically to cask-conditioned real ale from breweries 'that are concerned above all with quality'.[16] SIBA were also using it to refer to their members, who did not produce exclusively real ale.[17] Later that same year, it seems to have been taken up by Bill Dwan, with the headline accompanying an interview he gave with a journalist at the *Financial Times* being the earliest instance we have found of 'craft beer' being used to mean bottled and kegged microbrewery beer positioned as the *antithesis* of 'real ale':

> [Dwan] believes that microbrewing is handicapped by its associ-
> ations with real ales. In contrast to real ale, which is conditioned
> and fermented in the cask, and hand tapped, Dwan beers are
> pressurised and bottled or sold in kegs. Where real-ale enthu-
> siasts are concerned with how a beer is stored, microbreweries
> focus on the quality of the hops.[18]

In Leeds in 1997, what was arguably the UK's first 'craft beer bar' opened for business, though it was not, at first, described as such. It scaled down the cool of Mash And Air to fit a derelict shop unit; toned down the emphasis on dining and added more and better beer, creating a template which has since been much imitated.

The founders of North were John Gyngell and Christian Townsley, from Stockport and Sunderland respectively, who had come to Leeds to study at the university but dropped out. Gyngell, a few years older than his business partner, is tall and angular, wears dark-framed glasses and has black hair that makes him look somewhat Mediterranean. He might be described as sardonic. Townsley, on the other hand, seems cheerfully dazed, almost as if he might still be feeling the after-effects of the loved-up 1990s, and smiles constantly, though he is now in his late thirties and grey-haired.

They met while working together as barmen at the Town and Country Club. As Townsley told us, they began to feel frustrated that even a cosmopolitan city like Leeds had nowhere to go for a drink before moving on to a nightclub at a respectably late hour.

> Leeds just didn't have anywhere to hang out, except pubs, and pubs weren't what we wanted. There was maybe Mojo, which opened before us, and the Arts Café. There were a few coffee shops. That was it.

Like many of their generation, they found pubs old-fashioned and soporific, and Gyngell in particular missed Manchester's thriving bar 'scene'. It had grown up alongside the music scene popularly known as 'Madchester', and in response to a drive by the city's council to create a European-style, twenty-four-hour culture as part of its regeneration programme. Entrepreneur and broadcaster Tony Wilson, co-founder of Factory Records and manager of the Hacienda nightclub, opened Dry Bar in his home city in 1989. Its look and atmosphere were directly inspired by European café culture and by ultra-stylish bars such as Barcelona's Nick Havanna.[19] According to one expert on the Manchester scene, Dry Bar met a need among young people for 'a different kind of drinking establishment, not like the kind of place their big brothers went . . . where you could go in and order a cappuccino at 9 p.m. on a Friday night with no qualms.'[20] John Gyngell acknowledged that, in turn, Dry Bar was a key inspiration for his venture in Leeds.

Both Gyngell and Townsley were particularly eager to underline the fact that they had never intended to target 'anoraks', and Townsley repeated this point several times:

> It was never about beer . . . just about offering something different and better, as part of the whole range. First and foremost, we want it to be somewhere good to drink.

They found a derelict hardware shop – 'Knobs and Knockers'. It was in an unappealing part of central Leeds, according to Gyngell:

> People thought we were making a mistake opening a bar on
> Briggate. This was kebab alley. I remember driving past here
> with my mum and showing her the site and she just said: 'What
> the hell are you doing?'

To pay for the refit, as David Bruce had done in 1979, they took
loans from a bigger brewery – Yorkshire giant John Smith's of
Tadcaster, who distributed Kronenbourg lager and other such highly
advertised brands in the region.

Because the premises wasn't licensed to sell alcohol, they had to
make a case to the local magistrates, as Townsley recalled:

> We literally had to draw a map with circles to show that there
> were no other bars or pubs nearby. There's a theatre here with
> with a licensed bar, there's that pub, and so on – drawing circles
> with compasses to show the area they covered. It was really
> tedious, the whole process, but we saw it through.

After North Bar opened on 26 June 1997, the two faced a
depressing six months: no one came. 'We'd be sat in the window with
drinks, trying to make it look busy to people walking past,' recalled
Townsley. Worse, those who weren't indifferent to North Bar seemed
offended by the very idea, perhaps with a fixed impression of how a
'pub' should look, as Gyngell remembered with evident chagrin:

> I once came to open up and found two people, just ordinary,
> nice-looking people, looking through the window. I thought,
> great, customers! Then I heard the bloke say, with sort of *disgust*:
> 'What the *fuck* is that?' I was mortified. You want people to like
> you, don't you? And he really hated what he was seeing.

The bar did find its customers, however, though in those early
days, it was the party atmosphere that brought them in rather than
the beer. 'We were the biggest Kronenbourg account in the North
of England at one point,' Townsley told us with a mixture of pride

and embarrassment. 'It was considered the classy option then,' added Gyngell. '"Premium", and we thought it tasted pretty good. We had Beamish Irish Red for a while . . . John Smith's, Foster's.'

At some point – nobody can recall exactly when – either they approached import company James Clay, or were approached by them. Founded in 1980 as a partnership between Peter Clay and his son Ian, by the early 1990s James Clay was one of the major importers of American 'craft beer', notably from Anchor and New York's Brooklyn Brewery.[21] Having been drinking the influential American IPA Anchor Liberty at the Atlantic Bar and Grill and at Mash in Manchester – 'a real landmark beer' – they began stocking it at North, along with Chimay and Duvel from Belgium. They are proudest, though, of being among the first outlets in the UK, and almost certainly in Leeds, for Erdinger Weissbier from Bavaria:

> It got to the point where, when the John Smith's [sales repre-sentative] came round, we were standing there trying to conceal the number of beers from other breweries we had on. Eventually we just wanted to get rid of Kronenbourg, so we paid the loan off early.

From here on, beer – 'something different' – became a central part of North Bar's appeal. Others, too, were looking for ways to distin-guish their 'offer'.

❧

At the height of its hipness, in 1998 André Plisnier and Denis Blais sold Belgo and moved on. By that time, Belgian beer was every-where, and there were several specialist cafés. L'Abbaye in London's Smithfield served twenty-eight types of Belgian beer and resembled, according to Roger Protz, 'a Low Countries "brown café"'.[22] The Dove on Broadway Market in Hackney, east London, might have been transplanted whole from a backstreet in Brussels. Den Engel (The Angel) in Leek, Staffordshire, established by Geoff and Hilary Turner in 1996,[23] proved that the craze wasn't restricted to London.[24] Even mainstream chain pubs began to stock Leffe 'abbey' beers and

Hoegaarden wheat beer. Under the stewardship of Luke Johnson, who had turned Pizza Express into a high-street chain, Belgo continued to expand around the world, and gained two spin-off 'Bierodrome' Belgian beer bars in London in 1999.

In May 2001, brothers Jeff and Steve Pickthall opened Microbar in London. Cumbrian natives, they were inspired by both the world beer at Nigel Stevenson's Mason's Arms, and, more immediately, by Jeff's holidays in San Francisco in the late 1990s:

> What I found . . . was that good beer was everywhere . . . [and] the people drinking these beers were the very people that the real-ale businesses at home found hard to sell to: young people and women . . . This trip, and a return visit the following year, convinced me that the struggles and complaints of marginalisation in the world of real ale were simple failures of marketing rather than incontestable laws of nature . . . Back home, Steve and I became evangelists for a new way of selling beer . . . We wouldn't be anti-lager or anti-keg, acknowledging that CAMRA's proposition – real ale good; everything else bad – just ain't true.[25]

The Pickthall brothers, like Brendan Dobbin before them, were 'enchanted by Sierra Nevada Pale Ale' in particular. The bar was on Lavender Hill in Battersea, south-west London, and occupied a shop unit rather than a traditional pub building. Its name was written over the door in chromed sans serif letters alongside a logo that might have sat more easily on the headed notepaper of a research laboratory. A year after they opened, *The Sun* featured Microbar in one of its perennial articles on the price of beer, citing its £3.80 pints of Anchor Liberty Ale (a strong IPA imported from San Francisco) as the 'priciest' pint in Britain.[26] They distanced themselves from 'real ale' at every turn, as Steve Pickthall recalled in a recent interview: 'We didn't sell a lot of British beer because it had stories about dwarves and things on the label and we couldn't sell it to trendy Claphamites.'[27]

They adopted the term 'craft beer', which they'd come across in

California, as reported by Nicki Symington for the *Daily Telegraph* in 2001:

> The chiller cabinet behind the bar in the Microbar's aubergine-coloured interior is stuffed with variously sized bottles with bright esoteric-looking labels, bearing pictures of fruit or monks or both. At first glance, most of the beers appear to be Belgian, American and Czech, but there is a respectable number of British-made beers in the line-up, all made by 'craft' (i.e. small) brewers.[28]

Like Bill Dwan, the Pickthalls used 'craft beer' as an antidote to what they viewed as a poisonous 'real ale' culture. The latter, they felt, focused on dogma and technicalities at the expense of flavour: too many cask-conditioned beers were bland, conservative and barely distinguishable from one another, but, as long as they were 'real', CAMRA would promote them over fundamentally far more interesting products from bottles or kegs. And they had a point. When CAMRA was founded in 1971, cask-conditioned bitters *were* the most characterful beers available, so fighting for 'real ale' and 'good beer' were one and the same thing. By the late 1990s, the scene had become much more complicated, and, in the eyes of some, CAMRA had become part of the problem.

Microbar did not work out for the Pickthalls – a common fate for pioneers – but, in August 2006, after they had sold the bar and moved back to Cumbria, another 'craft beer bar' opened in London. The Rake is in London's Borough Market, a five-minute walk from the site of the former Becky's Dive Bar, and not much further away from the site of David Bruce's Goose and Firkin. It was founded by Richard Dinwoodie and Mike Hill, who had been selling beer from a stall in Borough Market since December 1999, branching out into wholesale a few years later. The bar ('we have never claimed to be a pub') was intended to act as a 'shop window', but, in a city then well supplied with both CAMRA kosher 'real ale pubs' and stylish bars with bog-standard beer, The Rake was an immediate success in its own right.

Occupying what had been a 'greasy spoon' café serving fried breakfasts to market traders on a narrow side road, at thirteen by seven feet[29] it is too small to have its own toilets – customers are obliged to use the public lavatories next door – and has no kitchen. When it became a 'must visit' destination for trendsetters as well as beer geeks, its size only emphasised overnight just how crowded it became, with people spilling out onto the pavement and into a 'garden' (actually an artfully decorated area of decking out of a side door).

Its location put beer – Belgian, American, German, British – right at the centre of 'foodie' London, just in time to showcase the products of another growth spurt in British alternative brewing.

THIRTEEN

INNOVATION, PASSION, KNOWLEDGE

While Kenneth Clarke, his predecessor, sipped whisky
at the despatch box, Mr Brown refreshes himself with
Highland Spring mineral water.

Financial Times, 1999[1]

Throughout the 1990s, SIBA continued to campaign for prefer-
ential tax breaks for small brewers. This felt like unfinished
business from the Beer Orders; it was frustrating to have had what
the Society's leadership saw as a vital reform scuppered by lobbying
from big beer. Paul Soden handed over leadership of SIBA to David
Roberts in 1992, having remained in place hoping to see the introduction of a 'sliding scale'. Meanwhile, in 1995 the Society changed its
name to the 'Society for Independent Brewers', losing 'the pejorative
word "small"'.[2]

Soden's sucessors kept up the pressure,[3] and there were hopes
that the new Labour government, elected in May 1997, would be
warmer towards the idea. In 1999, SIBA's leadership thought they'd
convinced the Chancellor, Gordon Brown, to include a sliding-scale
tax break in his March Budget, only to be disappointed when no
such commitment appeared in his speech.[4] The tone of their lobbying

became ever angrier – Gordon Brown was 'the smugglers' friend', his policies seen to encourage illegal imports of cheap beer and spirits from the Continent[5] – but to no avail.

More than twenty years after SIBA's founding, what finally made the difference was pure politics, as Gordon Brown's Treasury team sought some good news to liven up his April 2002 Budget speech. A sliding scale for small brewers wouldn't cost much to implement, but allowed him to make the following munificent-sounding statement:

> To encourage one group of small businesses, the nation's small breweries – often village pubs, some two centuries old – I have decided that the duty paid on their own beer will be halved. This is a cut equal to 14p off each pint, to be implemented . . . by this summer – in time for the World Cup. It will also be available in Scotland, Wales and Northern Ireland.[6]

However, it skirted around the fact that, as Robin Young observed in *The Times*, it would 'affect only one pint in fifty',[7] and larger brewers grumbled. SIBA were, of course, delighted, and there was a euphoric response to the culmination of twenty years of campaigning.[8]

The minute what was christened 'Progressive Beer Duty' (PBD) came into force, small brewers producing fewer than 30,000 hecto-litres a year were able to halve their tax bills on the first 50,000 litres. It saved some from closure and allowed others to expand. Alastair Hook, whose Meantime brewery was then only two years old, told us that it came at just the right time, allowing him to invest a further £100,000 in the business.[9] Dipam Patel, the entrepreneur behind ZeroDegrees, a Mash-style brewery bar which began trading in Blackheath, south London, in 2000, had joined calls for PBD ahead of the 2002 budget.[10] After PBD, he and his business partners were able to invest in growing their empire, opening a second branch in Bristol in 2004.[11]

Like the 1989 Beer Orders, PBD had some unintended conse-quences, though in this case less severe: Hertfordshire family brewers McMullen wound up a contract brewing operation to bring themselves under the limit for tax relief, leaving them rattling around a huge facility. Others, such as Peter Austin's Ringwood, seen as the epitome of the successful small brewery, were given no incentive to grow. As a result, in 2004, after a review of the policy, the threshold was moved upward to include breweries making up to 60,000 hecto-litres per year.

On the whole, though, PBD had an electrifying effect on British brewing. For many who had dreamed of founding their own breweries, it provided the final necessary incentive, and, between 2003 and 2005, more than a hundred new firms came into existence.[12]

It was during this period that two very significant new concerns emerged, sharing the same DNA: Thornbridge of Derbyshire and BrewDog of Aberdeenshire. So interconnected are many of the dominant breweries of the last decade that, some time ago, and inspired by Pete Frame's *Rock Family Trees*, we put together a diagram to help us understand the connections. What became clear was that, though they arose squarely from the 'real ale' tradition, with connec-tions to Dave Wickett's Sheffield-based Kelham Island Brewery, both Thornbridge and BrewDog quickly changed as a result of taking on influences from 'world beer' and, most especially, beer from the United States. In so doing, they generated a new excitement around British beer that triggered a completely new 'scene', one that is often described using the contentious term 'craft beer'.

Thornbridge, founded in Derbyshire in 2004, was, after the model of Alastair Hook's breweries in the 1990s, a marriage between wealthy backers and skilled brewers. In this case, the money came from two local businessmen, Simon Webster and Jim Harrison. We met Webster at Thornbridge's offices in Bakewell in June 2013, in the open-plan, bright-and-breezy visitor lounge (the building was once a car showroom). Forty-four years old, dressed in jeans and an expensive-looking formal shirt, he has a confident manner and a bluntly Northern, down-to-earth charm: 'I met Jim Harrison through football – we're both Sheffield Wednesday fans, unfortunately.'

Jim Harrison (left) and Simon Webster in the grounds of Thornbridge's Riverside Brewery.

We did not meet Jim Harrison, though towards the end of our visit, we did see his vast black Range Rover sail through the car park and caught a glimpse of him at the wheel – tweed-jacketed, long hair swept back, hand raised in a rather regal wave. The heir to a successful industrial manufacturing business, SPG (Seals, Packings and Gaskets), based in Barnsley, Harrison and his independently wealthy wife, Emma, bought Thornbridge Hall, a country house near Bakewell, in 2002.

Harrison had the idea that the house, with its many outbuildings and workshops, would make a good base for 'artisanal' food production. For some years Webster had been a director at Henderson's, whose Worcester sauce-style 'Relish' has a cult following in Sheffield, and so it was perhaps inevitable that their first venture would be producing pickles and condiments.

At this point, competing versions of events are told: the official Thornbridge story is that Harrison, looking at real ale in and around Sheffield with a critical eye, decided to step in: 'The market for beer is very fragmented and microbreweries seem poor at marketing . . . This looked like a real opportunity.'[13] At first, he and Webster considered buying in beer brewed elsewhere, to which they could apply the Thornbridge brand, but they couldn't identify a suitable supplier.

They approached a business contact, Dave Wickett, for advice, as Webster recalled:

> We'd been selling pickles to Dave, for the Fat Cat. He was a catalyst in a lot of what's happened in brewing in Britain, and especially in Sheffield over the last twenty years, but he did have his fallings-out with people. Dave was very strong-minded but was also a visionary.

Dave Wickett is another candidate for the title of 'father of British microbrewing'. Wickett, who died in 2012, was involved in the industry from 1981, as owner of Sheffield real-ale 'exhibition' pub the Fat Cat, in a former industrial area, Kelham Island, on the River Don to the north of Sheffield's city centre. His brewery, also called Kelham Island, was founded in 1990 in an outbuilding in the yard of his pub, not far from the site of the Tennant Brothers brewery, the huge entrance gates of which still dominate Bridge Street. Kelham was (and is) a classic 'real ale' brewery producing cask ale to service the thriving CAMRA-led scene in the city. Many brewers passed through Kelham before going on to found their own brewing companies (Pat

The Fat Cat, Sheffield.

Morton, the first head brewer, founded Abbeydale and Bob Lawson, head brewer from 1994 to 1997, founded the Ossett Brewery) and its reputation grew until, by 2002, it was highly regarded by many 'real ale' enthusiasts.

Wickett did not want to brew beer for Thornbridge, and gave beer writer Pete Brown a different version of how the idea to brew at the Hall came about:

> It was beautiful, like walking onto a film set . . . So I said to Jim, 'What you need out here is your own brewery!' And he replied, 'Come round sometime, we'll find a building to put one in!'[14]

Whoever came up with the idea, it was certainly Wickett who advised Webster and Harrison on how to set up their own brewery. He located and helped to install a second-hand, ten-barrel brewing kit from Marston Moor Brewery[15] in a slightly too small converted workshop with exposed stone and brick walls near the Hall's vegetable gardens, along a narrow track. Harrison and Webster themselves had no ambitions to get their hands dirty, and advertised for brewers towards the end of 2004.

In January 2005, they made a rather surprising appointment: not an experienced British 'real ale' brewer from Yorkshire or Derbyshire, but a young Italian, Stefano Cossi, who had a degree in food science from the University of Udine and some experience of working at German-style breweries in Italy. He had spotted the advertisement on an online message board and travelled to the UK on a whim. Described by friends and colleagues as 'a perfectionist' and 'fastidious', photographs from around this time show a lean, dark-eyed youth with hollow cheeks and dressed in a shiny blue tracksuit, as if he has just stepped off a basketball court.

He was joined, shortly afterwards, by twenty-three-year-old Martin Dickie from Fraserburgh in Aberdeenshire, who had just graduated from Heriot-Watt University in Edinburgh with a degree in brewing and distilling. During his time there, his interest had switched from whisky to beer: 'With distillation, you have to wait a very long time before you can actually sample the product. With brewing, you don't have to wait so long.[16]

Both men had the kind of technical training which, thirty years earlier, might have seen them join the ranks of the white-coated brewing staff at Whitbread or Watney's. At Thornbridge, however, there was no such stuffiness, and according to Pete Brown, the pair seemed to be 'a beery equivalent of Liam and Noel Gallagher'.[17]

Webster identified their appointment, with hindsight, as an important decision: 'What we had done by hiring an Italian and Martin straight out of Heriot-Watt was get people who weren't weighed down by tradition.' The first beers they developed and brewed, however, were not especially remarkable, according to Webster:

> By March that year, we were brewing Lord Marples, which we still brew, and Blackthorn, a golden ale. They were classic real ales, not that different to what everyone else in this area was making. The company motto, Innovation, Passion, Knowledge . . . well, that wasn't necessarily there right at the start, but we worked towards it.

What was there from the beginning was Thornbridge's intent to set itself apart from other breweries in the region with a highly polished brand identity. Rather than the faintly amateurish cartoon images and novelty names beloved of real-ale breweries (including, it must be said, Dave Wickett's Kelham Island), or the faux Victoriana of the established large regional companies, it employed tasteful typography and abstract designs that wouldn't seem out of place on designer wallpaper. This was not superficial. Rather, it was a core part of Jim Harrison's business plan. But the beer itself did not quite live up to the promise of the brand, and so Harrison issued a friendly ultimatum: 'I want a beer that's gonna take the world by storm.'[18]

Dickie and the 'fastidious'[19] Cossi continued to seek inspiration, and they found it in an American beer being imported by James Clay. Simon Webster: 'Let's be honest, they'd probably been drinking Goose Island IPA the night before.' (It seemed apt that the song blasting from the brewery's shop-floor stereo on our visit was 'Born in the USA' by Bruce Springsteen.) Their reaction to this boldly flavoured, highly perfumed beer was perhaps similar to that of beer writer Pete Brown during the US road trip he wrote about in his book, *Three Sheets to the Wind*: 'The first time you experience beers like this it's like tasting in colour and realising that you've only had black and white until now.'[20]

India pale ale has a complicated history, the details of which historians debate endlessly and often with considerable stridency. The term appeared during the nineteenth century and, put simply, it refers to pale ales exported to India, brewed specifically for export to India or which were marketed in Britain as being of sufficient quality that they *could* be exported to India. By the time the Campaign for Real Ale emerged in the 1970s, there were few beers being described as IPA, and most of those were indistinguishable from any other pale ale, or 'bitter' as it is generally known these days. From the 1970s onward, however, brewers and enthusiasts on both sides of the Atlantic, intrigued by what came to be regarded as a 'lost style', attempted to revive it.

In 1976, Dr John Harrison and the Durden Park Beer Circle published their book *Old British Beers and How to Make Them*. Based on extensive research into the records of various breweries, it included this passage:

> Indian pale ales are still produced today but do not compare with the old, original versions. When it was decided to supply British troops in India with home-brewed beer in the early 1800s, it was soon found that beer of ordinary strength would not survive the long journey through the tropics. Hodgson's of London were the first to discover that raising the OG to 70 and increasing the hop rate to 2 to 3 oz per gallon produced an overhopped beer that would arrive in India in good condition.[21]

Much of the history recounted therein has been discredited – early nineteenth-century IPAs weren't unusually strong, and it was the middle classes, not troops, which made up the bulk of the Indian market – but even so, it presented an exotic-sounding alternative to mild and bitter, couched in cosily conservative, nostalgic terms.

In America, at around the same time, a handful of brewers were developing a fascination with new hop varieties and British brewing techniques, such as 'dry hopping' (letting the fermenting or maturing beer sit on yet more hops to pick up fresh aroma and flavour). An old brand, Ballantine's IPA, brewed in New York from the 1800s, once famous for its immense hop aroma and strength but much diminished by the 1970s, also served as a template for the first US 'new generation' IPAs which began to appear from the middle of the decade.[22] These included San Francisco brewery Anchor's Liberty (not described as an IPA on the label), first brewed in 1975; and Bert Grant's Yakima Brewing IPA, which emerged in 1983[23] and was the first beer from a new American brewery to bear the appellation on its label. Dosed with citrusy-smelling Cascade, a hop which did not exist in the nineteenth century, and drunk fresh, rather than mellowed by months at sea, these remarkably aromatic beers represented something quite new, despite their claims to historical authenticity.

It wasn't until 1990 that IPA really began its revival in the UK, thanks largely to the efforts of Mark Dorber, manager of the White Horse in Parson's Green, west London. Long obsessed with Burton pale ales, in 1990 he held a successful seminar on the subject for an inner circle of brewers, historians and writers. In 1993, for a follow-up event, he went further, working with Bass to brew an India pale ale to an historic recipe:

> Something went wrong, however, and it had far higher alpha acids than we'd planned, and we also dry-hopped the hell out of it in the cellar. It was more or less undrinkable, but massively aromatic . . . I kept a couple of casks back for the next year, 1994, when we had a follow-up seminar. That was a real meeting of minds from the US and Britain, and everyone went away very enthused about IPA.

Key figures on both sides of the Atlantic set about brewing their own IPAs, or writing about them at every opportunity.[24] In Britain, word spread until, by the time of the 1995 Great British Beer Festival, *The Times* was able to report that the year's 'special fad is for resurrected India pale ales (IPA) brewed to original recipes'.[25]

The craze continued apace for the remainder of the decade, as evidenced by Michael Jackson's coffee-table book *Great Beer Guide* (2000), which offers an excellent snapshot of what was hot in the late 1990s. It lists '500 classic brews', among them not only several old-fashioned British IPAs indistinguishable from any other bitter, but also numerous American and British new-generation or revivalist beers, such as Bert Grant's India pale ale (US, 4.1 per cent) – 'unusually pale', with Cascade hops – and Burton Bridge Empire Pale Ale (UK, 7.5 per cent).

In 2003, IPA fever went mainstream when Goose Island IPA (a notably bold and aromatic interpretation brewed in Chicago) became available in the high-street supermarket chain Safeway.[26]

Jackson observed in 2002 that American brewers who had been inspired by British traditions were, by that time, returning the favour: 'I believe that the experience of [American beer festivals] has greatly encouraged the more open-minded among British ale brewers . . . It is not possible in every case to say where the American influence has been the parent of a new product, but in some instances, it seems obvious.'[27]

In June 2005,[28] Alastair Hook's Meantime brewery in south-east London released two 'historic' beers in 750ml champagne-style bottles – a 'London porter' and an 'authentic' India pale ale. Most of that was shipped to the States where, Hook said at the time, 'consumers appreciate the quality, authenticity and heritage, and are prepared to pay a fair price for it'.[29] It represented only a small part of Meantime's large range of beers, most of which were German-inspired lagers of one kind or another. IPA, for most British breweries, continued to be an oddity or seasonal speciality – a niche product that might bring kudos and help market the more accessible bitters or lagers which made up the bulk of their sales.

It was in that context that, on 7 July 2005, Thornbridge brewed their first batch of 'Mystery Blonde' (named in honour of a local woman), a 5.9 per cent India pale ale, light in colour and characterised by the use of large amounts of distinctive American hops to provide aroma and flavour. 'Once we tasted it,' said Webster, 'we all knew that, yes, this was it – this is what we ought to be doing.' Thankfully, the name 'Mystery Blonde' fell by the wayside and, picking up on the colonial history of India pale ale, it was renamed after the city in Rajasthan, India, where Harrison's marriage was held: Jaipur. In the short term, it would win awards from the local branch of CAMRA, before going on to trigger the most recent and substantial phase of a slow-burning obsession with IPA among beer geeks.

Jaipur was far from being the first 'new style', American-hopped, strong British IPA, but what made it different was that it became, rather than, say, Lord Marples, their 4 per cent traditional bitter, the core product. They resisted calls, too, to reduce Jaipur's strength to bring it in line with the hugely successful Deuchars, as Simon Webster recalled:

> People would taste it and say, wow, that's fantastic, and then they'd say, 'You know, if you got that down to 4.2 per cent, you'd be able to sell a lot of it.' But we didn't want to do that. That's when we began to think in terms of challenging the drinker. We wanted people to taste our beer and say, 'Wow, I'll have another of those!' What we came to realise was that a lot of people don't like intensely flavoured beer, and that's fine. We're not selling to everyone.

Thornbridge has had many brewers since 2005, but Jaipur has remained a constant. As Webster made clear, there is some unease about that within the company:

> It's become a proper brand. People have a few and say they've been 'Jaipured' the next day, that kind of thing. We could easily turn this into a Jaipur factory, but we never will. We can't

supply everyone who wants it – we just can't make enough. It does, maybe, overshadow some of the other things we do, and I joked a couple of years ago on the eve of GBBF that if it won the competition we would 'kill it' – anyway it lost and saved us the decision.

Jaipur turned a small country-house real-ale brewery in Derbyshire into the subject of excited admiration from beer enthusiasts and writers across the country, winning numerous awards both within the industry and outside of it. Scarcely out of university, Dickie and Cossi found themselves fêted and on the radar of beer-writer royalty.

In 2005, at an intimate dinner at the White Horse in west London hosted by Mark Dorber, Cossi and Dickie were introduced to Michael Jackson. The great beer writer was then in his sixties and rather shrunken, secretly battling Parkinson's Disease, as he had been for a decade. He asked them about their latest creation, a beer called Kipling, which took the Jaipur formula but with the added twist of a new variety of New Zealand hops called Nelson Sauvin.[30] Starstruck, Cossi and Dickie asked for Jackson's autograph.[31]

This was an important moment for Dickie in particular: as Sean Franklin, another pioneer, had done a quarter of a century earlier, he got from Jackson the encouragement he needed to go it alone. His new venture would share certain similarities with Thornbridge – American-influenced beer, slick branding – but would differ in one important way: instead of working within the Campaign for Real Ale's infrastructure of beer festivals and awards, BrewDog would define itself by going to war with CAMRA and, by extension, the whole of the 'real ale' culture.

FOURTEEN

REBELLION INTO MONEY

I think they are the breath of fresh air that was required in the UK. Props to them for having more balls than me, and for thinking big and not giving up despite the negativity sometimes shown towards them. Like it or lump it, everyone is still talking about them and this *sells beer* and is engaging a whole new segment of the beer market in the UK.

Jeff Rosenmeier, Lovibonds Brewery[1]

Martin Dickie met James Watt at comprehensive school in Peterhead, a North Sea fishing town in the far east of Scotland. Watt was born into a wealthy fishing family and first went to sea on a trawler with his father at the age of six. As a teenager, he was not only academically gifted but also a keen athlete – a Scottish junior swimming champion[2] – and, even today, he is broader-shouldered and apparently more outgoing than his friend. He and Dickie stuck together throughout higher education, Watt studying law and economics at Edinburgh University while Dickie attended Heriot-Watt in the same city. They shared a flat for a time where, it seems, they did some home brewing together. And though they were obliged to go their separate ways after graduating, they kept in touch.

While Dickie went away to work in England, Watt gave office work a fortnight before deciding that, regardless of his degree, he needed more stimulation and fresh air, and started working on his father's fishing boat, catching mackerel and herring. He enjoyed the thrill of being at sea – 'It is dangerous, but I've grown up with it. If you grow up here, you just get used to it" – and in 2005 gained a fishing-vessel captain's qualification. Throughout, though, he harboured another plan. He had seen in his friend's obvious talent for brewing the perfect opportunity to be his own boss, on dry land.

From here on, disentangling what actually happened from the official BrewDog legend, carefully managed by James Watt and his PR team, becomes tricky. For example, the narrative they repeat, with variations, in interview after interview, omits any mention of Thornbridge or Heriot-Watt:

> When Martin and I were considering starting our brewery, we were fortunate enough to be given the opportunity to meet him [Michael Jackson]. At the time we were home brewing together and really keen to quit our jobs and follow our dream. It was a pretty big risk for a couple of twenty-four-year-olds with no previous experience of running a business to consider taking. However we were extremely passionate about craft beer, and were keen to put everything on the line to pursue our passion. We decided to let Michael Jackson taste our home-brewed beer and get his advice on whether we should start our brewery or not. [The beer he tasted was] a batch of Paradox, which was brewed in late 2006 in Martin's garage and aged in a single Islay whisky cask.[4]

Of course, Dickie already knew Jackson, and the job he was keen to quit was that of successful brewer. It is also perhaps no coincidence that in 2005, Cossi and Dickie took a batch of Thornbridge's St Petersburg Imperial Stout and put it into three different whisky casks to mature, bottling it in mid-2006. That first embryonic BrewDog beer that Jackson tasted can scarcely have been very different to the Thornbridge St Petersburg Islay Whisky Reserve.

At any rate, Jackson was encouraging, and so, towards the end of 2006, Dickie left Thornbridge. He had been instrumental in brewing Jaipur, Kipling and St Petersburg, and had learned to operate a small commercial brewery, and took with him not only know-how but also a reputation as 'one to watch'.

Back in Fraserburgh, north of Aberdeen, he and Watt set about building a brewery, using, like so many small brewers before them, second-hand equipment. Combining their savings, which added up to £30,000,[5] and a £22,000 loan from the local council's Aberdeenshire Business scheme,[6] BrewDog began trading officially in November 2006. At first, there was little to indicate quite the impact they would have on the brewing industry, or how big the company would become in future. A correspondent for *The Scotsman* recounted a visit to their first premises on the Kessock Industrial Estate: 'At the edge of town, turn left and head for the desolate industrial estate . . . Ignore the discount carpet warehouse and park among the weeds and abandoned lorries.'[7] In March 2007, Watt's rhetoric, though perhaps a little belligerent, did not sound very different to what you might hear from the Campaign for Real Ale or an affiliated brewery:

> We want to do something that the area can be proud of, something different. I know we were fed up drinking over-marketed fizzy yellow beer and wanted to offer something of a far higher quality.[8]

People who met them at this time recall them as young, diffident and nervously seeking approval for beers they weren't sure people would like. In an interview with Per Nielsen of the Evening Brews blog, Tom Cadden, who, in 2007, was managing Glasgow's Black-friars pub, recalled:

> I tried the Punk IPA, on cask. My reaction was, 'Oh my God, someone finally made this kind of IPA, in Scotland, I can't believe it.' James Watt kind of edged over and shyly asked, 'Do you like that?' I was like, 'It's amazing, I work at Blackfriars and

I want this beer.' So we were their first ever customer. We got
invoice 001 from BrewDog.[9]

Norwegian beer blogger Knut Albert Solem, who has followed
their progress since being introduced to the pair in person by
Cadden in 2007, underlined the point that what they were doing
then, especially in Scotland, seemed very exciting: 'They were like the
Beatles in Hamburg.'

The plaudits they received, including a young entrepreneurship
award for James Watt,[10] gave them some confidence and they soon
began to develop a rather brash 'shtick':

> We are not a faceless corporate monstrosity. We have no
> mind-numbing automatic production line.
>
> We are just two guys trying to make the best beer we can, and
> trying to make other people as passionate about fresh, natural,
> full-flavour beers as we are.
>
> We have no multimillion advertising campaign trying to fool you
> into thinking drinking cheaply made, bland beer will change
> your life.[11]

Behind the scenes, they had been studying the business models
and practices of American breweries, through which they became
aware of San Diego's Stone Brewing Company, the straight-talking
evangelist spokesman for which is co-founder Greg Koch. Having
studied business in Los Angeles in the 1980s and attempted to make
it as a rock star, Koch went into brewing with a musician friend,
Steve Wagner. Wagner learned the technical side of brewing while
Koch was the manic ideas man, marketing genius and square-
jawed, outspoken figurehead for the company. At times, especially
when he is in a 'beard' phase, he resembles a cult leader, and his
pronouncements, frank to the point of bluntness, on the evils of
big beer and other subjects, only endear him more to his and his
brewery's fans.[12]

James Watt would take on the same role at BrewDog, and is open in his admiration for Koch and for Stone Brewing[13] and the influence is, at any rate, entirely obvious. Stone are perhaps best known for their Arrogant Bastard Ale, first launched in 1996, the label copy on which reads:

> This is an aggressive ale. You probably won't like it. It is quite doubtful that you have the taste or sophistication to be able to appreciate an ale of this quality and depth. We would suggest that you stick to safer and more familiar territory – maybe something with a multimillion-dollar ad campaign . . .

Compare that to BrewDog's Punk IPA:

> This is not a lowest common denominator beer . . . This is an aggressive beer . . . We don't care if you don't like it . . . It is quite doubtful that you have the taste or sophistication to appreciate the depth, character and quality of this premium craft-brewed beer.

In April 2008, BrewDog won two medals at the World Beer Cup,[14] an American-dominated, industry-run event, and continued to be fêted as a shining example of Scottish small business. A campaign of outreach to influential beer writers and bloggers, who, at any rate, were already inclined to be excited by a brewery doing something interesting, was paying off, with favourable mentions online. Everything was going remarkably well. Then, Watt and Dickie hit an obstacle: the alcohol industry's voluntary advertising regulatory body, the Portman Group, funded by the biggest producers. Portman were concerned that the language on the upstart brewery's labels might promote aggression, implied nutritional value or health benefits and was otherwise generally 'irresponsible'.

Whether out of sincere youthful rebelliousness or, like the Campaign for Real Ale more than thirty years earlier, spoiling for a publicity-generating David and Goliath battle, Watt refused to submit to Portman's demands that the labels be changed. 'It's ironic that a body funded by the UK's leading alcohol producers,' he said, 'those responsible for the supermarket pricing debacle, have decided to target a small craft-beer producer for the apparent evils beyond imagination contained on our labels.'[15] The story was covered by national tabloids such as *The Sun* and generated a buzz in the 'beer community'.

After months of arguing, and a petition raised by beer writer Melissa Cole on BrewDog's behalf,[16] the Portman Group dropped their case in December of the same year. It was welcomed by many as a victory for small brewers over the might of their industrial competitors, and Watt seized the opportunity to take a Churchillian stance:

> It is a victory for common sense, the intelligence of the consumer, small independent producers and freedom of speech; it is a victory that BrewDog had to fight tooth and nail for. We refused to roll over and be bullied into changing our packaging by what is basically a cartel funded by our larger competitors. We were determined and stood our ground to keep our dream and our business alive.[17]

In the meantime, BrewDog's profile had been raised enormously, and Watt had realised the publicity value of provoking 'the establishment'. The previous summer, while the initial Portman complaint was still being debated, he and Dickie had conceived and launched a beer provocatively named Speedball, containing legal stimulants and depressants (guarana, kola nut and California poppy). In January 2009, mere weeks after backing down on the previous complaint, Portman launched another, pointing out that 'Speedball' was slang for a potent mix of heroin and cocaine and accusing the brewery of 'profiteering from the scourge of illegal drugs'. BrewDog fought back once again, even going as far as to sue Portman for defamation, but this time commentators who, a month earlier, had been entirely on their side, began to ask questions, as in this blog post from Pete Brown:

Love the beer, love the brewery. Agree with the point the lads are making. But at the same time, I'm not sure it was a great idea to launch this beer with the specific intention of getting this result. Yes, it gives them an opportunity to put a case forward, but in an attention-deficient age where most people read the headline and skim the rest of a story, I worry that if you just get the barest facts or read reports like this one halfway, then you're going to walk away on Portman's side. Am I being an old fart about this?[18]

Eventually, BrewDog backed down and renamed the beer 'Dogma' (another dig at Portman), but not before they'd garnered even more headlines, television appearances (including on Oz Clarke and James May's *Drink Britain*) and many online blog and forum posts. For BrewDog, it seemed, there really was no such thing as bad publicity. Watt would take this idea to its logical conclusion later the same year. Meanwhile, they were beginning to develop a distinctive, almost cult-like company ethos,[19] and gathering about themselves people with more than a passing interest in their beer: BrewDog, like a football team or band, had *fans*.

They weren't the first brewery with keen followers, but Watt and Dickie were far more effective in capitalising on the enthusiasm of their customers than any who had preceded them. The concept of 'fan service' comes from the world of Japanese comics and animation and is now used more widely to refer to material intended specifically to excite the most obsessive fans. BrewDog were masters of 'fan service'. They produced a startling number of new beers, many of them in limited runs, such as Tokyo, a 12 per cent 'imperial stout', first released in June 2008 in a batch of 2,000 bottles. Such collectors' editions served as market research tools, good PR and canny business rolled into one.

Atlantic IPA offers an excellent case study. It was brewed to a historic recipe, and then James Watt took eight barrels of it to sea on a North Atlantic fishing boat. The finished product bore a label intricately drawn by illustrator Johanna Basford (Watt's girlfriend,

BrewDog founders Martin Dickie (left) and James Watt promoting the second round of 'Equity for Punks' in the City of London in 2011.

now his wife). It was released through specialist retailers such as Beer Ritz in Leeds and Utobeer in London, where it sold at around £9 for a 330ml bottle[20] at a time when their Punk IPA was available in Tesco for 99p. To publicise the beer, they released stunning video footage of the fishing boat, *Ocean Quest*, being battered by storms, and seized the opportunity to slam supposedly less historically authentic rival IPAs such as Caledonian's Deuchars. All of this gave their small but increasingly fanatical army of followers something to get excited about, and, we assume, they also made a profit on every bottle.

But that wasn't enough for BrewDog. They seemed to thrive on conflict, perhaps for the purposes of publicity, but perhaps also because they were young and genuinely impetuous. In July 2009, they released Tokyo* at 18.2 per cent, a stronger version of the previous year's strong stout (which had itself generated complaints from alcohol control bodies in Scotland) and announced that it was 'Britain's strongest beer'. Scottish Parliamentarians began a petition to have it banned. The Portman Group reared its head again, too, only this time there would be a twist.

In October 2009, their fans feeling well and truly serviced, and their numbers ever increasing, BrewDog began to drop hints that something amazing was about to happen:

> We are back, this time with a proposal of epic proportions that will truly revolutionise the beer industry. Never one to shy away from challenges, confrontation or cats, BrewDog is about to make dreams come true ... We can't give too much away yet ... but what we can tell you is that we are about to embark on something that has never been attempted before: it will provide a basis for the revolution against the corporate industrial brewers and it will help BrewDog in a way that no other company would ever have the audacity to try.[21]

When they announced 'Equity for Punks' in the same month, the gulf between their fans and their critics widened: the former were excited at the opportunity to buy a single 0.001 per cent share in the company for £230, entitling them, among other benefits, to a lifetime discount from the online shop and the right to attend annual general meetings at the brewery in Scotland. (It was an exercise in crowd-funding rather than a public issue, though, so there was no way for buyers to sell or trade the shares.)

Others, meanwhile, asked yet more questions. Beer writer Pete Brown was unimpressed at the disconnect between the hype and the reality and argued that the share price hugely overvalued the company,[22] while sceptics muttered variants of 'Equity for punks? Equity for mugs, more like.'[23] BrewDog's creators found themselves trying, on the one hand, to respond to critics, who wondered just how 'punk' and 'revolutionary' a share issue could be, while on the other, convincing potential investors that they were serious businessmen.

For the share issue to go ahead, they were required to sell £500,000 worth by the middle of January 2010. With uptake sluggish, it is perhaps no coincidence, then, that James Watt chose November 2009 to reveal the punchline to the continuing Tokyo* battle with the Portman Group and others. After months of newspaper articles,

TV news interviews, outrage from their fans and advocacy by beer writers, he confessed: in order to ensure Portman would wade in, Watt had himself written the initial letter of complaint which triggered their investigation.[24] It had been, after all, a row manufactured for PR purposes, and some beer enthusiasts who had defended BrewDog felt humiliated. Beer writer Zak Avery:

> I'd been made a pawn in their publicity machine, and vowed never to write anything about them again. Looking back, I still think it was a pathetic stunt, and when I explained to a friend what had happened, his response was, 'Christ, what a douche'. Yes, my friend is American, but he's also right.[25]

Even so, Equity for Punks was successful, reaching its target by 9 January 2010, demonstrating BrewDog's growing mastery of critiquing corporate behaviour while also being very good at it. The share funding paid for preliminary work on plans for a new eco-friendly brewery, and for what would turn out to be a chain of bars, the first of which opened in Aberdeen in October 2010. At this point, while BrewDog were still brewing cask-conditioned 'real ale', their own bar sold only beer dispensed from kegs. This caused concern among some enthusiasts, but was very much in line with the way their thinking had been developing in the preceding months:

> Although the industry standard for craft beers around the world, this is almost unheard of in the UK with 99.5 per cent of Britain's craft brewers sticking exclusively to cask ... We feel a lot of the beers we brew are better suited to being carbonated and served colder from keg as opposed to dispensed as real ale from a cask. It is a great way to serve craft beer, and hopefully an area which will develop in the UK the same way it has in the US.[26]

This break with CAMRA orthodoxy might, to some extent, have been influenced by their occasional collaborator, Pete Brown, whose 2006 book *Three Sheets to the Wind* was as much manifesto as travelogue. In it, the Barnsley-born former advertising executive recounted an eye-opening experience drinking American 'craft beer' and meeting evangelical American brewers, concluding with a call to arms:

> British beer drinkers need a better champion than the Campaign for Real Ale (CAMRA) in its current state. When CAMRA was founded, the only beer that tasted of anything was real ale; everything else was bland and dodgy. If you were going to champion decent beer, it made perfect sense to focus on cask-conditioned ale. But this is simply no longer true. By getting caught up in how the beer is made rather than how it tastes, CAMRA has become increasingly parochial.[27]

Brown was voicing the feelings of a number of beer drinkers – those who were excited by the intensity of flavour of many American beers compared to the typically more restrained and 'balanced' British brews – and was only the latest in a long line of complainants, including some CAMRA members, who felt the Campaign was focusing on technicalities rather than whether the beer actually tasted good.[28]

Over the preceding two decades, CAMRA had become less 'radical' (more like the National Trust than CND) and had successfully broadened its appeal so that, by 2005, it had around 77,000 members – more than twice the number of its previous late 1970s peak. In order to maintain that growth, they would have to ensure that both impassioned activists at regional level and casual members signing up at beer festivals were not alienated. As a basic and very sensible marketing technique, that required keeping the message simple and unambiguous – cask-conditioned good, everything else bad. For many, though, the mantra was not just simple but simplistic, and invited if not contempt, then certainly ridicule.

BrewDog went further than Brown, and a discussion that had at first been civilised began to get personal, not least after Watt's speech at the opening of the Aberdeen bar:

I don't think cask is an appealing way to get people into beer
... Cask is more sleepy, stuffy, traditional, and just has this kind
of stigma attached to it which isn't going to get young people
excited ... It's all CAMRA, beards, sandals, beer bellies, hanging
out at train stations at the weekend. We think keg beers could be
the future of craft beers in the UK.[29]

Of course, many of the beer enthusiasts who recognised
BrewDog as energetic, interesting and a 'good thing' had learned to
appreciate beer through that 'sleepy, stuffy' framework established
by CAMRA – festivals and pubs selling 'real ale' – and they felt
insulted. Suddenly, a row between broad-minded but novelty-
obsessed 'craftophiles' and 'real ale' dogmatists, which had been
bubbling since the 1990s, boiled over.

FIFTEEN

THE CULT OF CRAFT BEER

1   Only use distilled otter's tears.

2   Use only barley that's been warmed by the breath of kindly owls.

3   Craft beer cares, so only use hops that have been flown halfway around the world.

4   You can have it any colour you like, as long as it's not brown. Unless it's an Indian Brown Ale.

5   Beards allowed only if they're ironic.

6   It's not 'inconsistent', it's 'experimental'.

7   It's not 'hiding faults', it's 'barrel-ageing'.

8   It's not 'gone off', it's 'challenging preconceptions of sour beer'.

9   Ensure that the branding costs more than the brewhouse.

10 Collaborate every month with an international brewer, a blogger, a celebrity and a musician.

11 There are only seven ingredients in Craft Beer: hops, malt, water, yeast, YouTube, Twitter and Facebook.

12 Our overriding mantra – Craft Beer Is AWESOME!!!!!

Simon H. Johnson, 'The Craft Beer Manifesto'[1]

As BrewDog rose to prominence, their influence, and that of American breweries whose products were now more readily available in the UK, began to be felt, at least within the closeted world of beer enthusiasts. One result was that a handful of newer British brewers who had defaulted to 'real ale' as the standard-bearer of 'alternative' beer culture began to align themselves more with the idea of 'craft beer'. It was, as preached by BrewDog at least, the antidote to a stifling ('boring') CAMRA-led culture.

One case study of such a transition is that of brewer Stuart Ross, who was born in Sheffield in 1981.[2] Bearded and shaven-headed, Ross has a dry sense of humour, and when we spoke to him he seemed to be living on chilli-sauce-drenched Mexican-style burritos. These days, he usually drinks kegged 'craft beer' in half-pint measures, with the occasional imported bottle. But he began his drinking career as a confirmed 'real ale' man: 'When I was young, everyone else drank lager, but I never did: I always drank Stone's or Tetley's bitter . . . Back then, I didn't like cold, fizzy beer.'

Having trained in horticulture, he drifted into a career in brewing in 2004: 'I used to play crown-green bowls and, through that, got to know Paul Ward, who was head brewer at Kelham Island. We got on well, and then, one day, he asked if I'd be interested in coming to work with him.' Being employed by local brewing legend Dave Wickett could occasionally be difficult, Ross admitted, but the fact that he could be 'a bit of a nightmare' also created opportunities: there was a remarkable turnover of staff at Kelham Island, and, when Paul Ward left to go to the Bradfield Brewery, Ross was made head brewer by default.

Wickett's connections with the Brooklyn Brewery in New York gave Ross opportunities to collaborate with Brooklyn's celebrity head brewer, Garrett Oliver. Wickett also owned a pub in Rochester, New York, which Ross visited, and drank American beer on its home turf. But for Ross, there was no sudden conversion to 'the cause': 'To be honest, I found a lot of the beer over there too hoppy, back then.'

Ross was at Kelham Island when its Pale Rider – a 'pale and hoppy' bitter after the Sean Franklin model – was declared Champion Beer of

Britain at the Great British Beer Festival in 2004. The Kelham Island Brewery premises are now much expanded, but still only amount to a brick outhouse and a couple of repurposed cargo containers. Back then, the brewery was unable to supply the sudden demand for their beer the prize generated. As Thornbridge stepped in to help, Ross had the chance to brew on their premises alongside Martin Dickie and Stefano Cossi, with whom he remains in contact today: brewing is a small world, the world of 'craft beer' even more so.

Eventually, Ross left Kelham Island for another equally frustrating experience at Acorn of Barnsley: desperate to brew, he found himself driving a delivery van most of the time. It was in this period, however, that he first drank Sierra Nevada Pale Ale and suddenly 'got' American beer and hops, finding it 'a bit of an eye-opener'.

Finally, in 2007, he got the chance to be head brewer once again, this time at the Crown Brewery, in the basement of the Hillsborough Hotel outside Sheffield's city centre. The hotel owners contacted Acorn looking for a brewer who might be willing to help them reopen their on-site brewery, which had fallen into disrepair. Ross got the job.

Though he was beginning to feel the urge to experiment, he was obliged, at first, to produce straightforward, traditional (or perhaps old-fashioned) 'real ale'. 'The first few brews were made to fit these expensive pump clips they'd already ordered,' he told us. The brewery itself was small, damp and mouldy, the kit 'botched together'. When he commenced brewing in the summer of 2008, he was forced to ferment at less-than-ideal warm temperatures. Eventually, he got to know the kit and to improve on it, and then he got creative.

He spoke with particular pride of an early experiment, 'Wheetie-bits', a 4.5 per cent, German-inspired wheat beer. When one of the organisers of the Copenhagen Beer Festival who happened to be staying at the Hillsborough tasted the beer, he invited the Crown Brewery to attend. 'I ended up doing a meet-and-greet thing at the Ambassador's residence,' Ross recalled, 'and tried loads of different beers.' He followed Wheetie-bits with Ring of Fire, a strong barley wine fortified with 'a load of cheap chilli peppers' he bought at his local supermarket; a 6.5 per cent Belgian-style wheat beer and a smoked 'Oktoberfest' beer.

Pete Brown became an early champion after tasting Ross's beer at a beer writers' dinner in Sheffield, declaring him 'runner up' in his ranking of the country's best brewers in 2009: 'I don't think he knows how good a brewer he is.'[3]

Though he had been 'mostly drinking bitter' in 2009, Ross found himself brewing more beers showcasing American hops; one in particular, Brooklyn Heights, was a 5.8 per cent pale ale brewed in imitation of Sierra Nevada. 'Everyone loved it and wanted more,' he recalled, 'so I kept brewing it.' At the end of 2010, Matt Gorecki, the manager of North Bar in Leeds and an influential figure in 'craft beer', especially in the North, wrote gushingly of its brilliance:

> Crown's Brooklyn Heights is also an utter winner this year – now
> this is no lie – I haven't heard anyone mention this wonderful,
> bright hoppy ale without waxing lyrical about its brilliance.
> SERIOUSLY! Good fucking work, Stu, please, someone, get this
> man a bigger brewery![4]

Richard Burhouse's family ran a successful business based in Huddersfield selling gemstones, crystals and fossils, but he had been looking for a business opportunity relating to his interest in beer. Burhouse set up a mail-order beer company, but that did not quite scratch the itch. He wanted to start a brewery, and needed a skilled, experienced brewer. For some time he had been coming to the Hillsborough Hotel with a refillable keg to buy Brooklyn Heights in bulk and had got to know Ross quite well, sharing bottles of American beer with him from time to time. The next step was obvious.

A firm believer in the power of social media, Ross announced his departure from the Crown Brewery in December 2011 in two places. First, he quietly changed his Twitter username from '@crownbrewstu' to '@magicrockstu'; then he posted a comment on Matt Gorecki's blog, quoting Gorecki's praise and adding: 'They did!!!!!!'[5]

At first glance, there is very little about Magic Rock Brewing to suggest that it is a British company at all. The flagship beers are American-style pale ales, India pale ales and 'red ales', rather than bitter or mild, and Ross put to one side his usual taciturnity when he spoke of a recent research road trip in the US. His laptop was full of photographs of him and Richard Burhouse in tasting rooms at various American breweries, or on brewery tours on which they

Label for Magic Rock Cannonball IPA designed by Richard Norgate.

were treated as VIPs. His obsession when we spoke to him was Russian River Brewing's Pliny the Younger 'triple IPA', a homage to which, under the name Un-Human Cannonball, Magic Rock had just released as a 'limited edition', to the delight of the beer geeks who queued outside bars for a chance to taste it.

Ross acknowledged that, closer to home, BrewDog loomed large in Magic Rock's approach:

> We didn't realise until we had it pointed out to us, but our first beers looked just like BrewDog's range, with the same colour labels. They had Punk IPA with a blue label and we had High Wire; they had 5 a.m. Saint in red and we had Rapture in red because what other colour can you use for a red ale? And then Hardcore IPA and our Human Cannonball were both similar beers.

Perhaps because he knew Martin Dickie personally when they were both very young brewers, he has nothing but good things to say about BrewDog, and gives them a great deal of credit: 'There's no doubt that BrewDog opened up the market.'

That sentiment was echoed by many people in the industry to

whom we spoke, from brewers to writers to PR men. BrewDog have succeeded in doing something which bigger or more traditional brewers, or both, have failed to do, despite their best efforts: selling beer to affluent, fashionable under-twenty-fives – a group which has been more interested in recent years in flavoured ciders. BrewDog have achieved this not despite their apparent arrogance, but precisely because of it.

Some who have come in BrewDog's wake aped James Watt's rhetoric just as he himself had aped Greg Koch's of Stone Brewing, as this blog post, entitled 'CAMRA – the Campaign for Real Alienation', from Holmfirth's Summer Wine Brewery, reveals:

> The beer world is changing, fast! If CAMRA does nothing, they will be marginalised over time and seal their own demise with the attitudes played out above. The alternative is to move on with our dynamic, eclectic, exciting, fast-paced industry and become a useful force instead of hankering after past glories; the term 'real ale' no longer encompasses what we as brewers are doing. We are progressive, not regressive; we are innovative, not traditionalists; we package beer in new ways; we dispense in new formats. Stop trying to rein in our activities; if you persist, then we are better off without you![6]

In some cases, the influence of BrewDog runs more deeply and subtly. Irishman Evin O'Riordain, founder of London's Kernel Brewery (2007), has hippyish long hair and a beard, and seems altogether more easy-going than the ever-ambitious Watt and Dickie. For all that, he acknowledged, in an interview with Per Nielsen of the Evening Brews blog, that it was BrewDog that inspired him to take the plunge and begin brewing:

> There was this 'yap yap yap' from Scotland. The tone of what they're saying and how they go about things is completely different to anything I would do, but the message I understood. Now, are you going to make the beer to back this up? Punk IPA

back in those days, that was it. It was clean, fresh and bitter as
fuck. Just the fact that that beer existed was enough. There were
people who were doing a similar thing, and making beer I like,
in a style I want to drink.[7]

Similarly, Hardknott, based in Cumbria, began life as a small 'real
ale' brewpub, but, in the wake of BrewDog, and with advice from
Watt and Dickie, reinvented itself with edgy graphic design and
increasingly vocal criticism of CAMRA. It even had its own rather
contrived dispute with the Portman Group.[8] Its owner, Dave Bailey,
was, until recently, frank in his admiration for BrewDog.

Meanwhile, the running feud between BrewDog themselves and
CAMRA culminated, in the summer of 2011, in a row over their
attendance at CAMRA's Great British Beer Festival. BrewDog's side
of the story was that they'd been 'banned' at the last minute because
CAMRA changed their minds over allowing them to serve keg
beer and used petty technicalities to back out of the deal.[9] CAMRA
responded by suggesting that BrewDog had engineered the dispute
for publicity purposes in failing to meet the terms agreed in the
contract. Letters were made public, accusations were fired back and
forth and observers chose which story to believe depending largely
on their personal prejudices.

As with the debate within CAMRA about 'top pressure' in the
late 1970s, this argument seemed baffling and boring to many. But
it did help BrewDog to distinguish their approach more clearly
from that of potential rivals from the world of 'real ale': in 2012
they announced with a flourish their intention to stop producing
cask-conditioned ale altogether.

Since 2010, the term 'craft keg' has been in circulation, intended to
distinguish kegged beers produced by 'craft brewers' from, say, John
Smith's 'smooth' bitter or Carling lager. The former beers are often
unpasteurised, sometimes unfiltered, or at least filtered using gentler
methods, which are supposed to leave more 'flavour' in the beer. The

trend took a long time to arrive, no doubt arrested to some extent by the Campaign for Real Ale's domination of 'beer appreciation' in the UK and the anti-keg stance that was their founding principle. But was it kegging that made Watney's Red so unpalatable to connoisseurs, or was it the recipe, the ingredients and the pasteurising and filtering that took place before it reached its sealed container?

Way back in the 1980s, Peter Austin considered kegging beer at Ringwood; Sean Franklin at Rooster's thought about it, but was held back by the cost of the equipment and the technical challenge, which he felt was beyond him.[10] Alastair Hook was annoying CAMRA by insisting on using kegs at Meantime long before BrewDog. But it was BrewDog who turned kegging into a statement – a sign of a 'young', open-minded brewery.

American Jeff Rosenmeier, owner of Lovibonds of Henley-on-Thames, is a vigorous advocate of kegging and an outspoken critic of both cask-conditioning and CAMRA. He argues that kegging is more suitable for German-style wheat beers, for instance, which typically come with a huge head of foam. More than that, he finds traditional casks fundamentally disgusting:

> [When] the publican is pulling a pint, that pint is replaced in the firkin with a pint of cellar air. If you have ever been in a pub cellar you will know that they are probably one of the most unhygienic environments you could find, with beer spoilers [bacteria] being blown around in the air by the cellar-cooling fans. Often you have the chef storing vegetables and other food products in the cellar, and all of this is going into the beer. To me, this makes no sense whatsoever, and I cannot believe that every brewer in the land hasn't revolted against the dire treatment of their labour of love ... Our kegs are a closed system. If we have done our job properly in the brewery and packaging hall, then when our kegs come back they have nothing left in them but a splash of micro-biologically clean beer and 100 per cent CO_2. This is a very harsh environment for any living thing, and that's the way I like it.[11]

The fact is, however, that despite trendy branding and 'innovative' recipes, many in the industry express a lingering fondness for tradition, and very few small British breweries keg any beer. Among those who do, fewer than a handful completely eschew cask-conditioning. Stuart Ross of Magic Rock, though these days he himself can barely stand to drink cask-conditioned beer, said:

> We would never 'do a BrewDog' and abandon cask . . . Richard [Burhouse] is very committed to it, as that's what got him into beer, through hoppy ales from Ossett, Mallinson and Saltaire.

Simon Webster of Thornbridge, another Yorkshireman who grew up on cask-conditioned bitter, seemed similarly ambivalent:

> At first, keg was maybe 10 per cent of the business; now, it's forty. The market's come to us; it's not something we've pushed or wanted to do, especially, but there's huge demand for it.

Dominic Driscoll, a senior brewer at Thornbridge, went further:

> Personally, I'm a cask ale drinker – I've been a CAMRA member since I was a teenager – I think the balance here has maybe gone a bit too far towards keg. It's so tempting, though, because you've got pub landlords ringing up complaining about the one cask they've bought, which they probably haven't looked after, and on the other line, someone from Scandinavia wanting to buy two pallets of keg Jaipur.

Jeff Rosenmeier is in no doubt that kegging has helped his business find new customers: 'We are not converting beardie weirdies into drinking our craft beer ... they walk in, see the fonts and walk out. What we are doing is converting the people that have been drinking cold, shit beer.'

In practice, whether a beer is kegged or cask-conditioned makes very little difference to its flavour in itself, as there are many other more important variables, from the ingredients to the brewing process to the conditions in which it is kept and served at the point of sale.

Cask ale can be a victim of the dirt and bacteria Rosenmeier so despises, and doesn't last long at peak condition – a matter of days – so can suffer if careless or unscrupulous publicans continue to sell it past its best. At the same time, like ripening cheese or well-hung steak, these ales also benefit from being allowed to begin the process of spoiling as air replaces liquid in the cask, gaining a 'funky' note, which, at the right dosage – barely perceptible – is extremely pleasing.

Keg beer, too, can be mishandled – over-chilled and over-pressurised, leaving it, as the real-ale crowd would say, 'cold and fizzy'. A little more carbonation and a slightly cooler serving temperature, on the other hand, though many CAMRA loyalists would disagree, has a distinct intrinsic appeal: it is more 'refreshing'. Bold American-inspired beers, especially IPAs, can seem muddy when cask-conditioned and benefit from extra carbonation. In most cases, they are big enough in flavour for whatever subtlety gained from the cask process to be imperceptible. Kegging also works well, in our view, for lagers and other Continental styles, where a certain crispness is a key part of the appeal.

Perhaps an appropriate analogy is the difference between the 'warmth' of music on vinyl and the 'sheen' of digital: neither is categorically 'better' than the other, but some people have a strong preference for one, while others are able to appreciate both.

⁂

With the new market for kegged 'craft beer' has come a new type of drinking establishment. Where once there was North Bar and The Rake, now there are beer-focused bars (as opposed to 'real ale' pubs), if not in every town, then at least in every corner of the country. Many of these new bars are part of two small chains, which emerged at around the same time.

First, there was Pivo Beer Café and Bar, which opened in December 2007 in a half-timbered building in the medieval centre of the rather genteel walled city of York. Like The Rake, it was a 'shop window' for a beer import concern whose primary business was distributing a well-regarded Czech lager called Bernard in the UK. It had more than fifty different bottled beers, three cask ales and around twelve kegged 'world beers'. It also sold beers from Alastair Hook's Meantime – then one of the few British 'craft' breweries packaging any beer that way. Pivo gained a cult following, becoming a 'must visit' for beer enthusiasts travelling in the region, and it won an industry award for its beer selection.[12] The owner, Jamie Hawksworth, who was in his early thirties, started thinking about where he might open another bar.

Meanwhile, in London in the summer of 2009, Cask Bar and Kitchen opened in Pimlico, south-west London. Occupying an unpromising corner site in a block of red-brick flats on a backstreet parallel to Vauxhall Bridge Road, it had previously been a run-down pub of no particular distinction: The Pimlico Tram, owned by large regional brewer Greene King. Martin Hayes, who had previously run a pub for Punch Taverns, a national pub company, approached Greene King and pitched 'an unusual concept' – something 'different', focused on 'good beers'.

In its first months, Cask was a modest 'real ale' pub augmented with some imported bottled beers, struggling to 'gentrify'. When we visited not long after it opened, we found Hayes – a big man with prematurely white hair and ruddy cheeks – dealing forcefully with drunks and verbally aggressive eccentrics who had previously been regulars and who refused to find somewhere else to drink. But before long, a bank of keg 'fonts' had been installed, at first dispensing German, American and Belgian beers. More refrigerators were fitted, and the range of bottles grew, too, until by the middle of 2011 there were ten cask-ale handpumps, fourteen keg lines and 500 different bottled beers. It won several local CAMRA awards and was declared 'best tenanted/leased pub' by the *Publican* magazine, all of which encouraged Hayes to expand.

Back in the North, Jamie Hawksworth and his business partners had staged something of a coup, negotiating the lease on the abandoned bar and restaurant in Sheffield's central railway station. After a substantial restoration job, the Sheffield Tap opened for business in December 2009. It stocked similar beer to Pivo, but with more of everything: the Edwardian decor – tiles, brass, polished wood and leather seating – was more impressive, and journalists and beer writers loved the unusual juxtaposition of a top-notch pub and a functional, twenty-first-century railway station.

Hawksworth then set about turning two bars into a chain, and the 'Taps' into a brand. Recognising that part of the appeal of the Sheffield Tap was the location and its architectural oddity, his next venture was in London, occupying one of the surviving lodges which had flanked the long-demolished Euston Arch. It opened in November 2010. While the Euston Tap lacked the Sheffield branch's easy-going atmosphere – it is small, cramped and often crowded with commuters – London's beer geeks, and those from elsewhere, passing through, welcomed it. (Just around the corner, The Bree Louise, once one of London's best-known 'real ale' pubs, began to seem a little shabby and old-fashioned by comparison.)

The month before the Euston Tap opened, BrewDog joined the fray with their first bar in Aberdeen – just one outcome of their 'Equity for Punks' share scheme. Perhaps unsurprisingly, it served nothing but kegged beer, whereas both Hawksworth and Hayes had a lasting commitment to cask-conditioned beer. It was a statement of intent on BrewDog's part. Once again unknowingly echoing David 'Firkin' Bruce, they 'de-decorated' an unloved property in the city centre, stripping it back to bare brick with exposed pipes and furnishing it austerely. From the off, it was obvious that this was a corporate style which would be easy to roll out to more branches, and, with an Edinburgh bar under development, they made it known that they were looking for likely locations for a third and fourth bar.[13]

Martin Hayes was also gearing up to expand, and to create a brand of his own. 'Cask', which had seemed a reasonable enough name in 2009, seemed a little unfortunate by 2011, with BrewDog stoking a craze for 'craft keg', and so the second pub, on Leather Lane in Clerkenwell, was christened 'The Craft Beer Co.' It was from day one what Cask had slowly evolved into, but more so: an exhibition of beer (to borrow the words of CAMRA in 1978) which included cask-conditioned 'real ale', a dazzling array of bottles from around the world and a vast number of keg beers. There was no Guinness, Stella Artois or John Smith's Extra Smooth. Despite occupying a Victorian pub building, it was distinctly un-pub-like, with a whitewashed interior and high-backed seating around the walls.

Perhaps just too busy, or maybe recognising that a middle-aged man behind the bar might not appeal to the target audience of students and twentysomethings, Hayes installed a smart young manager, Tom Cadden. Still only in his mid-twenties, Cadden, a Scot, had already worked at The Rake and for BrewDog, and was well connected. He described the Craft Beer Co.'s opening day to Per Nielsen: 'I went outside because there were four policemen there, who asked me why there were three hundred and fifty people standing outside the pub.'[14]

Since 2011, new bars have been opening with remarkable regularity. There are now five branches of the Craft Beer Co. in London (Cask in Pimlico, the original Craft Beer Co. in Leather Lane, one in Islington, another in Brixton and the newest in Clapham) as well as one in Brighton. The York Tap opened in yet another abandoned station building in November 2011,[15] and, though they have so far been unsuccessful, Jamie Hawksworth has ambitious plans to open 'Taps' in Bristol, Cambridge and elsewhere. He also has a hand in other bars not under the Tap brand, such as the Holborn Whippet.

Thornbridge, with twelve pubs in total, entered the 'craft beer bar' market with the Dada in central Sheffield in December 2011. Simon Webster:

> Dada ... wasn't ever really a pub, it was a wine bar. We took it
> because the rent was affordable for the city centre, and we use
> it to showcase our keg beers. Sheffield is a big weekend market,
> so we have DJs and it's all about Friday and Saturday night, the
> younger market.

Confusingly, Tap East, which opened at the Westfield London Shopping Centre in Stratford, east London in 2012, is nothing to do with Hawksworth and is actually a spin-off of Utobeer and The Rake. It also has its own small, on-site brewery.

As of August 2013, BrewDog have thirteen bars in Aberdeen, Birmingham, Bristol, Edinburgh, Glasgow, Leeds, Nottingham, Newcastle and Manchester, and four in London. Several more are in the pipeline.

Finally, alongside these three relatively large chains there are one-offs, such as the Hand Bar in Falmouth, Cornwall, run by a former North Bar employee, Pete Walker (2010); Port Street Beer House in Manchester (also 2010); and the Teign Cellars in Newton Abbot, Devon (2013).

When we visit most of these bars, especially BrewDog's, being in our mid-thirties we tend to feel rather old. It is not unknown to see older drinkers, especially on a quiet midweek afternoon when the music is down low, there is space to breathe and the chance of a seat, but it seems clear that they are not really the intended audience.

More common are students scraping together money for pints of IPA or 'craft lager', because these bars, regardless of the beer on offer, are cool. (They are also, on occasion, caught smuggling in bottles of Budweiser.) There are young professionals – what might once have been called yuppies, though this generation wouldn't be seen dead in a suit – who think nothing of spending £8 on a pint of beer, or more than £20 on a bottle of something rare and exclusive.

It is not unusual to see people working on laptops or posting photos of their beer on Instagram and Twitter. Those among the clientele who aren't especially interested in beer are liable to find themselves being educated by well-trained bar staff, or picking at random from huge printed menus.

Anecdotally, it seems the new breed of beer exhibition is also more popular with women (certainly young women) than 'real ale' pubs have been. Where there is a lingering sense that pubs are an essentially 'male' space into which women have intruded or been invited, stylish bars are too new to have attracted such prejudices.

What all of these bars require to stay ahead, however, is a constant supply of beers with the whiff of rarity, novelty and exclusivity about them. India pale ales, once a showcase for the unusual and hard to come by, are ten a penny – Michael Jackson's list of 500 great beers from 2000 included thirteen IPAs; when Zak Avery undertook a similar project in 2010,[16] his 500 included no fewer than forty IPAs. So where is the cutting edge now?

SIXTEEN

THE OUTER LIMITS

A burly navvy was holding a mug of ale up to the light.
'Wot's this 'ere?' he asked again, gruffly.
A glance was enough to show me what was wrong . . .
'Hmm – it is cloudy, isn't it!' I muttered.
I drew off two or three pints and tried again. It was
worse.

Tom Berkley, *We Keep a Pub*, 1955[1]

If Hop Back, Brendan Dobbin and Sean Franklin showed that British beer could be pale and perfumed, and Alastair Hook made lager respectable, then the most recent generation of British brewers have gone even further in questioning assumptions, creating niches within what is already a small part of the beer market. That perfectly clear beer is always best is the kind of belief that might be up for challenge. The following passage by Dr Keith Thomas from the CAMRA *Good Beer Guide* 1995 summarises the received wisdom:

> Before paying for a pint, quickly check its clarity. This will indicate whether the beer has been handled correctly and whether it might be infected. Real ale contains live yeast and does have the potential to be served cloudy. However, a very yeasty pint will have a quite different taste from a clear one and should be refused, and any excuses about it being 'natural' or a 'healthier pint' should be rejected.[2]

There are various ways to make beer clear, from mechanical filtering to the addition of ingredients which attract suspended particles of protein and yeast before being removed from the beer. In Britain, the most traditional approach is the use of the euphemistically named 'isinglass finings', a substance made from the dried and powdered swim bladders of sturgeon, or 'fish guts', as Dickie and Watt of BrewDog have called it.[3]

In recent years, several brewers have begun to question the need for this process. If mechanical filtering is frowned upon, why is this acceptable? Aren't 'additives' something to be avoided in 'artisanal' products? And anyway, isn't clarity a merely superficial characteristic? Justin Hawke of Moor Beer is arguably the most vocal champion of what have come to be known as 'unfined' beers, though he does understand the obsession with clarity in the UK:

> It's cultural. In this country, for a long time, cask ale would sit in the pipes, which hadn't been cleaned in God knows how long, and when you ordered a pint, you got warm, cloudy vinegar. Pretty disgusting, and it would upset your stomach, but it wasn't yeast or haze that did that.

Hawke's questioning of that culture is perhaps to be expected: he is an outsider – an American who has made Britain his home. His brewery is housed in a rather plain-looking, 'rural industrial' building with walls of corrugated metal and without any signs to advertise its presence. What would be the point? It sits on a single-track lane leading off into the green flatness of the Somerset Levels, where grasshoppers are the loudest sound for miles. Once we had found our way in by banging on an unmarked door, we discovered Hawke supervising the end of a brew. His eyes were trained on his team of young brewers as he barked safety warnings and instructions: 'That spent grain is hot! Is that tap off? Tell him to make sure the tap is off.'

He is a dark-haired and somewhat intense character who salts his speech with turns of phrase that sound odd with an American accent

– 'That does my head in.' The contradiction between his casual dress and occasionally stiff manner made sense when he talked about his childhood in California in the 1970s and his journey to Europe:

> I grew up with Michael Jackson's books – various editions of the *Pocket Guide to Beer*. My dad had them all and he would seek out these interesting beers, in all the different styles, and share them with me. I was young, so just small amounts, obviously, but enough to give me an education.

After studying at the United States Military Academy at West Point, he was stationed with the US Army in Frankfurt in the early 1990s, and took the opportunity to visit great beer-producing centres such as Prague, Munich and Belgium. German breweries often promote their unfiltered beers, opaque with suspended yeast, as a kind of health food, with talk of 'enzymes' reminiscent of yogurt advertisements and their 'friendly bacteria'. For Hawke, it was all about the flavour: 'During my time living in Germany the best beers I would drink in the local brewpubs were all unfined and very hazy, even the lagers.' He returned to California in the mid-1990s and absorbed what had become a booming 'craft beer' culture: 'I went to San Francisco and learned to brew. This was the peak time for the growth of American craft beer, and I learned a lot from breweries like Speakeasy and Burlingame Station.'

His final move was to Britain, where he fully embraced the CAMRA-led 'real ale' culture, working at the Great British Beer Festival as a volunteer, helping to run the Champion Beer of Britain award competition. Managed through 'blind tasting', in which the judges do not know which beers they are drinking as they assess them, the contest has generally included the clarity of the beer among the quality criteria, with elaborate procedures for assessing it.[4]

Hawke spent years planning to buy or start a brewery and finally got the opportunity in 2006 just as, elsewhere in the country, Thornbridge was getting on its feet and BrewDog was gestating. Moor Beer, an award-winning, well-established brewery in Somerset, founded in

1996 by Arthur and Annette Frampton, came up for sale as a 'lock, stock and barrel' proposition, and Hawke snapped it up. It wasn't, however, quite the bargain he had thought:

> I realised, once I'd taken over, that it needed a lot of work. The place wasn't up to the standards of hygiene I wanted – it was a converted dairy, like a lot of 'real ale' breweries, but it really was improvised kit sort of jumbled together. The brewery, the recipes and the branding all needed to be completely redone.

Since then, the brewery has moved to a new location, and only two beers are still in production using names – but not recipes – from before the takeover. The reinvention of Moor is a powerful example of how, with a few simple changes, a traditional 'real ale' brewery can become a poster boy for 'craft beer'. 'I've got a soft spot for CAMRA,' Hawke told us. 'They can't keep plugging away with the same rhetoric; they have to change.' After overseas importers began to demand kegged beer for sale in foreign markets, Moor was among the first UK breweries to use 'ecokegs', so that, as demand for kegged craft beer grew, the company was well placed to respond.

The move to unfined beer, however, was prompted, he insists, by his own taste buds: 'It wasn't driven by a desire to be "different" or annoy anyone, and it's not about "whole food" – it just tastes better. It's natural.' In a walk-in storage room at the brewery, shelves are stacked with plastic sacks of beer – samples drawn off so that the quality of the beer can be monitored without interfering with the huge stainless steel fermenters which reach up to the ceiling. These samples, because they weren't for sale, did not need to be perfectly clear and so were never fined: 'I was taking these home to carry out quality assurance testing – you've got to quality-control your own beer, right? – and I found that I preferred the beer without finings. It just tasted better to me.' Having come to that conclusion, Hawke began, cautiously at first, to apply it across the brewery's range: 'First, the dark beers, because you can't see if it's hazy anyway. Then the strong beers, because they're for a niche market. Then the hoppy beers, for the same reason. Now, *everything* is unfined.'

That doesn't mean, necessarily, that the beers are cloudy or even hazy. Given time, yeast will settle naturally, especially if the particular strain has been selected for that characteristic. Among other changes Hawke made at Moor was the development of a yeast, in collaboration with Mark Tranter, formerly of Dark Star Brewing, and Eddie Gadd of the Ramsgate Brewery, with characteristics similar to those used in Californian pale ales such as Sierra Nevada. On our visit, Hawke held up a bottle of beer to the light: 'You can't actually *get* much clearer than that.'

Even so, depending on its age, temperature and how it is served, Moor's beer may well be less than 'pin bright', as the jargon would have it, and there has been more than a little work done in getting people to judge the beer on its taste rather than on its appearance. 'The consumer isn't the barrier,' Hawke told us. 'It's pub landlords. They're very risk averse. A good landlord, on the other hand, who educates people and reassures them, won't have any trouble selling this beer, and people love it when they try it.'

One wall of the brewery is covered in framed award certificates from CAMRA and SIBA. When we visited, the most recent were from a festival that had taken place in Devon the week before. Hawke pointed them out with pride: 'I campaigned to get SIBA to change their competition judging rules so that a beer which tasted incredible but was hazy couldn't be knocked out. This year, at the Tucker's Maltings festival, we won three prizes, in tough categories, with unfined beer.'

Moor Beer is not, according to Hawke, making him rich, but nor is it any longer a struggling company. Unfined beer might be a niche product, but it has a market, and other breweries are not only following Moor's example but are going even further.

At Evercreech, near Shepton Mallet, only thirty minutes along the road from the Moor brewery, another Californian is also brewing unusual beer. The Wild Beer Co. operates out of a converted industrial unit on the grounds of a dairy farm, next door to a cheese maker. Walking across the concrete car park, past sheds with corrugated roofs and through a plain white door, visitors are assailed by an aroma reminiscent of the famous Cantillon Brewery on a side street in Brussels: dust,

The label for Wild Beer Co.'s 'non-beer', Ninkasi.

wood, mould and the tang of something like sherry. Cantillon is an old brewery, cobwebbed and creaking, yet the paint on the Wild Beer Co. sign is barely dry. The comparison is appropriate, though, because the Belgian brewer is a major influence.

'I guess you could say we're brewing in the Belgian tradition, via California, with some inspiration from the more intense end of British beer,' says Andrew Cooper. A burly, bearded, Somerset native educated at nearby Millfield public school, he is the company's spokesman and business manager, as well as one of the major investors. Brett Ellis, the head brewer, is tall and fashionably bespectacled, and somehow makes his very practical orange heavy-duty work wellingtons and overalls look like hip accessories. Having lived in Bristol for several years, his Californian accent has blurred around the edges.

Before they'd brewed a drop of beer, WBC's advance publicity machine – Cooper admits, sheepishly, that he worked hard to create the hype – had the attention of beer geeks with a mention of 'wild' yeast. The following, from a news story accompanying the brewery's launch, is typical:

> We believe exceptional brewing stems from imagination and
> passion ... It's not just a process ... Brewing doesn't need to be

confined by rules, tradition or ingredients ... Modus Operandi
will be an untamed beast that thrives on the unpredictability of
wild yeast and the subtlety and complexity of maturation in oak.[5]

The yeast used in most breweries is anything but wild. It is refined
and cultivated in laboratories, isolated from contamination at every
stage and discarded when it shows signs of mutation or infection.
Different 'strains' that produce unique flavours are maintained in
banks. Most brewers want their yeast to perform the same way,
under the same conditions, to produce consistent beer. Some Belgian
breweries, however, such as the above-mentioned Cantillon, operate
in wilful opposition to those principles: after boiling the sugary 'wort',
they leave this proto-beer in an open tank and wait for whatever yeast
is drifting invisibly in the air to settle on the surface. The resulting beers
are often sour and 'funky' – exactly the kinds of tastes which British
beers drinkers have, on the whole, been taught to take as warning signs.

Wild yeast flavours are not anathema to West Country cider
drinkers, whose farmyard 'scrumpy' is more often than not fermented
with whatever happens to be present on the skins of the apples when
they are pressed. That's what Cooper and Ellis have in mind as their
ultimate aim, as Cooper explained:

> [We] hope, soon, to start using an old milk vat as a *koelschip*[*]
> to collect wild yeast. That will be a really local ingredient, right
> out of the Somerset air. There are orchards reasonably nearby,
> so we'll see what happens. If we find something that works, we
> might have it refined in a lab and then that will become one of
> our primary yeast strains.

They are far from being the first of the current generation of British
breweries to experiment with wild yeast, but few others have made it
the cornerstone of their business in quite the same way.

---

[*] In Belgian breweries which use wild yeast, a flat, open tank in which beer sits after
brewing but before transfer into fermenting vessels.

Another source of wild yeast can be the brewery buildings themselves – old beams and unhygienic-looking wall surfaces – and wooden barrels, in which a type of yeast known as *Brettanomyces* often lurks. Arthur Millard and the founders of the Society for the Preservation of Beers from the Wood would no doubt be surprised to discover that, as a result, there is now a widespread interest in beers matured in wood, or at least which taste as if they have been.

Whether from the wood or through deliberate inoculation with lab-grown material, *Brettanomyces* makes its presence known not by creating sourness, but rather by imparting a sort of dry 'funkiness'. It is most obvious in the famous Belgian Trappist beer Orval: an acquired taste. Several newer UK breweries have also experimented with 'Brett' in recent years.

The Wild Beer Co. brewery, though it is freshly painted and has brand-new, stainless steel conical fermenters, is also well stocked with barrels, each almost a metre from end to end, that were previously used for bourbon, sherry or wine. As well as contributing wild yeast, the lingering remains of their previous contents also add flavour to any beer which is aged in them. Such is the demand for barrels in brewing today that Andrew Cooper admits to being secretive about his sources: 'That's the one thing that we guard a bit jealously – we've got a little black book of contacts, and we don't share it.' Ellis is excited by the possibilities presented by barrels, each of which has its own history. Looking as if he might snap in half under its weight, he hoisted one up, popped out its bung and said, with gleaming eyes: 'This one was used for Pedro Ximenez – here, smell it!' The fumes from the empty vessel, which once contained a sweet Spanish fortified wine made with dried grapes, were, perhaps unsurprisingly, reminiscent of Christmas pudding.

One of WBC's flagship beers, Modus Operandi, is an 'old ale' in the English tradition, partly inspired by Gale's Prize Old Ale, famous for its sherry-like aroma and flavour when aged over extended periods. This connection, Ellis insists, is not superficial:

> At the one end, we have these beers which overlap with cider, and at the other with sherry and wine. But it's not just that they sort of taste and smell *like* cider or sherry – they're literally made with the same ingredients, processes, and undergo the same chemical changes during fermentation and ageing.

Though they never say it in front of beer geeks, for fear of being laughed out of the room, Cooper and Ellis have been known to describe some of their brews as 'beer but not as you know it'. Ninkasi, for example, is made with a proportion of apple juice and fermented partly with a yeast usually used to make champagne. The resulting beer is hazy yellow, dry and slightly sour, with a prickling fizz, and is served from a 750ml bottle with a waxed cap. 'Some people might say that Ninkasi is "not really beer"', said Cooper, 'and we're fine with that.'

Though this might seem to be as far from the mainstream as it is possible to get in British brewing – a sideshow to the sideshow, while the majority of people continue to drink internationally branded lager, if they drink beer at all – it is, like Moor's unfined beer, finding a market. 'We set this up as a business,' said Cooper. 'We've both got young families, so it needed to pay us a wage from day one . . . What we didn't want was to be the people who wait for other people to prove there's a market for something and then jump on the bandwagon – we wanted to be taking the risk and, if not creating a new market, exactly, then being among the first.'

Much of their beer is bottled, and most of what is sold in keg or cask – usually the former – is snapped up by the small but growing network of 'craft beer bars' around the country and the specialist distributors, such as Liberty Beer, which have emerged to supply them. Cooper expressed a certain frustration over the beer geeks and their constant demand for 'something new'. In the longer term, the intention is to find a more sustainable market by 'converting' people who don't drink beer at all: 'What we want to do is reach out to those people, who are probably wine drinkers at the moment, who don't really think about drinking beer.' Wine drinkers, of course, rarely drink by the pint, and prefer a more elegant vessel.

❀

The pint has become synonymous with British drinking habits, to the point where Nigel Farage of the UK Independence Party uses a pint of bitter as a prop in reference to fears that the European Union will, at some point, enforce metric measures in the UK. (In 2007, when the EU passed a resolution requiring the traditional crown symbol on pint glasses to be replaced with a standardised CE mark, there was uproar and the tabloids rushed to 'defend our Great British Pint from the meddling Euro-prats'.[6]) When British people meet their friends, they 'go for a pint', regardless of whether both are drinking half-pints, bottled beer or even cocktails. There are people – mostly men – who not only won't drink halves themselves, but won't buy them for anyone else: to do so would be emasculating. In this context, where 'a pint' means much more than a measure of liquid, conversations about whether smaller or alternative servings might be better for some beers have tended to become rather fraught.

The way for smaller measures and more elegant glassware was paved, perhaps, by ladies drinking bottled stout in the lounge – the room in the pub where men wore their Sunday best and refrained from spitting. It was then furthered by the rise of 'national brands', especially lagers, with glassware custom-designed to evoke Continental sophistication: Carlsberg's UK advertising from the early 1960s featured images of slender, vase-like vessels topped with white foam and bearing the company logo.[7] With Michael Jackson and 'world beer' came a new opportunity for fetishism:

> Like Frenchmen drinking wine, Belgians are inclined to order *le ballon*. Belgium's *ballon* will vary in shape depending on the beer which it is meant to hold. Each brewer has his own style … delicate glasses which might suit a fine brandy; chunky goblets; tall-stemmed bowls worthy of medieval castles.[8]

In 1998, Jackson launched his own range of specially designed 'tasting' glasses, produced by Ritzenhoff, each of which was engraved with a portrait of the man himself and advertised with the slogan: 'The Right Glass at the Right Time'.

During the 'noughties', Alastair Hook, a devotee of Jackson who knew Belgian and German beer well, stocked the Meantime brewery tap – the Greenwich Union – with glassware distinctly at odds with the English tradition. Though pints were on offer, they came in German-style 'willybecher' glasses; and, at any rate, drinkers were positively encouraged to drink by the half-pint from stemmed, elegantly curved 'cervoise' glasses. Bottled beers were often delivered in delicate Belgian-style goblets with intricate screen-printed designs. On the one hand, this was a way of establishing Meantime's place in the market; on the other, it reflected the fact that some of the beers were strong enough to warrant smaller measures.

When more 'craft beer' bars began to appear from around the middle of the first decade of the twenty-first century, most made a virtue of their glassware, matching branded glasses to imported bottled beers, perhaps with a view to increasing their perceived value as drinkers handed over ever more startling amounts of money compared to the prices asked for 'real ale' or 'cooking lager'. As 'drink less but drink better' became a rallying cry, the half-pint measure became, in these bars at least, perfectly respectable, and perhaps even fashionable.

Oddly, it took CAMRA, by now seen as rather fuddy-duddy, to take another look at the 1988 Weights and Measures Order and notice that, though the permissible measures were strictly controlled, there was a legal measure even smaller than half a pint.° At the Great British Beer Festival in 2006, drinkers were given the option of third-pint glasses, which were so popular they ran out. Thereafter, CAMRA began to lobby the pub industry to offer thirds in pubs, although, with some irony, the call was only really heeded to any noticeable extent by CAMRA-ambivalent 'craft beer bars'.

In 2011, the government amended legislation under pressure from the industry, including BrewDog, who sent a dwarf to protest outside

Parliament, and made two-thirds of a pint a legal measure. Some were furious: it was neo-prohibitionism, they said – 'a back-door health measure' designed to drive down alcohol consumption.[10] Others were concerned that the new glasses would allow unscrupulous publicans to charge pint prices for the new, slightly smaller measure, perhaps in deceptively designed glasses.

In reality, there has been very little take-up by 'ordinary' pubs, but the beer-geek end of the market has welcomed the change. 'Many of the specialist beers we represent just don't suit being served in pint or half-pint glasses,' said Ian Clay of James Clay and Sons.[11] BrewDog in particular have embraced the two-thirds measure, recommending it for medium-strength beers which might be too heady in full pints.

In 2012, however, in the run-up to its opening, the proprietors of a new specialist beer outlet in Edinburgh announced, with something of a flourish, that they would go a step further: they would not be serving any measure larger than two-thirds of a pint. Chris Mair, the co-owner of the Hanging Bat Beer Café, explained:

> Calum [Carmichael, the manager] and I agreed from the outset that neither of us enjoyed drinking pints any more. We always drink halves, and wish more people served the kinds of beers we enjoyed in two-thirds, largely due to ABV as [well as] freshness. We were both sick of getting to the bottom of a beer and finding it warm and flat. The session-beering, sink-seven-pints days are slowly going. Not because these kinds of beers aren't good, but because I genuinely believe that people's attitudes towards drinking, and in particular drinking beer, are changing.[12]

He insisted that the decision hadn't been at all political – that there was no conscious attempt to do as Oliver Peyton had done twenty years before and ostentatiously reject 'real ale' culture – but it is nevertheless a statement, as is calling the establishment a café rather than a pub.

SEVENTEEN

ECUMENICAL MATTERS

In beer (as in wine, cheese, bread and numerous other foods) there is a growth in interest in products of quality, character and tradition, and at the other end of the market, a demand for bland, light flavours; the middle ground is vanishing.

Michael Jackson, 1986[1]

The last fifty years have seen the monolith that was 'beer' split in two. On one side are the mass-produced 'monopoly beers' (to borrow a 'real ale' Campaign slogan), and on the other, what Michael Jackson sometimes used to call 'beers of character'. Though 'big beer' seems to be struggling, there is plenty of energy and excitement on the latter side of the fence, and new breweries continue to open while better-established ones keep growing. Now that 'alternative' category is in the process of subdividing yet again, this time into two broad camps: 'real ale' and 'craft beer'.

Some generalisations: 'real ale' brewers are more likely to have as their flagship product a sub-5 per cent ABV cask-conditioned bitter. They are more likely to have been founded before 2005. Their names will crop up time and again at CAMRA festivals and on the bars at CAMRA-friendly pubs. They tend to be resolutely and proudly British.

'Real ale', as a cultural phenomenon, is now more than forty years old, and has become a well-established national institution. Despite constant fretting over the loss of 'community locals', there is scarcely a corner of the country where cask-conditioned beer is not now easier to find than it was in 1975. Norwich, once Christopher Hutt's favourite example of a city whose beer culture had been ruined by Watney's, now hosts an annual 'City of Ale' event where pilgrims travel from far and wide to enjoy its unusually wide range of highly rated, CAMRA-friendly pubs. Those who like to drink straight-forward cask-conditioned bitter made with English hops are spoilt for choice, as CAMRA founder Michael Hardman observed with some impatience:

> You hear people say now, oh, free houses only ever have the same old suspects – London Pride, Adnams – but it would have been really great to find that in 1971. I certainly would never have dreamed of a place like this in every town.

'This' refers to the JD Wetherspoon pub where he had chosen to meet us. Entrepreneur Tim Martin's chain of pubs is a high-street version of the 'beer exhibition', in a compromised form, and demon-strates how mainstream real ale has become. The business was founded at around the same time as David Bruce's Firkins, in 1979, at the height of the 'real ale craze', and focused on cask-conditioned beer for which Martin could see a huge demand but which the Big Six seemed reluctant to service. The philosophy of the company was supposedly inspired by George Orwell's vision of the perfect English pub in his 1946 essay *The Moon Under Water*: resolutely Victorian, no irritating music and a good, solid lunch 'for about three shillings'. Wetherspoon pubs are now on every high street. They are a boozy equivalent of McDonald's or Kentucky Fried Chicken – wipe-clean, good value, impressively efficient. Many occupy beautiful old buildings – cinemas, banks – cleverly repur-posed to maximise drinking and serving space. The bigger branches offer more cask ales at any one time than even St Albans' legendary

Barley Mow in its pomp, and at around a pound a pint less than most other outlets.

As for the Campaign for Real Ale, it is in rude health. After a long period during which membership languished below its 1970s peak, it now has more than a 150,000 members – it is larger than the Conservative Party. That remarkable growth has been achieved steadily, with membership creeping up year on year, rather than skyrocketing as it did in the period between 1973 and 1978. Many members have been tempted into signing up at local and national beer festivals in exchange for discounted entry and freebies for new customers. Helpful too has been the introduction of automatically renewing direct-debit payments for membership – it is more trouble to leave CAMRA than to stay – as have the wedges of discount vouchers for Wetherspoon's pubs that arrive with each renewal.

More positively, joining CAMRA has also become something of a rite of passage for beer enthusiasts – a way of announcing 'conversion to the cause'. The general boom in beer in the last decade, in which CAMRA are far from the only players, has probably helped: a third of the current membership joined after 2009.

In becoming large, CAMRA has also become more complex, with its own politics and subcultures. Today, its central office is staffed by professionals from various fields and is calmly corporate, with a professional chief executive providing continuity and measured management. Chairs are still elected from the membership but, for the last twenty or so years, have tended to be not young firebrands but middle-aged veteran campaigners, who often remain in post for many years at a time. The current chair, Colin Valentine, though often plain-speaking, is no revolutionary.

If the centre is corporate, the branches are a mixed bag. Some produce glossy, professional-looking magazines and are run with admirable commitment to due process; others less so. Relations between local branches and the publicans and brewers they are expected to deal with are not always harmonious. Though unsurprising – unpaid volunteers can only be expected to do so much

– this is sometimes a problem simply because CAMRA has become a national institution and is extremely influential. When it declares its Champion Beer of Britain, the winning brewery is invariably required to expand to meet the resulting demand. When it tells its members to sign a petition lobbying government, they sign, and various groups, sometimes in competition with each other, lobby the Campaign for its support. Inclusion in CAMRA's annual *Good Beer Guide* can give a pub a much-needed boost, while delisting can be a severe blow.

Arguably, CAMRA has become, to borrow Christopher Hutt's description of Watney's, et al., 'entrenched and powerful' – a Goliath where once it was David –which is perhaps why it is vulnerable to so-called 'CAMRA-bashing'. A good deal of that bashing comes, unfortunately, from another group of beer lovers, sometimes derisively described by CAMRA loyalists as 'craftophiles'.

To generalise once more: 'craft beer' brewers often don't produce a bitter at all. If they do, to avoid the stigma of such an old-fashioned term – 'boring brown bitter' is a 'craft beer' mantra – it might be disguised as an 'amber' or 'red' ale. Their beer will probably be stronger, on average, and will look to the US or Europe for inspiration. It will probably be marketed with reference to 'New World' hops and is extremely unlikely to contain those British stalwarts, Fuggles and Goldings. These breweries are likely to have been founded after 2005, inspired either by BrewDog, or perhaps, more directly, by American breweries such as Russian River or Stone.

'Craft beer' overlaps neatly with the American-inspired 'street food' trend of the last few years: both movements are simultaneously discerning and self-consciously informal. In London, Manchester, Leeds and other urban centres, it seems every other twenty- or thirtysomething is a food critic, unwilling merely to consume other people's reviews when they can generate their own with a smart-phone camera and a free blogging or Twitter account. The gourmet burger and craft beer go hand in hand, both expressions of a kind of democratic snobbery: if you have as little as £10 in your pocket and you are 'in the loop', you can buy the best burger in town, or one of the world's most sought-after beers.

While, unlike 'real ale', the term 'craft beer' has no clearly defined meaning, people are getting on with building a culture around it. In the last two years, from 2012, there have been several successful 'alternative' gatherings such as the Independent Manchester Beer Convention ('IndyManBeerCon'), Birmingham Beer Bash ('BCubed') and the London Craft Beer Festival. Daniel Brown, one of the organisers of 'BCubed', explained what motivated him and his colleagues:

> [We] had all started to ask the same question – why has craft beer not hit Birmingham? Why is our city always the last to know? David [Shipman] and I had both written blog posts bemoaning the lack of a Birmingham Tap, especially when smaller cities seemed to have been afforded much better 'craft' access. We jokingly said, 'If no one else is going to make things happen, we'll have to do it ourselves.' Then we realised we were serious. The beers we wanted weren't available at CAMRA festivals! We knew there was a whole developing scene out there, but CAMRA weren't interested, so we couldn't wait for them to bring the beers to us.

That is not so different to what drove CAMRA members to organise festivals in the mid-1970s. There are likely to be even more such events in the years to come.

Though it is much newer than the 'real ale' culture, there are signs that 'craft beer', too has the potential to become a British institution. BrewDog are almost a household name, perhaps even a global one: thousands of people walk past their boldly branded city-centre bars every day, and, in the summer of 2013, James Watt and Martin Dickie filmed a series, *BrewDogs*, for American cable TV. Magazines with 'craft beer' in their names have begun to appear in newsagents, and the *Guardian* ran a 'beginner's guide' to craft beer in June 2013[2] – a sure sign, as some wags have observed, that it is no longer 'cool'.

Some bigger British brewers usually associated with 'real ale' are certainly convinced that 'craft beer' is a game worth playing. In the United States, several craft breweries are actually subsidiaries of multinational companies, either created from scratch or bought out. In the UK, that process has only just begun. A notable example is Brain's of Cardiff, who launched Brain's Craft Brewery with its own distinct branding in 2012. The parent company, founded in 1882, has a reputation for being rather traditional, and exudes Victorian respectability. The 'craft' spin-off, by contrast, uses modern typography and quirky illustrations rather reminiscent of the work Richard Norgate produces for Magic Rock. The beers are Belgian- and American-inspired, and make a virtue of using, variously, unusual hop varieties, fruit, Belgian yeast and barrel-ageing.

They are not alone. Bath Ales (a solid 'real ale' brewery) has set up 'Beerd' as a separate concern. Thwaites of Blackburn has its 'Crafty Dan' spin-off. Shepherd Neame of Faversham launched 'The Faversham Steam Brewery' in 2013. In Southwold, Suffolk, Adnams are producing beers with names like Innovation, their labels bearing the name 'Jack Brand', looking just like they've been imported from the US, despite being based on a 100-year-old design. Hyde's of Manchester have 'The Beer Studio'. In August 2013, St Austell announced their intention to open a microbrewery and bar in a warehouse in Exeter. Even those breweries which have not gone quite so far have begun to slap the word 'craft' on their products with gay abandon: Fuller's, for example, have Frontier, a 'craft lager'.

Opinion is divided as to whether these offshoots are a good thing. On the one hand, don't beer geeks want more choice and variety? On the other, there does seem to be something underhand about a well-established business pretending to be otherwise – reminiscent, perhaps, of Watney's return to 'real ale' in the late 1970s. It certainly irritates Andrew Cooper of the Wild Beer Co., though it does not worry him:

> If something's hot, they want in, but having tasted a few . . .
> they're no threat, not to what we do. It's not what they do best
> and their hearts aren't in it. They're using the wrong yeasts, a

lot of the time – trying to make beers which put the hops up front but then using very fruity yeasts that totally overwhelm the hops. But it does show how useless the label 'craft' can be.

Fergus Fitzgerald, head brewer at Adnams, bristled somewhat when we suggested their Innovation brand might be exploiting a trend:

> I tend to avoid the craft tag but, in essence, Adnams and many of the older breweries are the original craft brewers. There is little doubt that the current beer movement in the UK is inspired by the US craft beer renaissance, but that in turn was inspired by, among others, the UK cask beer breweries. So if we are jumping on the bandwagon, then it's the same wagon that brewers like Adnams helped build and sent across the Atlantic. Fair enough, it's been 'pimped' now, and has more horsepower, some shiny new banners and has been fitted with a 'banging' sound system so you can hear it coming, but it's still the same wagon.[3]

It would be wrong to imply a great deal of antagonism between the 'real ale' and 'craft beer' camps. There are plenty of 'craftophiles' who are also members of CAMRA, and, within the Campaign, a vocal minority struggles to reconcile cask-ale conservatism with the keg-friendly world of 'craft beer'. They are opposed by a hardcore which continues to lambast 'fizz', and argues vehemently that CAMRA should never do anything to promote or support brewers of keg beer. The debate is riddled with prejudices on both sides, and complicated by political intricacies, which preclude any quick fix.

The problem is slowly being worked through, with small gestures – a few keg beers appearing at 2013's east London CAMRA 'Pig's Ear' beer festival, for example – and competing motions at the annual general meeting. The central secretariat, after some misfires, have settled on a diplomatic line calculated to avoid offending either the old guard or the new:

> CAMRA is committed to choice. We want pub-goers to have
> access to a range of quality and interesting real ales. Our role is
> to promote real ale as our national drink, but that doesn't prevent
> brewers producing other beer products for their customers.[4]

❧

For all its increasing diversity and apparent health, there are anxieties
in the world of 'alternative beer'. Several people we spoke to in the
industry say they are braced for a shake-out: there are too many
breweries, they say, and many are brewing downright bad beer, which
they are selling too cheaply, thus undermining the whole market.

Another concern is that, in a market where the buzz is around the
latest and weirdest beer, there might be nothing new left to discover.
As the previous chapter demonstrated, British brewers (or at least
those based in Britain) are exploring the outer reaches of what might
be expected to find a market, even among self-proclaimed, novelty-
obsessed geeks. Beers cannot get any stronger than those produced by
BrewDog, or much weaker than the 2.8 per cent low-alcohol 'session
pale ale' released by Magic Rock in 2013. Camden Town Brewery and
Meantime have lager covered. In recent years, we have seen beers
made with cucumber, rhubarb, bacon and almost any other kitchen
ingredient, which might make you think, what happens when the
cupboard is bare? We have no doubt that brewers will continue to
surprise us. There are long-forgotten historical styles yet to be fully
explored, obscure yeast strains and experimental hop varieties creeping
onto the market in limited amounts and under cryptic codenames. But
it has got to be harder to innovate now than it was ten years ago, when
brewing a beer of any distinguishing character whatsoever was enough
to garner the attention of pundits and enthusiasts.

Finally, the latter part of 2013 saw a growing concern about the
basic quality of 'craft beer'. While brewers such as Justin Hawke
are producing subtly hazy 'unfined beer', others are using the
same rhetoric to justify beer which is simply poorly made and
unpleasantly yeasty. Similarly, it is difficult, sometimes, to tell

whether a beer is sour because the brewer intended it to be so or because it has become infected. 'Shitloads of hops' and high alcohol content can hide a multitude of sins. Some new breweries seem, at best, overambitious, and at worst are utterly cynical in exploiting the enthusiasm of neophytes.

One indicator of the health of this sector of the market might be the fortunes of the Campaign for Really Good Beer (CAMRGB). A somewhat mischievous, free-to-join group with, as of July 2013, some 700 fully signed-up members,[5] it was founded in 2011 by musician and graphic designer Simon Williams in the wake of CAMRA's spat with BrewDog. It does not really campaign for anything, there is no 'national executive' – Williams is the sole leader, in the loosest sense of the term – and, so far as it has meetings, they are 'Twissups' ('piss-ups' organised through Twitter). It has an active blog, where Williams and others review beers without great pretension. It has T-shirts (designed by Williams), which mark out members in the wild. CAMRGB also has Twitter followers – almost 6,000 – many of whom, as far as we are able to tell, are CAMRA members making a passive-aggressive protest in the face of the older Campaign's perceived conservatism.

If 'craft beer' is anything other than a fad, and 'alternative beer' as a whole is experiencing something more than an unsustainable bubble, then we might expect CAMRGB to get bigger and, as CAMRA did forty years ago, become more serious in its intent. Otherwise it will simply fade away, or perhaps, if it is lucky, become a keg-friendly equivalent of the Society for the Preservation of Beers from the Wood.

THE BEER FROM THE WOOD MEN

London, 10 June 2013

The Society for the Preservation of Beers from the Wood is still going, if not exactly going *strong*, almost fifty years on from its founding in 1963, and, as they do on the second Monday of every month, members of the National Executive of the SPBW are gathering for their committee meeting. The venue is the Royal Oak on Tabard Street, Borough, the primary London outlet for family brewers Harvey's of Sussex, and a perfectly traditional pub with plenty of brown wood, net curtains and a large central bar, which looks as if it has been there for ever but was actually installed as part of a refurbishment in the late 1990s. Today, it is serving a 'light mild' as a seasonal special – a type of beer which is almost extinct but which hangs on, thanks to the efforts of a few nostalgic brewers and drinkers.

One by one, SPBW men arrive, mingling in the bar for an hour before the meeting commences. The famous pinstriped suits and once-compulsory embroidered ties fell by the wayside in the 1970s when the membership ceased to be made up largely of middle-class City men: these few stalwarts are dressed casually.

Roger, who is first to arrive, wears a brand-new polo shirt embroidered with a discreet fiftieth anniversary logo, and has been a member since 1977. He edits the Society's newspaper and is the closest thing it has to an official historian. 'The archive is on top of my wardrobe,' he confesses, slightly embarrassed that all that history does not have a more suitable home. From a carrier bag, he brings an artefact to show us: a small red leather-bound book with thick pages bearing the signatures of the seven founder members, inscribed above the date, 6 December 1963, which is written in an elaborate calligraphic style.

Next to arrive is John, long-haired and bearded with bright blue spectacle frames. He wears a scarlet T-shirt given out to volunteers at the 2004 Campaign for Real Ale Great British Beer Festival. Like most of his fellows, John is an active CAMRA member. Then comes Gary, a softly spoken civil servant. He comes closest to the Arthur Millard dress code in his suit, polished shoes and shirt, and is ribbed by his colleagues for it. Even Gary is not wearing a tie, though he has brought £12.50 with the intention of buying one that evening. Mike, the fourth arrival, was once also a civil servant, but is now retired. Though he bears the grand title of National Chairman, he is also the target of most of the good-natured banter, which he shrugs off with avuncular tuts and chuckles. Bill, long-haired and in a bright yellow T-shirt, arrives last, his arms full of official paperwork in binders.

After a few more pints of mild, and once it has been established, with some irritation, that no one else is expected, they make their way to the function room upstairs, which the landlords of the pub let them use for free. On the way, notes are compared on cures for gout – 'I ate a pound of cherries today, so it should be under control' – and aches and pains are reported. When they arrange themselves around the conference table, each, of course, has a pint in front of him. Minutes are distributed and the discussion commences. It is revealing.

CAMRA has almost 150,000 members; the SPBW has only 331. CAMRA has 37 employees;' the SPBW has none: every aspect of the Society is managed by keen (and sometimes not so keen) unpaid volunteers, who use what spare time they have after work and after local CAMRA duties have been fulfilled. Whereas CAMRA elects its National Executive thanks to a complex internal democracy, the SPBW's executive body is decided more or less by a show of hands at the annual general meeting. At various points, there are slips of the tongue: 'As we in CAMRA know ...' Rigorous care is taken over a discussion of financial matters, though the sums involved are small; and a discussion on the sales of branded products concerns individual shirts and tankards, pounds and pence.

The SPBW exists because these men – and they are all men, though the names of a couple of female members do come up in discussion – are determined to keep it alive, though it must be sorely tempting, at times, to give up. They describe how their annual London 'pub of the year' competition took a hiatus for many years because it was difficult to organise, and are proud to have brought it back from the dead. The same goes for the newsletter, *Pint in Hand*, which Roger Jacobson took on in 1982, frustrated that it was not being taken seriously.

At no point does anyone discuss campaigning, and there is some rolling of the eyes at how much CAMRA spends on lobbying Government over one issue or another. The SPBW, just as Terry Pattinson, Chris Hutt and Michael Hardman found forty years ago, is not about rocking the boat. 'Nowadays, we're about *promoting* good beer and good pubs,' says John. 'Quality beer and traditional pubs,' adds Mike.

The real purpose of the SPBW becomes clear when, business matters out of the way, the conversation turns to the social calendar, which is especially busy in this anniversary year. There are visits to friendly breweries and elaborate pub crawls planned, and opportunities for far-flung members of the loosely knit, decentralised organisation to get together in the North and the Midlands. Towards the end of the year, a pilgrimage to The Rising Sun in Epsom is scheduled, as is, on 6 December, fifty years to the day since Arthur Millard and his friends drew up the constitution, a grand anniversary dinner in a central London pub.

They would like more members, and they would like more members under fifty, too, but realistically have neither the appetite nor the budget to go chasing them. They can no longer afford to run stands at the largest CAMRA festivals, and especially not at the GBBF. ('They think we're a bunch of wankers, anyway.') They try their best with social media and the internet, but it's an uphill struggle. 'Our members are not the sort of people who use Facebook and Twitter, to be honest,' says John with a resigned sigh.

There is some discussion about whether 'beer from the wood' might be due for a revival. Though the Society gave up beating that drum in the 1960s, accepting the inevitability of metal casks, there is still a lingering attachment to the idea, especially given the recent trend towards barrel-ageing.

And what of 'craft beer'? When the term is first uttered, it is with a hint of sarcasm – 'sort of semi-keg, isn't it?' – but there is no hostility. 'We go on trips to those Craft Beer Co. pubs and places like that, mostly because they have a lot of good cask ale,' says Mike, 'and it's good to see so much choice.'

Then he snaps his fingers and frowns. 'What's that place up there by Shoreditch Tube station?'

He means the BrewDog bar.

'That's it! Now, you go in there, and it's not really a pub, but it's *packed.*' He gives a wide-open shrug. 'And I just think it's good to see all those youngsters in there, taking a real interest in beer.'

APPENDIX I

THE BIG SIX

The Big Six in 1959[*]

Ind Coope and Taylor Walker, Watney Mann, Courage and Barclay, Bass Ratcliffe Gretton, Whitbread, Scottish Brewers

Brewery mergers/takeovers 1960–67

Courage Barclay + Simonds = Courage Barclay and Simonds (1960)

Scottish Brewers + Newcastle Breweries = Scottish and Newcastle (1960)

Ind Coope + Taylor Walker + Ansells + Tetley Walker = Ind Coope Tetley Ansell (1961)

Ind Coope Tetley Ansell = Allied Breweries (1963)

Bass + Mitchells and Butlers = Bass Mitchells and Butlers (1961)

Charrington United + Bass Mitchells and Butlers = Bass Charrington (1967)

The Big Six in 1967[†]

Bass Charrington, Allied Breweries, Whitbread, Watney Mann, Scottish and Newcastle, Courage Barclay and Simonds

Mergers/takeovers/name changes after 1967

Courage Barclay and Simonds = Courage (1970)

Watney Mann + Truman Hanbury and Buxton (owned by Grand Metropolitan Hotels) = Watney Mann and Truman (part of Grand Metropolitan) (1973)

---

[*] 'What the Brewery Merger Means', *Financial Times*, 4 June 1959, p. 11.

[†] *Beer: A Report on the Supply of Beer*, Monopolies Commission, 1969, table IV, p. 5.

Allied + J. Lyons = Allied Lyons (1978)
Bass Charrington = Bass (1983)

The Big Six in 1989[*]
Allied Lyons, Bass, Courage, Grand Metropolitan, Scottish and
  Newcastle, Whitbread

The Big Seven
As above, plus Guinness

Mergers/takeovers/name changes after 1989
Allied Lyons + Carlsberg-Tetley (1992)
Scottish and Newcastle + Courage = Scottish and Newcastle (1995)
Grand Metropolitan + Guinness = Diageo (1997)
Interbrew + Bass (1999)
Molson Coors + Bass Brewers = Coors Brewers (2002)
Carlsberg/Heineken + Scottish and Newcastle = Heineken UK (2009)

---

[*]   The Suppply of Beer, Monopolies and Mergers Commission, March 1989, Appendix
   2.3, p. 238.

APPENDIX II

THE FIRST NEW BREWERIES 1965–78[*]

1965

Traquair House, Peeblesshire

1972

Selby, North Yorkshire

1973

Miner's Arms, Priddy, Somerset

1974

Litchborough, Northamptonshire; Mason's Arms, Oxfordshire

1975

Pollard's, Stockport, Cheshire; Fighting Cocks, Corby Glen, Lincolnshire

1976

New Fermor Arms, Rufford, Lancashire; Miskin Arms, Pontyclun, Mid Glamorgan; York Brewery, Boroughbridge, North Yorkshire

1977

Smiles, Bristol; John Thompson Inn, Stanton-by-Bridge, Derbyshire; Blackawton, Devon; Penrhos, Herefordshire; Ribblesdale Arms, Gisburn, Lancashire; Godson's, London

1978

Butcombe, Bristol; Mendip, Bristol; Broughton, Biggar, Borders; Hawthorne, Gloucester; Bourne Valley, Andover, Hampshire; Ringwood, Hampshire; Studley, Warwickshire; Goose Eye, Keighley, West Yorkshire

[*]   Sources: *Twenty-five Years of New British Breweries*, Ian Mackey, 1998; *CAMRA New Beer Guide*, Brian Glover, 1988; editions of the CAMRA *Good Beer Guide*, 1974–79; editions of CAMRA newsletter *What's Brewing*, 1972–78.

APPENDIX III

BRITISH BREWING FAMILY TREES

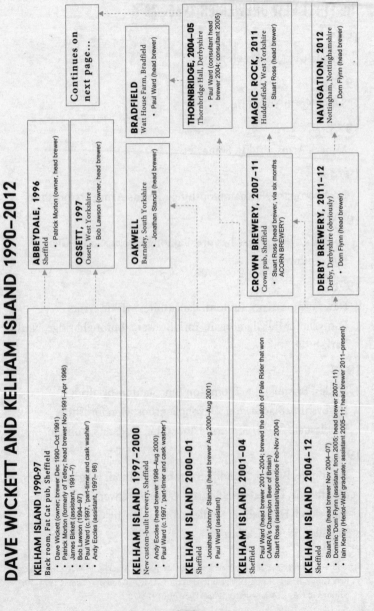

DAVE WICKETT AND KELHAM ISLAND 1990–2012

KELHAM ISLAND 1990–97
Back room, Fat Cat pub, Sheffield
- Dave Wickett (owner; brewer Dec 1990–Oct 1991)
- Patrick Morton (formerly of Tetley; head brewer Nov 1991–Apr 1996)
- James Birkett (assistant, 1991–?)
- Bob Lawson (1994–97)
- Paul Ward (c.1997, 'part-timer and cask washer')
- Andy Eccles (assistant, 1997–98)

KELHAM ISLAND 1997–2000
New custom-built brewery, Sheffield
- Andy Eccles (head brewer 1998–Aug 2000)
- Paul Ward (c.1997, 'part-timer and cask washer')

KELHAM ISLAND 2000–01
Sheffield
- Jonathan 'Johnny' Stancill (head brewer Aug 2000–Aug 2001)
- Paul Ward (assistant)

KELHAM ISLAND 2001–04
Sheffield
- Paul Ward (head brewer 2001–2004; brewed the batch of Pale Rider that won CAMRA's Champion Beer of Britain)
- Stuart Ross (assistant/apprentice Feb–Nov 2004)

KELHAM ISLAND 2004–12
Sheffield
- Stuart Ross (head brewer Nov 2004–07)
- Dominic 'Dom' Flynn (assistant, from 2005; head brewer 2007–11)
- Iain Kenny (Heriot-Watt graduate; assistant 2005–11; head brewer 2011–present)

ABBEYDALE, 1996
Sheffield
- Patrick Morton (owner, head brewer)

OSSETT, 1997
Ossett, West Yorkshire
- Bob Lawson (owner, head brewer)

OAKWELL
Barnsley, South Yorkshire
- Jonathan Stancill (head brewer)

BRADFIELD
Watt House Farm, Bradfield
- Paul Ward (head brewer)

THORNBRIDGE, 2004–05
Thornbridge Hall, Derbyshire
- Paul Ward (consultant head brewer 2004; consultant 2005)

CROWN BREWERY, 2007–11
Crown pub, Sheffield
- Stuart Ross (head brewer, via six months ACORN BREWERY)

MAGIC ROCK, 2011
Huddersfield, West Yorkshire
- Stuart Ross (head brewer)

DERBY BREWERY, 2011–12
Derby, Derbyshire (obviously)
- Dom Flynn (head brewer)

NAVIGATION, 2012
Nottingham, Nottinghamshire
- Dom Flynn (head brewer)

Continues on next page…

Brewdog might seem a million miles from a 'real ale' brewery like Sheffield's Kelham Island, but really, there are only a few degrees of separation as these two 'family trees' show.

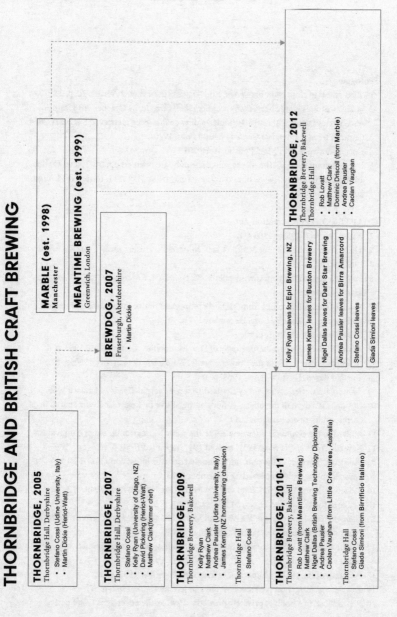

THORNBRIDGE AND BRITISH CRAFT BREWING

THORNBRIDGE, 2005
Thornbridge Hall, Derbyshire
- Stefano Cossi (Udine University, Italy)
- Martin Dickie (Heriot-Watt)

MARBLE (est. 1998)
Manchester

MEANTIME BREWING (est. 1999)
Greenwich, London

BREWDOG, 2007
Fraserburgh, Aberdeenshire
- Martin Dickie

THORNBRIDGE, 2007
Thornbridge Hall, Derbyshire
- Stefano Cossi
- Kelly Ryan (University of Otago, NZ)
- David Pickering (Heriot-Watt)
- Matthew Clark(former chef)

THORNBRIDGE, 2009
Thornbridge Brewery, Bakewell
- Kelly Ryan
- Matthew Clark
- Andrea Pausler (Udine University, Italy)
- James Kemp (NZ homebrewing champion)

Thornbridge Hall
- Stefano Cossi

THORNBRIDGE, 2010-11
Thornbridge Brewery, Bakewell
- Rob Lovatt (from Meantime Brewing)
- Matthew Clark
- Nigel Dallas (British Brewing Technology Diploma)
- Andrea Pausler
- Caolan Vaughan (from Little Creatures, Australia)

Thornbridge Hall
- Stefano Cossi
- Giada Simioni (from Birrificio Italiano)

THORNBRIDGE, 2012
Thornbridge Brewery, Bakewell
Thornbridge Hall
- Rob Lovatt
- Matthew Clark
- Dominic Driscoll (from Marble)
- Andrea Pausler
- Caolan Vaughan

Kelly Ryan leaves for Epic Brewing, NZ

James Kemp leaves for Buxton Brewery

Nigel Dallas leaves for Dark Star Brewing

Andrea Pausler leaves for Birra Amarcord

Stefano Cossi leaves

Giada Simioni leaves

NOTES

Prologue

1 'Bass group to close eight breweries', Ross Davies, *The Times*, 9 April 1970, p. 23.
2 'Joule's – Stone's iconic beer', *Stone and Eccleshall Gazette*, 24 October 2013, http://www.stonegazette.co.uk/2013/10/joules-stones-iconic-beer/, retrieved 8 January 2014.
3 Cuttings from *A Complete Guide to Bristol Pubs*, 1970s.
4 Correspondence with Nigel Poustie, April 2013.
5 E.g., in stories such as 'The places where the pubs are boarded up', BBC News Online, 14 August 2013, http://www.bbc.co.uk/news/magazine-21713311, retrieved 14 August 2013.

CHAPTER ONE: Preservation Act

1 Nairn, *Outrage*, 1955, p. 365–71.
2 'On the Move: the Militant Middle Class', Michael Parkinson, *Daily Express*, 17 May 1961, p. 10.
3 In 'Not a keg to stand on', Christopher Ford, *Guardian*, 6 March 1971, p. 10, Millard gave his age as 53.
4 Much of this detail comes from Millard's retirement notice in the Bank of England staff magazine, *The Old Lady*, December 1971.
5 *Guardian*, 6 March 1971, p. 10.
6 Table III, *Beer: a report on the supply of beer*, Monopolies Commission, 1969, p. 4.
7 'Towards Larger Units in the Brewery Trade', *The Times*, 19 February 1960, p. 17.
8 *The Red Barrel*, Hurford Janes, 1963, p. 163.
9 'Flowers Breweries', statement by Bernard Dixon, *Financial Times*, 24 January 1956, p. 4.
10 Unpublished draft of the official history of the SPBW by Roger Jacobson, shared in correspondence on 1 August 2012.
11 Millard in the *Guardian* interview 1971: 'the society just grew up out of bar chatter'.
12 Keverne, *Tales of Old Inns*, 1939; revised 1947, reprinted 1951, p. 16.
13 Blog post, 'Pevsner in the pub', http://susieharries.wordpress.com/2011/01/14/pevsner-in-the-pub/, retrieved 22 December 2013.
14 Review of John Piper's *Buildings and Prospects*, *Observer*, 10 April 1949, p. 3.
15 Letter to the editor, *The Times*, 20 February 1951, p. 5.
16 *Guide to the Manuscripts in the National Maritime Museum: Public records, business records and artificial collections*, R.J.B. Knight, 1980, p. 67.
17 Paddle Steamer Society website, http://www.paddlesteamers.org.uk/index.htm, retrieved 29 August 2012.
18 'A Breath of the Halls in Hoxton', *The Times*, 6 November 1963, p. 22.
19 *Epsom: a pictorial history*, Trevor White and Jeremy Harte, 1992, p. 27.
20 Reproduced in a booklet privately printed c. 1998 by the Sovereigns Golf Society,

dedicated to the memory of Boyes Lee, supplied by John Keeble.

21 'History', Friends of the Froth Blowers, 2007, http://frothblowers.co.uk/aofbhist.htm, retrieved October 2012; *The London Gazette*, 22 May 1931, p. 43.

22 'It's a very sober society', Paul Hughes, *Daily Mirror*, 18 December 1961, p. 5.

23 'Mike and hero pals leapt to defend pub life as keg beers arrived in 50s', *Derby Telegraph*, 13 June 2011, http://www.thisisderbyshire.co.uk/Mike-hero-pals-leapt-defend-pub-life-keg-beers/story-12759771-detail/story.html#axzz2Qnm65yS6, retrieved 19 April 2013.

24 *Pint in Hand*, November 2008, p. 6.

25 Obituary in the SPBW newsletter *Pint in Hand*, No. 70, May 1999, pp. 10–11.

26 *Guardian*, 6 March 1971, p. 10.

27 'Beer battle', 29 April 1965, p. 11; 'Cheers! say beer from the wood brigade', 26 August 1965, p. 3; 'Keg or not to Keg – that is the question', Vincent Mulchrone, 13 September 1965, p. 8.

28 *The Death of the English Pub,* Christopher Hutt, 1973, p. 27.

29 *Pint in Hand*, No. 100, September 2006.

30 Correspondence with Alan Risdon, 25 September 2012.

31 Hutt, *Death of the English Pub*, p. 26.

32 *Daily Express*, 5 October 1971 , p. 10; Hutt, *Death of the English Pub*, p. 27.

33 *City of London Pubs*, Timothy M. Richards and James Steven Curl, p. 116.

34 'From the Wood', E.B. Lee, *The Times*, 21 March 1971, p. 9.

35 This caused a minor mutiny, with one branch, based at The Poplars pub in Wingfield, Wiltshire, protesting furiously against the change. SPBW unpublished official history, Roger Jacobson.

36 SPBW obituary.

37 *Guardian*, 6 March 1971.

38 'Men and Matters', *Financial Times*, 24 August 1972, p. 14, in summary of the government response to the 1967 representation.

39 *Financial Times*, 24 August 1971, p. 14.

40 *Daily Express*, 5 October 1971, p. 10.

41 'Miscellany: bitter draft', *Guardian*, 4 May 1971, p. 11.

42 *Guardian*, 6 March 1971, p. 10.

43 Ibid.

44 Hutt, *Death of the English Pub*, p. 27.

45 *Pint in Hand*, May 2010.

46 'Cheers! It's Draught Day', *Daily Mirror*, 11 September 1972, p. 11.

47 'Ale and farewell', Iain Murray, *Observer*, 24 September 1972, p. 18.

48 Display advertisement by The Beer Festival, Ilford in *Observer*, 14 May 1972, p. 30.

49 *The Times*, 19 September 1972, p. 12.

50 *Daily Express,* 5 October 1971, p. 10.

51 'On here for the real stuff!', *Hornsey Journal*, 27 October 1972, p. 1.

52 *Morning Advertiser*, 23 October 1972, p. 16.

CHAPTER TWO: The Campaign for the ... Something ... of Ale

1 'Nickel Beer: rejoice it's here – but give a thought to the woes of its sponsor', p. 42.

2 Chapter 2, 'Parallel Universe: social movements before 1970', *British Social Movements*

Since 1945: Sex, Colour, Peace and Power, Adam Lent, 2001.

3 '40th anniversary founders' crawl', Chester and South Clwyd CAMRA website, http://myweb.tiscali.co.uk/hardpeg/founder.htm, retrieved 12 September 2012; email correspondence of 10 September 2012 with Gary Chester, who took part in that anniversary pub crawl.

4 Graham Lees quoted in 'Camra at forty', Claire Garner, *Canny Bevvy: the magazine of Tyneside and Northumberland CAMRA*, Spring 2012, p. 20.

5 'The birth of a drinker's revolution', *CAMRA News*, July 1975, p. 1 (insert to *What's Brewing*, July 1975).

6 'The Glory that is Beer', Vincent Mulchrone, *Pub*, ed. Angus McGill, 1969, p. 34.

7 In 'Founding Fathers', *Called to the Bar*, 1992 Michael Hardman refers to the pub as 'Patrick O'Neill's' for reasons unknown; it has been Kruger Kavanagh's in subsequent retellings, and Kavanagh's does indeed claim to be the most westerly pub in Europe.

8 'Discovering Dingle', collected in *Sunrise with Seamonsters*, 1976, p. 142.

9 See note 12 below on confusion over the dates of the trip to Ireland.

10 *CAMRA News*, July 1975.

11 'The sobering truth about the British pint', *Sunday Mirror*, 21 March 1971, pp. 24–5.

12 *What's Brewing*, December 2011, pp. 8–9: Mellor actually claims to have read this story on the way *to* Ireland, which would mean that Hardman's recollection of their dates of travel and of the founding of CAMRA is incorrect and might suggest that the article was the trigger for the Campaign's founding.

13 *What's Brewing*, December 2011, pp. 8–9.

14 'Pubs Learn to Take the Pressure Off', *Guardian*, 6 December 1975, p. 8.

15 Hardman sometimes says six months later (*Financial Times*, 31 July 2001); nine months later (*Morning Advertiser,* 16 March 2011); and sometimes 'Almost a year later' ('Founding Fathers', *Called to the Bar: an account of the first 21 years of the Campaign for Real Ale*, ed. Roger Protz and Tony Millns, 1992).

16 Hutt, *Death of the English Pub*, p. 30.

17 Hardman, 'Founding Fathers', *Called to the Bar*, p. 35.

18 Mellor speaking in the documentary *The History of CAMRA*, Lagoon Media/British Local Histories, 2011.

19 The Rose Inn is invariably described as 'the birthplace of CAMRA', as in this article from the *Daily Telegraph*, 4 October 2012, http://www.telegraph.co.uk/sponsored/foodanddrink/top-100-famous-pubs/8041513/The-Rose-Inn.html, retrieved 11 September 2012.

20 *Morning Advertiser*, 2011.

21 Hardman, 'Founding Fathers', *Called to the Bar*, p. 35.

22 'Anti-keg group is ailing in numbers', Roy Derry, *Nuneaton Observer*, 4 May 1972, p. 14.

23 'Pubs Learn to Take the Pressure Off', Michael Hardman, *Guardian*, 6 December 1975, p. 8.

24 Hardman, 'Founding Fathers', *Called to the Bar*.

25 'In brief', *What's Brewing*, June 1972, p. 2; interview with Michael Hardman.

26 'Liberals and their sparking plugs', Francis Boyd, *Guardian,* 25 September 1967, p. 6.

27 http://www.camra.org.uk/camrahistory, retrieved 27 August 2012.

28 *What's Brewing*, December 2011, pp. 8–9.

29 Flyer – 'Festival of Fraud: facts you should know', The Beer Campaign, October 1972.
30 SPBW obituary.
31 'What if CAMRA had never existed', Martyn Cornell, *What's Brewing*, May 2011, pp. 10–11.
32 Quoted in the *Evening Standard Guide to London Pubs*, Martin Green and Tony White, 1973, p. 14.
33 Correspondence, July 2013.
34 SPBW obituary.
35 'It's business – not booze', *What's Brewing*, October 1972, p. 3.
36 October 1972, p. 2.
37 Minutes, as shown in *The History of CAMRA*, Lagoon Media, DVD, 2011.
38 Letter: 'Beer the public wants', E.C. Handel, *Financial Times*, 23 June 1973, p. 16.
39 *What's Brewing*, December 2011, pp. 8–9.
40 Spelling as per the minutes shown in the *History of CAMRA*; in *What's Brewing*, September 1973, p. 2 it is spelt 'Linley'.
41 'CAMRA men', *What's Brewing*, September 1973, p. 2.
42 *Watch Out!: My Autobiography*, Jeremy Beadle, 1998, pp. 75–96.
43 Interview with Michael Hardman in *What's Brewing*, June 1973.
44 Hansard, 20 April 1971, Vol. 815.
45 Obituary, Michael McNay, *Guardian*, 23 December 2006, http://www.theguardian.com/media/2006/dec/23/pressandpublishing.guardianobituaries, retrieved 9 September 2013.
46 'Beyond the Ale', Dennis Barker, *Guardian*, 3 August 1974, p. 11.
47 Hutt, *Death of the English Pub*, p. 71.
48 'Boston on Beer', Richard Boston, *Guardian*, 3 November 1973, p. 11.
49 'Good Spirits', Edmund Penning-Rowsell, *Financial Times*, 6 December 1973, p. 19.
50 'Boston on Beer', Richard Boston, *Guardian*, 8 December 1973, p. 9.
51 'An Obituary?', *Brewing Review*, November 1973, Vol. LXXXVIII, p. 579.

CHAPTER THREE: CAMRA Rampant

 1 Interview conducted by the authors on 14 March 2013.
 2 Interview, 14 March 2013.
 3 Biographical information about Ted Handel from a conversation with Nick Handel, 13 June 2013.
 4 Hardman, 'The Right to Know', *Called to the Bar*, p. 62.
 5 It was trailed on Saturday, 22 June and first appeared on 29 June on p. 7.
 6 *Sunday Times (Weekly Review)*, 30 June 1974, p. 33.
 7 'Anti-CAMRA writer is paid by big brewers', *What's Brewing*, October 1974, p. 3.
 8 'Good Beer Guiding: 25 Years On', Barrie Pepper, *CAMRA Good Beer Guide 1998*, p. 12.
 9 Interview with Terry Pattinson, 13 March 2013.
10 Mentioned by Victor Watson in the book *The Waddingtons Story*, 2008, pp. 27–8, and in an interview conducted by Juliana Vandegrift for the Museum of Childhood in 2012, http://www.museumofchildhood.org.uk/collections/british-toy-making-project/oral-histories, retrieved March 2014.
11 'New Guide will list 1,500 pubs', *What's Brewing*, September 1973, p. 1.
12 Correspondence, 8 March 2013.

13 '"Sabotage" claims over guide to Britain's ale', *Daily Mail*, 11 March 1974, p. 11.

14 *What's Brewing*, December 1973.

15 'Time Please! But Still They Marched', *Stone Newsletter*, 9 November 1973, p. 1.

16 'Beer used to come from breweries; now it comes from profit centres', Richard Boston, *Guardian*, 10 November 1973, p. 11.

17 Interview with Terry Pattinson; *Stone Newsletter*, 13 September 1973.

18 Interview with Terry Pattinson.

19 'Bad Weather Waters Down Bitter Protest', *Barnsley Chronicle and South Yorkshire News*, 6 September 1974, p. 1.

20 'Crowded rooms and protest marches: is this what CAMRA members want?', Brian Sheridan, *What's Brewing*, July 1975, p. 5.

21 *What's Brewing*, September 1974, p. 3.

22 Ibid.

23 Additional details here from contemporary photographs by David A.L. Davies; a memoir by Paul Bailey at his blog, http://baileysbeerblog.blogspot.co.uk/2012/11/the-covent-garden-beer-exhibition-1975.html, retrieved 23 January 2014.

24 'The Covent Garden Beer Festival', Hardman, *Called to the Bar*, p. 59.

25 D.M. Thomas, 'Letters to the Editor', *Guardian*, 15 September 1975, p. 10.

26 Ibid.

27 'Ale festival looks set to get bigger', *What's Brewing*, October 1975, p. 1.

28 'Only here for the beer', 14 September 1975, p. 3.

29 'Real ale drinkers are on the right beat', Gareth Parry, *Guardian*, 9 September 1975, p. 6.

30 *What's Brewing*, October 1975.

31 'Blood, sweat and tears at St Albans', John Green, *What's Brewing*, October 1974, p. 3.

32 'Business diary', *The Times*, 6 March 1975, p. 19.

CHAPTER FOUR: Lilacs Out of the Dead Land

1 Gordon Thorburn, 26 September, p. 10.

2 See *Country House Brewing in England 1500–1900*, Pamela Sambrook, 1996.

3 Sambrook, *Country House Brewing*, p. 248.

4 History of Traquair House and family, http://www.traquair.co.uk/brief-history-traquair-and-family, retrieved 29 August 2012.

5 Correspondence with his daughter, Catherine Maxwell Stuart, currently 'lady Laird' of Traquair.

6 'Scotland's most unusual lady laird, Catherine Maxwell Stuart', Heraldscotland.com, 16 August 2010, http://www.heraldscotland.com/life-style/real-lives/scotland-s-most-unusual-lady-laird-catherine-maxwell-stuart-1.1048599, retrieved 29 August 2012.

7 Obituary, *The Times*, 17 February 1990, p. 12.

8 'Brothers, a drink to your legacy', Michael Jackson, 1994, http://www.beerhunter.com/documents/19133-000784.html, retrieved 29 August 2012.

9 Obituary, Heraldscotland.com, 2 June 2007, http://www.heraldscotland.com/sandy-hunter-1.858984, retrieved 29 August 2012.

10 Video: 'Traquair', retrieved from http://www.merchantduvin.com/brew-traquair.php on 3 December 2012.

11 Lady Maxwell Stuart on video, 2008.

12 'One man went to brew, went to brew a barrel', Roger Protz, *Guardian*, 25 August 1979, p. 12; correspondence with Catherine Maxwell Stuart.

13 Correspondence with Martin Sykes, November 2012.

14 'Selby Brewery', Martin Sykes, in *Called to the Bar*, p. 56.

15 *Journal of the Institute of Brewing*, Vol. 74, 1968, p. 144.

16 *Guardian*, 11 July 1970, p. 12.

17 Correspondence with Martin Sykes, October 2012.

18 Hardman, *Called to the Bar*, p. 57.

19 Obituaries in *Guardian*, 5 December 1998, p. 23; and *Independent*, 8 December 1998, http://www.independent.co.uk/arts-entertainment/obituary-paul-leyton-1189995. html, retrieved 14 September 2012.

20 'New A. V. Roe chief engineer', *Guardian*, 18 May 1961, p. 22.

21 'Bus that Became a Home', *Picture Post*, 11 December 1948, pp. 18–19.

22 CAMRA *Good Beer Guide 1978*, p. 249.

23 'Leisure and Pleasure', John Arlott, *Law Guardian*, January 1967, p. 43.

24 'Height of Spring 1999', Jonathan Williams, http://jargonbooks.com/rjobit.html, retrieved 14 September 2012.

25 'Eating Italian style', Archestratus, *Guardian*, 6 March 1970, p. 9.

26 Correspondence with Julian Leyton, 23 October 2013.

27 'Boston on Beer', 2 August 1975.

28 Brian Glover, *The New Brewery Revolution*, 1988, p. 10.

29 Glover, *New Brewery Revolution*, p. 10.

30 p. 71.

31 Email correspondence with Peter Mauldon, a former colleague of Urquhart's, 18 August 2012.

32 Glover, *New Brewery Revolution*, p. 12.

33 Correspondence with Urquhart's daughter, Elspeth Urquhart, 21 August 2012.

34 Correspondence with Peter Mauldon.

35 Correspondence with Elspeth Urquhart, 14 September 2012.

36 A contemporary at Tollemache, Peter Scully, recalled being taken on at the Brook Street brewery 'as a kind of dogsbody pupil, going up to London University about three times a week, bashing the books like hell'. ('Tolly Cobbold: gone but not forgotten', *East Anglian Daily Times*, 24 June 2006).

37 *Journal of the Institute of Brewing*, Vol. 57, 1951, p. 76.

38 Glover, *New Brewery Revolution*, p. 12.

39 Email correspondence with Elspeth Urquhart, 19 August 2012.

40 Correspondence with Mick Bolshaw, former Northamptonshire CAMRA chair, 15 August 2012.

41 Frank Kenna, interviewed by Alaric Neville, http://www.phipps-nbc.co.uk/2.html, retrieved 28 March 2013.

42 See, for example, 'Use of Cold Detergents for Cleaning Enclosed Beer-Containing Systems', Institute of Brewing (Great Britain), Federated Institutes of Brewing, 1955, p. 240.

43 Correspondence with Alaric Neville of the revived Phipps Northampton Brewing Co., 21 August 2012.

44 Glover, *New Brewery Revolution*, p. 12.

45 'A History: P. Phipps, Northampton Brewery Company, Phipps NBC and beyond', http://www.phipps-nbc.co.uk/2.html.

46 Correspondence with Elspeth Urquhart, 21 August 2012.

47 Correspondence with Peter Mauldon, August 2012.

48 Alaric Neville recalled being told of this delegation by a veteran Phipps landlord, Dennis Wilmott, of the Bell Inn at Finedon.

49 According to Alaric Neville, who has spoken to Mike Henson.

50 The term was not used in *The Times* until 1991.

51 Correspondence with George Jenkinson, 15 August 2012.

52 Correspondence with Mick Bolshaw, 15 August 2012.

53 *Sunday People*, 10 November 1974, p. 13.

54 Correspondence with Elspeth Urquhart, 21 August 2012.

55 *Brewed in Northants*.

56 CAMRA *Good Beer Guide 1975*, ed. Michael Hardman, 1974, p. 173.

57 Richard Boston, *Beer and Skittles*, 1976, p. 197.

58 Correspondence with Elspeth Urquhart, 14 September 2012; CAMRA *Good Beer Guide 1979*, p. 281.

59 'Bill turns off the gas', *What's Brewing*, February 1978, p. 3.

60 CAMRA *Good Beer Guide 1978*, p. 248; interview with Frank Kenna, Urquhart's assistant brewer, by Alaric Neville, at http://www.phipps-nbc.co.uk/2.html, retrieved August 2013.

61 *Brewed in Northants*.

62 *Sunday People*, 10 November 1972.

63 Inland Revenue Act 1880, p. 6, http://www.legislation.gov.uk/ukpga/1880/20/pdfs/ukpga_18800020_en.pdf, retrieved 2 September 2013.

64 *Hansard*, 3 April 1963, Vol. 675, c459.

65 'A toast to the chancellor', *Financial Times*, 5 April 1963, p. 14.

66 'The growing army of home ale brewers', *Guardian*, 17 May 1963, p. 13.

67 E.g. 'In the kitchen', Syllabub, *Observer*, 21 April 1963, p. 30.

68 *Guardian*, 17 May 1963, p. 13.

69 'What is happening to the price of beer?', *Financial Times*, 27 July 1964, p. 9.

70 *Observer*, 21 April 1963, p. 30.

71 'The Durden Park Beer Circle', *Brewer's Contact*, January 1996, p. 5.

72 Correspondence with Tony Badger, August 2012.

73 *The Big Book of Brewing*, 1974; reprinted 2010, p. 11.

74 In, e.g., brewing supplement, *The Times*, 26 April 1971, p VI.

75 'CHEERS! Stars test the beers that cost just 6p a pint', Margaret Jones and Alasdair Buchan, 23 October 1978, p. 9.

76 Brian Glover, *CAMRA New Beer Guide*, 1988, p. 52.

77 'New Brew', *What's Brewing*, November 1977, p. 12.

78 'Fishy business in an East End brewhouse', *What's Brewing*, January 1978, p. 5.

79 Interview with David Bruce, 24 July 2013.

80 Probably 'London's vanishing breweries', Jo Parfitt, 30 July 1977, p. 51.

81 'New brewery for London', *What's Brewing*, October 1977, p. 3.

82 'Fishy business', *What's Brewing*, January 1978.

83 'A zany excuse for supping ale', *What's Brewing*, July 1976, p. 1.

84 'Voles of the world unite', Robin Lustig, *Observer*, 22 November 1977, p. 40.

85 'The global brewer', Brian Glover, *What's Brewing*, March 1986, p. 5.

86 *Diaries 1969–1979: The Python Years*, 2007, pp. 440–41.

87 'And now for the Monty Python pint', Tom Merrin, *Daily Mirror*, 13 April 1978, p. 23.

88 *Amber, Gold and Black*, Martyn Cornell, 2010, pp. 76–7.

89 'Beer fest is a walloping hit', Denis Palmer, *What's Brewing*, October 1978, p. 1; 'Porter takes another step forward', Brian Glover, *What's Brewing*, November 1978, p. 7; CAMRA *Good Beer Guide 1979*, p. 233.

CHAPTER FIVE: More an Exhibition than a Pub

1 Stanley Budd, 16 September 1975, p. 12.

2 We have not been able to find any specific record of its demolition.

3 The record of her marriage gives her maiden name as Dunne and the record of her death provides 1907 as her date of birth.

4 Quoted in *Guide to London Pubs* by Martin Green and Tony White, 1968, p. 131.

5 Dive Bar regular Chris Partridge in an email, 25 July 2012.

6 'Maximus Bibendus' in his poem 'Memories' at http://www.bibendus.org.uk/bm24. html, retrieved 15 August 2012.

7 Correspondence with Robert Willeter, Becky's step-grandson, October 2012.

8 Chris Partridge, Dive Bar regular.

9 Green and White, *Guide to London Pubs*, 1968.

10 According to both Bob Abel, *The Book of Beer*, 1976, p. 219, and Richard Boston, *Beer and Skittles*, p. 98.

11 *Guardian*, 18 May 1974, p. 9.

12 Bob Abel, *Book of Beer*, p. 220.

13 'Food' by Adrian Bailey, in *London Dossier*, ed. Len Deighton, 1967, p. 44.

14 See White Rabbit's blog post and also Bob Abel's *Book of Beer*, p. 219. Similar fibs are told about the cellars of the Viaduct Tavern opposite the former site of Newgate Prison in the City of London. In fact, there aren't many London buildings of any age that aren't popularly supposed to have dungeons, tunnels or nuclear bunkers beneath them.

15 '. . . And here's where to get it', Brian Schwartz, *Off Duty*, Europe edition, November 1975, p. 50.

16 *Daily Express*, 10 June 1969, p. 3. In this story, she suffers the indignity of being renamed 'Becky Wilder'.

17 *The Times*, 28 December 1970, p. 4.

18 Schwartz, *Off Duty*, p. 49.

19 'Becky's Dive Bar' http://ohdearohdearishallbelate.blogspot.co.uk/2008/03/beckys-dive-bar.html, retrieved 20 August 2012.

20 Correspondence, October 2012.

21 Ibid.

22 'CAMRA: the history', *Called to the Bar*, 1992, p. 38.

23 'Business and Money', Kenneth Fleet, *Sunday Express*, 16 May 1982, p. 24.

24 *A History of Stockport Breweries*, Mike Ogden, 1987, p. 24.

25 'CAMRA pub will open in New Year', *What's Brewing*, October 1974, p. 1.

26 *Pulling a Fast One*, Roger Protz, 1978, p. 78.

27 Ibid.

28 *Financial Times*, 11 April 1976, p. 11.

29 *Dear Boy: The Life of Keith Moon*, Tony Fletcher, 2005, p. 315; *Dazzling Stranger: Bert Jansch and the British Folk and Blues Revival*, Colin Harper, 2006, p. 232.

30 *Hertford Mercury and Reformer*, 18 December 1858, p. 3.

31 *Herts Advertiser and St Albans Times*, 20 June 1925, p. 4.

32 'The Barley Mow Story', *Pints of View*, Issue 241, June/July 2012, pp. 17–18.

33 *The Beverage Report*, p. 129.

34 'A Decade at the Barley Mow', *The Hertfordshire Newsletter*, Issue 92, April 1986, p. 1.

35 Much of the detail hereafter from correspondence with Barrie Pepper, June 2013.

36 'Town pubs of the 70s and 80s', Secret Leeds messageboard, http://www.secretleeds.com/forum/PrintMessages.aspx?ThreadID=168, accessed June 2013.

37 12 December 1975, p. 2.

38 'Eat, Drive and be Happy', *Daily Express*, 6 August 1978, p. 11.

39 Letters by Mike Day and P.R. Bailey under the heading 'These "exhibition pubs" harm real ale cause!', *What's Brewing*, February 1984, p. 2.

40 'Camaraderie back in the snug', Robert Waterhouse, *Guardian*, 3 October 1979, p. 10.

41 *Daily Express*, 6 August 1978.

42 'The Danger of Over-enthusiasm', *What's Brewing*, June 1974, p. 4.

43 Correspondence with the founder, Nick Winnington, December 2012.

CHAPTER SIX: The Empire Strikes Back

1 'Watney's Give Traditional Beer Big Boost', Michael Hardman, *What's Brewing*, April 1975, p. 1.

2 'Economies', minutes of the meeting of directors, 22 June 1968, held at the London Metropolitan Archive.

3 Ibid; also, for example, 18 May 1967.

4 'The whys and the whats of Watney's Draught Red Barrel', *Daily Mirror*, 15 May 1961, p. 10.

5 *Daily Express*, 15 November 1967, p. 12.

6 *Sunday Mirror*, 21 March, p. 1.

7 'Keg Beer', April 1972, p. 124–7.

8 Correspondence with Mike Cowbourne, 12 July 2013.

9 He was forty-six at the time of his death in January 1987, according to a short obituary notice by Michael Hardman in *What's Brewing*, February 1987, p. 16.

10 *What's Brewing*, March 1987, p. 4.

11 '. . . Real ale', *Financial Times*, 9 March 1975, p. 14.

12 'Watney test expanded', 3 December 1975, p. 18.

13 'Watney's Give Traditional Beer Big Boost', Michael Hardman, *What's Brewing*, April 1975, p. 1.

14 'Putting all your kegs in one basket', Richard Boston, *Guardian*, 16 November 1974, p. 9.

15 *What's Brewing*, May 1976, p. 3.

16 'A fresh recipe for Allied's customers', Kenneth Gooding, *Financial Times*, 23 August 1978, p. 9.

17 Confirmed by Chris Holmes in a telephone conversation on 16 June 2013.

18 'A right real ale row', Robert Head, *Daily Mirror*, 30 September 1977, p. 22.

19 'Pubs learn to take the pressure off', Michael Hardman, *Guardian*, 6 December 1975, p. 8.

20 'Eating Out', Richard Boston, *Guardian*, 9 July 1977, p. 12.

21 'Beer barons take heed', Roger Protz, *Guardian*, 4 September 1978, p. 16.

22 *Private Eye*, 24 June 1977, p. 3.

23 Ibid., 8 July 1977, p. 7.

24 E.g. ibid., 7 July 1978, p. 7.

25 Ibid., 15 September 1977, p. 7.

26 Ibid., 14 October 1977, p. 3.

27 Ibid., 28 October 1977, p. 8.

28 Interview conducted by the authors, 28 November 2012.

29 '"Leave it to branches" is decision on air pressure', *What's Brewing*, November 1977, p. 2.

30 'On the hop', 'Observer', *Financial Times*, 22 June 1981, p. 14.

31 'CAMRA celebrates its tenth birthday', Roger Protz, *Guardian*, 24 February 1981, p. 3.

32 April 1979, p. 11.

33 Letter: 'The S. West needs YOU', Ray Hodgins, *What's Brewing*, March 1984, p. 2.

34 'Brewers can't be bitter about lager', *Guardian*, 29 July 1976, p. 18.

35 *Food Standards Committee Report on Beer*, 1977, p. 21.

36 Table A10: 'BEER: UK Beer Sales Analysed Between Ale, Stout and Lager', *Statistical Handbook 2012*, British Beer and Pub Association, 2012, p. 17.

37 Ibid.

38 Roger Protz's argument and supporting data are in *Pulling a Fast One*, pp. 61–7.

39 Historical census data at http://www.ons.gov.uk/ons/interactive/vp1-story-of-the-census/index.html, retrieved 25 September 2013.

40 Protz, *Pulling a Fast One*, p. 62.

41 See, for example, a letter entitled 'To the Right Honourable Lord Cliff' by James Howells, 17 October 1634, in *Epistolae Ho-Elianae: the familiar letters of James Howell*, 1907, pp. 231–2.

42 'Britons Riot in Ostend', *Daily Mirror*, 31 March 1964, p. 1.

43 For example, 'Slim pickings', Simon Winchester, 26 March 1976, p. 13.

44 E.g. advertisements: 'Munich Beer Festival', *Daily Express*, 8 September 1972, p. 15; 'Weize beer festival', *Guardian*, 14 February 1976, p. 19.

45 'Beyond the Ale', Dennis Barker, *Guardian*, 3 August 1974, p. 11.

46 'Drink up chaps, we're only here for the sex', *Daily Express*, 6 August 1974, p. 1.

47 'Time Please!', Richard Boston, *Guardian*, 30 November 1974, p. 9.

48 Dedication, *Michael Jackson's Pocket Beer Book*, Michael Jackson, 1986.

49 'The Color Purple', *Slow*, August/September 2003, p. 12.

50 'The Unique Michael Jackson', Carolyn Smagalski, Phillybeerscene.com, August/September 2012, retrieved from http://www.phillybeerscene.com/2012/08/the-unique-michael-jackson/ in April 2013.

51 'Lending an Ear to the Beer Hunter', Clement Freud, *The Times*, 2 May 1992, p. 23.

52 An interview on video from August 2007 with Daniel Shelton, retrieved from http://www.youtube.com/watch?v=ZYSnoZqmNMc in April 2013.

53 'The Color Purple', *Slow*.

54 'Lending an Ear to the Beer Hunter', Freud.

55 'Christmas books: food and drink', Roger Baker, *The Times*, 25 November 1977, p. XIV.

56 'Beer Legends: part one', *All About Beer*, January 1997, p. 10.

57 'They're quietly steaming in Frisco', Frank Baillie, *What's Brewing*, October 1977, p. 3.

58 Ibid.

59 'No small beer at the palace', *Guardian* , 1 September 1979, p. 2.

60 'Why the Ally Pally girl took the 1040', Bryan Rimmer, *Daily Mirror*, 9 September 1979, p. 18.

61 Correspondence with Colin Gillespie, via Phil Lowry, 29 April 2013.

62 'Helping a damson in distress', Michael Jackson, *Independent*, 13 October 1990, http://www.beerhunter.com/documents/19133-000074.html, retrieved 12 August 2013.

63 E.g. *What's Brewing*, January 1984, p. 8.

64 For contemporary lists of regularly imported beers and specialist import companies, see 'Beers from abroad', a double-page spread in *What's Brewing*, March 1986, pp. 6–7.

65 'Godson's go Dutch, thanks to Denis', *What's Brewing*, May 1980.

CHAPTER SEVEN: Breweries, Breweries, Everywhere

1 Interview, 24 July 2013.

2 Interview, 24 July 2013.

3 Glover, *CAMRA New Beer Guide*, p. 7.

4 Editions of the *CAMRA Good Beer Guide* 1978–84; issues of *What's Brewing* from the same period; Glover, *CAMRA New Beer Guide*, 1988.

5 'Britain's redundancy payments for displaced workers', table 1, Lawrence S. Root, University of Michigan, *Monthly Labor Review*, June 1987.

6 'Where to buy your brewery', *What's Brewing*, October 1986, pp. 8–9.

7 *What's Brewing*, Oct 1986; 'Brewery Company News', *The Brewer*, February 1983, p. 82.

8 Glover, *CAMRA New Beer Guide*, p. 107.

9 'UK Beer Statistics', Ron Pattinson, http://www.europeanbeerguide.net/ukstatsn.htm, retrieved 15 August 2013.

10 CAMRA *Good Beer Guide 1979*.

11 Unless otherwise specified, information on David and Louise Bruce and the Firkin chain comes from interviews conducted on 24 July 2013.

12 Hutt, *Death of the English Pub*, p. 83.

13 'Popular return of the spit and polish boozer', Richard Gilbert, *The Times*, 3 February 1986, p. 10.

14 'The Renaissance of Real Ale', Mitch Pryce, *Illustrated London News*, 28 February 1981, p. 51.

15 'Men and matters', *Financial Times*, 20 February 1980, p. 22.

16 *Morning Advertiser*, 18 February 1979, p. 12.

17 *Capital Ale*, Roger Protz, 1981, p. 159.

18 Richard Gilbert, *The Times*, 3 February 1986.

19 'Cod tale of the Turbot and Tank', *What's Brewing*, May 1985, p. 8.

20 Parkes, *Financial Times*.

21 Michael Jackson, *Pocket Guide to Beer*, 1982, p. 76.

22 'Cod tale of the Turbot and Tank', *What's Brewing*, May 1985, p. 8.

23 Glover, *CAMRA New Beer Guide*; Mackey, *Twenty-Five Years of New British Breweries*; cross-referenced with various newspapers.

24 'The Phoenix Arises at Denmark Hill', Jeremy Bennett, *Illustrated London News*,

30 November 1985, pp. 52–3.

25 Glover, *CAMRA New Beer Guide*.

26 Richard Gilbert, *The Times*, 3 February 1986.

CHAPTER EIGHT: Taste the Difference

1 Interview, 26 March 2013.

2 *The Pub and the People*, Mass Observation, 1943, reprinted 2009, p. 36.

3 Andrew Campbell, *The Book of Beer*, pp. 92–3.

4 Ibid., pp. 199–200.

5 *Financial Times*, 27 March 1969, p. 20.

6 *Daily Mirror*, 4 August 1976, p. 11.

7 *CAMRA at 40*, pp. 57–66.

8 Boston, *Beer and Skittles*, p. 61.

9 '125th anniversary Review: The Role of Hops in Brewing', C. Schönberger and T. Kostelecky, *Journal of the Institute of Brewing* No. 117, 2011, pp. 259–67, http://onlinelibrary.wiley.com/doi/10.1002/j.2050-0416.2011.tb00471.x/pdf, retrieved 22 August 2013.

10 Correspondence with John Keeling, 19 March 2013.

11 'Hop Varieties', Gerard W.C. Lemmens, *Journal of the Institute of Brewing*, January 1983, p. 13.

12 Interview with Sean Franklin, 26 March 2013.

13 *London Characters and Crooks*, Henry Mayhew, ed. Christopher Hibbert, 1996, p. 376.

14 'Warre and Dow', *Financial Times*, 7 November 1962, p. 10.

15 'How French wine led an Englishman to love the hops of Oregon and Washington', *Independent*, 27 October 2001, via Newsbank.com.

16 'Good News from the Northwest', *New York Magazine*, 28 June 1982, p. 46.

17 *Land of Giants: The Drive to the Pacific Northwest 1750–1950*, David Lavender, 1979, pp. 436–7.

18 *The Fruited Plain: The Story of American Agriculture*, Walter Ebeling, 1979, p. 276.

19 'Tasting Beer', Sean Franklin, *Brewer's Contact*, Craft Brewing Association, November 2006, p. 3.

20 Correspondence with Gazza Prescott, 25 September 2012.

21 CAMRA *Good Beer Guide 1983*, pp. 10–11.

22 'A brisk little brew, don't you think?', *Daily Mail*, 17 February 1975, p. 3.

23 'The language of beer: a long journey', *CAMRA at 40*, p. 63.

24 'How it all began', CAMRA *Good Beer Guide 1993*, p. 11.

25 Interview, 5 September 2013.

CHAPTER NINE: Small Beer

1 Interview, 14 March 2013.

2 Unless otherwise specified, the main source for the history of SIBA is *A History of The Society of Independent Brewers 1980–2005* by Nicholas Redman, 2005.

3 Interview, 24 July 2013.

4 Ibid.

5 Unless otherwise specified, quotations from Peter Austin are from telephone conversations on 20 and 21 August 2013.

6 'Bourne drinkers visit brewery', Campaign for Real Ale Hertfordshire Newsletter, September 1979, p. 2, http://www.hertsale.org.uk/newsletter/HN20.PDF, retrieved 29 August 2013.

7 Quoted in Redman, *History of The Society of Independent Brewers*.

8 'So you want to set up a brewery?', Glover, *CAMRA New Beer Guide*, p. 121.

9 'Resilience Wins Bigger Share of Market', Gareth Griffiths, *Financial Times*, 4 March 1981, p. 14.

10 'SIBA – fighting for a far fairer deal', Elisabeth Baker, *What's Brewing*, June 1985, p. 5.

11 Ibid.

12 'Liddington ends 12 years of brewing', *What's Brewing*, October 1986, p. 9.

13 'Small beer crash', Brian Glover, *What's Brewing*, February 1984, pp. 6–7.

14 Ibid.

15 'As the "new wave" recedes', Brian Glover, *What's Brewing*, November 1984, pp. 6–7.

16 According to his autobiography *Lend Me Your Ears*, 1999, p. 264.

17 Here and elsewhere, we have relied on the definitive account of these events provided by *Government Intervention in the Brewing Industry* by John Spicer, Chris Thurman, John Walters and Simon Ward, 2011 (reprinted 2013).

18 'A submission of the Small Independent Brewers Association (SIBA) to the Monopolies and Mergers Commission (MMC) concerning the monopoly situation in the supply of beer in the United Kingdom', p. 7.

19 'The last days of the beerage', *The Economist*, 20 May 1989, pp. 105–6.

20 'The beer bores brewers', 20 May 1989, p. 106.

21 'Last orders for the local', George Hill, 24 March 1989, p. 11.

22 'Tonic in Pub War', *Daily Mirror*, 16 May 1989, p. 7.

23 SIBA submission to MMC on the supply of beer, p. 236.

24 John Spicer, et al., *Government Intervention in the Brewing Industry*, p. 109.

25 'Small Brewers a Tougher Breed', Elisabeth Baker, *Financial Times*, 17 April 1984, p. 37.

26 There were 188 in 1999, according to John Willman in 'Whitbread poised to acquire Allied pubs', *Financial Times*, 3 May 1999, p. 1.

27 'Little Cheer at the Fake and Firkin', Chris Arnot, *Guardian*, 22 May 1994, p. 15.

28 'Whatever happened to the Firkin pubs?', Good Beer Good Pubs blog, http://www. goodbeergoodpubs.co.uk/articles/what-happened-to-the-firkin-pubs/, retrieved 29 August 2013. The author of that piece confirmed via Twitter that he had heard the date first-hand from two former Firkin brewers.

29 Trevor Webster, 11 July 1989, p. 27.

30 Hansard, House of Commons debates for 10 July, 18 July, 14 December 1989.

31 Ibid.

32 Foreword, p .3.

33 'Home thoughts and abroad', pp. 4–6.

34 John Spicer, et al., *Government Intervention in the Brewing Industry*, p. 137.

35 'The future of the British pub', Ted Bruning, CAMRA *Good Beer Guide 1991*, pp. 9–10.

36 CAMRA *Good Beer Guide 1995*, p. 408.

37 See, for example, 'The Brewers' Case', *Beer: a report on the supply of beer*, Monopolies Commission, 1969, pp. 77–82.

CHAPTER TEN: Spicing Up the Relationship

1 'A beer for all seasons', CAMRA *Good Beer Guide 1995*, p. 23.

2 'CAMRA celebrates its tenth birthday', John Ezard, *Guardian*, 24 February 1981, p. 3.

3 'Join CAMRA or die!', CAMRA *Good Beer Guide 1987*, p. 319.

4 Glover, *CAMRA New Beer Guide*, p. 7.

5 *Amber, Gold and Black*, hardback edition, 2010, pp. 122–3.

6 Ibid., pp. 123–4.

7 'Brewery Profile: the Hop Back Brewery', James Godman (a brewer at Hop Back), *Brewer and Distiller International*, September 2012, pp. 36–8.

8 'Brewing up at the Hop Back', P.D. Wood and Alan Green, *What's Brewing*, September 1987, p. 6.

9 CAMRA Champion Beer of Britain archive, http://www.camra.org.uk/cbob, retrieved 28 August 2013.

10 'Beer judges savour task of choosing a champion', *Independent*, 5 August 1992, via Newsbank.com.

11 'Beers of the month', Michael Jackson, *Independent*, 19 June 1993, via Newsbank.com.

12 'A beer for all seasons', Roger Protz, CAMRA *Good Beer Guide 1995*, pp. 23–4.

13 Correspondence with John Keeling, 6 March 2013.

14 According to American home-brewing guru Charlie Papazian writing in the CAMRA *Good Beer Guide 1985*, p. 18.

15 Correspondence with Jim Schlueter, 29 February 2014.

16 The compound is 4-methylpentan-2-one, according to Stan Hieronymus, *For the Love of Hops*, pp. 18, 34.

17 E.g. 'Killing marks new dimension in "Gunchester" violence', Erlend Clouston, *Guardian*, 4 January 1993, p. 20; 'Children who die for kicks', John Burns, Norman Luck and Peter Hooley, *Daily Express*, 1 July 1993, pp. 12–13.

18 'Heroes of the Hop', Scoopergen.co.uk, 5 July 2008, http://www.scoopergen.co.uk/essay_hopheroes.htm, retrieved 30 September 2013.

19 Correspondence with Gazza Prescott, 29 September 2012.

20 CAMRA Champion Beer of Britain archive, http://www.camra.org.uk/cbob, retrieved 28 August 2013.

21 'Heroes of the Hop'.

22 CAMRA *Good Beer Guide 1994*, p. 465.

23 MikeMcG, mikemcg6363@my-deja.com, 'LONG:Beer bit - Rooster's', 8scfku$gh9$1@nnrp1.deja.com, in Usenet group uk.food+drink.real-ale, 15 October 2000.

24 'Beer: go with the grain – the aroma-rich world of beer remains unexplained by many. Tap into it', *Independent*, 29 November 1997, via Newsbank.

25 'A return to the best of British – Ales', Andrew Barr, *Sunday Times*, 17 August 1997, 'Style' section, p. 24.

26 Table A10: 'BEER: UK Beer Sales Analysed Between Ale, Stout and Lager', *Statistical Handbook 2012*, British Beer and Pub Association, 2012, p. 17.

27 'Lager market still frothy', Philip Rawsthorne, *Financial Times*, 11 January 1990, p. 10.

28 Advertisement, *Sussex Drinker*, February 1997, p. 2, http://www.aaa-camra.org.uk/Sussex%20Drinker/SD%205.pdf, retrieved 23 August 2013.

29 'Old, new, borrowed and green', CAMRA *Good Beer Guide 1997*, p. 18.

30 Mackey, *Twenty-Five Years of New British Breweries*, p. 219; CAMRA *Good Beer Guide 1980*, p. 233.

31 'Helping a damson in distress', Michael Jackson, *Independent*, 13 October 1990, http://www.beerhunter.com/documents/19133-000074.html, retrieved 12 August 2013.

32 *Beer: tap into the art and science of brewing*, Charles Bamforth, 2nd edn., 2003, pp. 74–5.

33 'Our Daily Beers', *The Beer Hunter*, Episode 4.

34 'Holy beer draws on spring of brewers' patron', 4 August 1995, http://archive.catholicherald.co.uk/article/4th-august-1995/1/holy-beer-draws-on-spring-of-brewers-patron, retrieved 22 July 2013.

35 http://www.camra.org.uk/cbob, retrieved 2 September 2013.

CHAPTER ELEVEN: Unreal

1 *Bar and Club Design*, 2002, p. 19.

2 Paul Hammersley, Saatchi & Saatchi, quoted in 'You can't top a premium lager', Emily Bell, *Observer*, 27 September 1990, p. 32.

3 'Stella's pearls swilled by swine', *Observer*, 22 August 1999, 'Media' supplement, p. 20.

4 Ibid.

5 Denis Blais and André Plisnier, *Belgo Cookbook*, 1998, p. 8.

6 Ibid.

7 'Ale fellows well met', *The Times*, 18 April 1992, 'Weekend' section, p. 6.

8 'Belgian banquet – tasters', Sian Roberts, *Sunday Times*, 12 April 1992, 'Features' section, pp. 4–5.

9 Blais and Plisnier, *Belgo Cookbook*, p. 11.

10 'Any drop to drink', Robin Young, *TheTimes*, 20 March 1993, 'Features' section, p. 35.

11 'The Age of the Megabite', Michael Bateman, *Independent*, 27 October 1996, http://www.independent.co.uk/arts-entertainment/the-age-of-the-megabite-1360550.html, retrieved March 2013.

12 'Three drop into the Atlantic', Helen Nowicka, *Independent*, 18 May 1994, http://www.independent.co.uk/life-style/three-drop-into-the-atlantic-this-seasons-hot-spot-is-big-and-beautiful-and-open-till-three-helen-nowicka-descends-1436674.html, retrieved May 2013.

13 'Mash hits', *Caterer and Hotelkeeper*, 28 November 1996, http://www.catererandhotelkeeper.co.uk/articles/28/11/1996/20939/mash-hits.htm, retrieved 30 September 2013.

14 'The new Peyton place in Manchester', 11 January 1997, via Newsbank.com.

15 Unless otherwise specified, material here is from an interview of 21 August 2012.

16 'Bavarian Beer Hunt', *Caterer and Hotelkeeper*, 15 September 1994, http://www.catererandhotelkeeper.co.uk/articles/15/9/1994/30304/bavarian-beer-hunt.htm, retrieved 4 September 2013.

17 'Beer price rise falls behind the rate of inflation', *Guardian*, 3 November 1994, p. 10.

18 'Just pull me a pint of Freedom', *Independent*, 6 May 1995, via Newsbank.com.

19 'That taste of freedom', *Guardian*, 6 May 1995, p. A53.

20 Mackey, *Twenty-Five Years of New British Breweries*, p. 127.

21 *Opening Times*, January 1997, p. 1.

22 *Manchester Evening News*, 10 January 1997, p. 47.

23 See, for example, 'DJ Cox dines with dog', *The Sun*, 24 May 2000, p. 15.
24 'Mash Hits', *Caterer and Hotelkeeper*, 28 November 1996, http://www.catererandhotelkeeper.co.uk/articles/28/11/1996/20939/mash-hits.htm, retrieved May 2013.

CHAPTER TWELVE: Neither Art Nor Science

1 'The lonely death of the British ale', *Guardian*, 29 June, p. 14.
2 *A Book About Beer*, p. 33.
3 'The Sections', *Journal of the Institute of Brewing*, May 1938, p. 252.
4 *Small is Beautiful*, p. 50.
5 *World Guide to Beer*, pp. 179–80, and p. 204.
6 'Beers with a lot of bottle', *What's Brewing*, May 1987, p. 8.
7 'SIBA Call for Help in Bar War', *What's Brewing*, May 1987, P.12.
8 See, for example, the Introduction to Michael Jackson's *Pocket Beer Book*, , p. 4.
9 CAMRA *Good Beer Guide 1990*, p. 58.
10 Correspondence cited in 'Who first used the words *craft* beer?', Stan Hieronymus, Appellation Beer blog, 9 July 2010, http://appellationbeer.com/blog/who-first-used-the-words-craft-beer/, retrieved 19 August 2013.
11 *Good Beer Guide: Brewers and Pubs of the Pacific Northwest*, p. 9.
12 Correspondence with Ian Garrett, 23 August 2013.
13 'Porter murdered by Al Gapone comes back from the dead', *Observer*, 27 November 1994, p. 23.
14 'The Mancunian Candidate', *Observer* magazine, 26 February 1995, p. 46.
15 Interview, 8 September 2013.
16 'Beer BC (Before CAMRA)', *The Taste*, May/June 1998, p. 20.
17 'Brewers Toast Watchdog for Beer Tax Move', David Blackwell, *Financial Times*, 12 December 1998, p. 6.
18 'Raise your glass to craft beers', John Murray Brown, *Financial Times*, 17 November 1998, p. 18.
19 'Club 30something', Martin Deeson, *Observer*, 23 January 1994, 'Life' section pp. 4–5; 'Posh bars with Becks', Louise Weston, *Observer Magazine*, 3 October 1999, p. 73.
20 Luke Bainbridge, editor Manchester's *City Guide*, quoted in 'The revolution starts at closing time', Paul Vallely, *Independent*, 27 January 2001, p. 4.
21 Correspondence with James Clay, 14 November 2012.
22 'My round: Six pubs for Belgian beer', *Observer*, 26 July 1998, p. C34.
23 'Pub of the Month', *Potters Bar* (CAMRA branch magazine for 'the Potteries', August/September 1999, http://community.fortunecity.ws/oasis/ozarks/197/pb88/pom88.html, retrieved 12 August 2013.
24 'The abbey habit – the only Belgian Trappists not to brew beer have succumbed to the demon drink', Michael Jackson, *Independent*, 18 July 1998, via Newsbank.com.
25 'Britain's first "craft beer" bar', Jeff Pickthall, *It's Just the Beer Talking* blog, 28 June 2011, http://jeffpickthall.blogspot.co.uk/2011/06/britains-first-craft-beer-bar.html, retrieved 12 August 2013.
26 'Best Bromwich', Grant Rollings, *The Sun*, 21 August 2002, p. 22.
27 'Experienced brewer is a man who knows his craft', Richard Fletcher, *The Journal*, 8 March 2013, http://www.thejournal.co.uk/news/north-east-news/experienced-brewer-man-who-knows-4395138, retrieved 12 August 2013.

28 'Strawberry beers forever', 25 August 2001, p. 15.

29 'Rake wins Time Out award', *Morning Advertiser,* 18 September 2007, http://www. morningadvertiser.co.uk/General-News/Rake-wins-Time-Out-award, retrieved 12 August 2013.

CHAPTER THIRTEEN: Innovation, Passion, Knowledge

1 George Parker, 10 March 1999, p. 4.

2 Redman, *History of The Society of Independent Brewers,* pp. 16–30.

3 See, for example, 'Tax puts brewers of real ale over a barrel', John Willman, *Financial Times,* 15 November 1997, p. 7; and 'Brewers toast watchdog for beer tax move', David Blackwell, 12 December 1998, p. 6.

4 'Pilgrim Searches for Progress in Independent Beer Market', John Willman, *Financial Times,* 7 June 1999, p. 9.

5 Letter from Peter Haydon, SIBA chair, *The Times,* 23 March 2000, p. 23.

6 Hansard, 17 April 2002, http://www.publications.parliament.uk/pa/cm200102/ cmhansrd/vo020417/debtext/20417-04.htm, retrieved 27 September 2013.

7 'Brown accused of serving brewers a short measure', 18 April 2002, p. 11.

8 Redman, *History of The Society of Independent Brewers,* p. 29.

9 Interview, 21 August 2012.

10 'Dirty words that take heavy toll on purveyors of purity', Matthew Beard, *Independent,* 25 March 2002, via Newsbank.com.

11 'Bristol Evening Post: London's finest hoping to lure real ale punters', *Bristol Evening Post,* 4 February 2004, via Newsbank.com.

12 'Crisis? What crisis', CAMRA *Good Beer Guide 2006,* p. 3.

13 'Business profile: The Thornbridge Brewery', Russell Smith, *Independent,* 3 March 2009, retrieved from http://www.independent.co.uk/news/business/sme/business-profile-the-thornbridge-brewery-1636075.html, June 2013.

14 From an extended, unpublished version of the Introduction to Thornbridge's *Craft Union,* 2012, kindly shared with us by the author.

15 http://www.thornbridgebrewery.co.uk/how_we_brew.php, retrieved 5 July 2013.

16 'Brewery venture is maturing nicely', Keith Findlay, *Aberdeen Press and Journal,* 28 March 2007, via Newsbank.com.

17 'Introduction', Pete Brown, *Michael Jackson: a Special Issue of the Journal of the Brewery History Society,* 2011, p. 3.

18 'He Brews, He Scores', Susann Forbes, *Imbibe,* May/June 2012, http://imbibe.com/ feature/he-brews-he-scores/14389, retrieved 5 July 2013.

19 http://beerevolution.wordpress.com/2010/07/15/uk-brewer-of-the-year-thornbridges-stefano-cossi/, retrieved 5 July 2013.

20 'Foreword', *Craft Union,* Thornbridge Brewery and Richard Smith, 2012, p. 10.

21 *Old British Beers and How to Make Them,* p. 3.

22 *IPA: Brewing Techniques, Recipes and the Evolution of India Pale Ale,* Mitch Steele, 2012, pp. 132–7.

23 Ibid, p. 146.

24 For a full first-hand account of the revival and especially the White Horse seminars, see *Homebrew Classics: India Pale Ale,* by Roger Protz and Clive La Penseé, 2001, pp. 39–46.

25 'Roll out the barrel, cask, bottle and glass', *The Times*, 29 July, p. 30.

26 'Goose Island India Pale Ale: Down in One', Roger Protz, *Guardian*, 4 January 2003, 'Weekend' section, p. 67.

27 'Brewing in the global village', CAMRA *Good Beer Guide 2003*, p. 17.

28 'Branded range from Meantime', *The Grocer*, 3 June 2005, via Newsbank.com.

29 'British brewer pulls in US market', Andrew Jefford, *Financial Times*, 2 July 2005, http://www.ft.com/cms/s/0/e858cefe-ea94-11d9-aa7a-00000e2511c8. html#axzz24CGeyKAH, retrieved 21 August 2012.

30 'Introduction', Pete Brown, *Michael Jackson: a Special Issue of the Journal of the Brewery History Society*, 2011, p. 3.

31 'Father of beer writing dead', Pete Brown, http://petebrown.blogspot.co.uk/2007/08/ father-of-beer-writing-dead.html, retrieved 13 August 2013.

CHAPTER FOURTEEN: Rebellion into Money

1 Comment on 'UK Brewing Industry Unfriendly? Really?', Melissa Cole, *A Girls Guide to Beer* blog, 30 January 2012, http://girlsguidetobeer.blogspot.co.uk/2012/01/uk-brewing-industry-unfriendly-really.html, retrieved 9 July 2013.

2 'Binge-drinking? Don't blame me', Gillian Blowditch, *Sunday Times*, 1 November 2009, 'Features' section, p. 9.

3 Ibid.

4 'BrewDog and Michael Jackson', James Watt, BrewDog blog, 3 May 2009, http://www. brewdog.com/blog-article/91, retrieved 9 July 2013.

5 'Interview: BrewDog founders James Watt and Martin Dickie' , *Scotsman*, 2 August 2011, http://www.scotsman.com/news/interview-brewdog-founders-james-watt-and-martin-dickie-1-1778421, retrieved 8 July 2013.

6 'Brewery venture is maturing nicely', *Aberdeen Press and Journal*, 28 March 2007, via Newsbank.com.

7 *The Scotsman*, 2 August 2011.

8 'Whisky ale renews Broch's link with Japan', *Aberdeen Press and Journal*, 17 March 2007, via Newsbank.

9 'Tom Cadden – gatekeeper of good beer', Per Nielsen, The Evening Brews blog, http:// www.theeveningbrews.co.uk/tom-cadden-gatekeeper-of-good-beer/, retrieved 12 July 2013.

10 'Broch brewer top dog in Livewire contest', *Aberdeen Press and Journal*, 24 April 2007, via Newsbank.com.

11 Brewdog.com home page, 16 July 2007, archived at http://web.archive.org/ web/20070716074028/http:/www.brewdog.com/, retrieved 10 July 2013.

12 Biographical information from *The Craft of Stone Brewing Co*, Greg Koch, Steve Wagner and Randy Clemens, 2011.

13 'Greg Koch's thoughts on bashah and Scotland', BrewDog Blog, 9 August 2009, http:// www.brewdog.com/blog-article/135, retrieved 10 July 2013.

14 Results listed at http://www.worldbeercup.org/wp-content/uploads/2012/03/2008_ winners.pdf, retrieved 2 September 2013.

15 'Brewery faces boycott over "aggressive" marketing', Brian Ferguson, *The Scotsman*, 15 May 2008, p. 23.

16 http://www.petition.co.uk/prevent-the-portman-group-from-stamping-out-humour-

in-british-brewing.html, retrieved 10 July 2013.

17 'Portman Group's Final Decision on BrewDog Announced', BrewDog blog, 22 December 2008, http://www.brewdog.com/blog-article/48, retrieved 10 July 2013.

18 'BrewDog rapped for Speedball beer drug connotations', http://petebrown.blogspot.co.uk/2009/01/brewdog-rapped-for-speedball-beer-drug.html.

19 See, for example, an early recruitment advertisement from 10 October 2007 which declared that 'buying into the BrewDog philosophy is perhaps more important than qualifications', now offline but archived at http://web.archive.org/web/20071011015907/http://www.brewdog.com/news.php, retrieved 2 September 2013.

20 'Atlantic IPA: is it worth it?', Martyn Cornell, Zythophile blog, 17 November 2009, http://zythophile.wordpress.com/2009/11/17/brewdog-atlantic-ipa-is-it-worth-it/, retrieved 11 July 2013.

21 'The time is almost upon us . . .', James Watt, BrewDog blog, 19 October 2009, http://www.brewdog.com/blog-article/180 , retrieved 11 July 2013.

22 'The earth didn't move. But that's OK', http://petebrown.blogspot.co.uk/2009/10/earth-didnt-move-but-thats-ok.html, retrieved 11 July 2013.

23 Various comments on blogs in this period, e.g. this one from 21 October 2009, http://real-ale-reviews.com/equity-for-punks-brewdog-shares-with-all/2009/10/#comment-343, retrieved 16 January 2014.

24 'Brewdog are Dead: Long Live Brewdog!, Are you Tasting the Pith blog, 26 July 2010, http://thebeerboy.blogspot.co.uk/2010/07/brewdog-are-dead-long-live-brewdog-26.html, retrieved March 2014.

25 'Mr Portman Bans Tokyo*, but who complained?', James Watt, BrewDog blog, 5 November 2009, http://www.brewdog.com/blog-article/197, retrieved 11 July 2013.

26 'Craft Beer in Kegs', BrewDog blog, 15 April 2010, http://www.brewdog.com/blog-article/287, retrieved 12 July 2013.

27 *Three Sheets to the Wind*, reprinted 2007, p. 449.

28 E.g. Letter: 'Campaign for real quality ale', Brian Sheridan, *What's Brewing*, July 1986, p. 6.

29 'BrewDog: keg is the future', Claire Dodd, *Morning Advertiser*, 28 October 2010, http://www.morningadvertiser.co.uk/General-News/BrewDog-Keg-is-the-future, retrieved 12 July 2013.

CHAPTER FIFTEEN: The Cult of Craft Beer

1 'Reluctant Scooper' blog, 5 February 2012, http://www.reluctantscooper.co.uk/2012/02/craft-beer-manifesto.html, retrieved 4 September 2013.

2 Unless otherwise specified, quotations and biographical material in this section are from interviews conducted on 24, 25 and 28 June 2013.

3 '2009: what the blazes was all THAT about? (Part Two)', blog post, http://petebrown.blogspot.co.uk/2009/12/2009-what-blazes-was-all-that-about_18.html, retrieved 20 August 2013.

4 'A bit of a year in beer', New Briggate Beer Blog, 28 December 2010, http://newbriggatebeerblog.blogspot.co.uk/2010_12_01_archive.html, retrieved 20 August 2013.

5 Comment on 'Golden pints', 23 December 2011, http://newbriggatebeerblog.blogspot.co.uk/2011/12/golden-pints.html, retrieved 20 August 2013.

6 James Farran, *Raising the Beer Bar* blog, 10 February 2012, http://raisethebeerbar. blogspot.co.uk/2011/02/camra-campaign-for-real-alienation.html, retrieved 12 July 2013.

7 'Brewmaster Series: Evin O'Riordain – The Kernel Brewery', 5 June 2013, http://www. theeveningbrews.co.uk/brewmaster-series-evin-oriordain-kernel/, retrieved 20 August 2013.

8 'Just the Tonic', Hardknott Dave's beer and stuff blog, http://hardknott.blogspot. co.uk/2011/12/just-tonic.html, retrieved 25 September 2013.

9 'CAMRA cancels BrewDog's GBBF Bar', James Watt, BrewDog blog, 19 July 2011, http://www.brewdog.com/blog-article/camra-cancels-brewdogs-gbbf-bar, retrieved 2 September 2013.

10 Correspondence with Sean Franklin, 5 July 2013.

11 Correspondence with Jeff Rosenmeier, 21 August 2013.

12 'Beer Range Pub of the Year 2009: Pivo Cafe Bar, York', *The Publican*, 18 November 2009, http://www.morningadvertiser.co.uk/General-News/Beer-Range-Pub-of-the-Year-2009-Pivo-Cafe-Bar-York, retrieved 21 August 2013.

13 'The Great Brew Dog Bar Hunt', 7 November 2010, http://www.brewdog.com/blog-article/398, retrieved 21 August 2013.

14 The Evening Brews blog, http://www.theeveningbrews.co.uk/tom-cadden-gatekeeper-of-good-beer/, retrieved 12 July 2013.

15 'New pub taps into the real-ale market', Gavin Aitchison, *York Press*, 16 November 2011, http://www.yorkpress.co.uk/news/9366138.New_pub_taps_into_the_real_ale_market/, retrieved 2 September 2013.

16 Zak Avery, *500 Beers*, pp. 182–95.

CHAPTER SIXTEEN: The Outer Limits

1 p. 72.

2 'The Bad Beer Guide', p. 26.

3 'BrewDog launch fake lager', 1 April 2013, http://www.brewdog.com/blog-article/brewdog-launch-fake-lager, retrieved 30 September 2013.

4 'Best Practice for Running and Judging CAMRA Beer Competitions', internal memo, CAMRA Technical Advisory Group, September 2007.

5 'Wild Beer launches new brewery', http://www.thisissomerset.co.uk/Wild-Beer-launches-new-brewery/story-17033976-detail/story.html, retrieved 3 September 2013.

6 'You tell Euro-prats: HANDS OFF OUR PINTS!', *Daily Star*, 4 January 2007, p. 9.

7 E.g. *Daily Mirror*, 22 August 1962, p. 9.

8 Michael Jackson, *World Guide to Beer*, 1977, p. 110.

9 http://www.legislation.gov.uk/uksi/1988/2039/made, retrieved May 2013.

10 'Government commits to two-third pint changes', John Harrington, *Morning Advertiser*, 4 January 2011, http://www.morningadvertiser.co.uk/General-News/Government-commits-to-two-third-pints-changes, retrieved May 2013.

11 http://www.jamesclay.co.uk/beer-suppliers/news/103-beer-industry-news-the-23rd-pint-glass, retrieved 26 September 2013.

12 Correspondence with Chris Mair, 14 May 2013.

CHAPTER SEVENTEEN: Ecumenical Matters

1   *What's Brewing*, May 1985, p. 3.

2   http://www.theguardian.com/lifeandstyle/wordofmouth/2013/jun/13/craft-beer-guide-beginners, retrieved 27 August 2013.

3   Correspondence with Fergus Fitzgerald, 28 August 2013.

4   Mike Benner quoted in 'Craft Keg in the United Kingdom', Adrian Tierney-Jones, *All About Beer*, January 2012, http://allaboutbeer.com/craft-keg-in-the-united-kingdom/, retrieved 17 December 2013.

5   CAMRGB. '5000 twitter followers, 700+ signed up members & a site that gets 8000 hits a month. Not bad for a 2 year old organisation. Cheers! #CAMRGB', 10 July, 2013, 8.48 a.m. Tweet.

EPILOGUE: The Beer from the Wood Men

1   Correspondence with CAMRA head office (@CAMRA_official) via Twitter, 3 September 2013.

Picture Credits

Advert for the Join the Watney's RED Army campaign, 1971 – 95

Author's Collection – 197

Originally in *The Belgo Cookbook*, Blais, Denis and Plisnier, André, 1997 – 171

Courtesy of Brewdog.com – 212

© Brewer Magazine (now the Brewer and Distiller International) taken from Brewers and Distillers – 62

Courtesy of CAMRA – 44

Cover of *The Death of the English Pub*, Christopher Hutt, 1973 – 36

Copyright Guardian News & Media Ltd 1971 – 8

Copyright Guardian News & Media Ltd 2006 – 35

© John Simpson – 29, 55

Courtesy of Martin Sykes of Selby Brewery – 91

By Miller Design for the Wild Beer Company – 237

© National Portrait Gallery, London – 174

Originally published in *PINT* magazine, (Summer 1982, p6) – 156

Designed by Richard Norgate for Magic Rock Brewing – 221

Courtesy of Tessa Musgrave – 54

Originally published in *What's Brewing*, (July 1975, *insert* page 1) - 24

Originally published in *What's Brewing*, (March 1975, p1) – 32

Originally published in *What's Brewing*, (October 1977, p1) – 77

Originally published in *What's Brewing* magazine, (Winter 1980–1, p18) – 70

Originally published in *What's Brewing*, (March 1986, p2) – 120

SELECT BIBLIOGRAPHY

Abel, Bob, *The Book of Beer*, Regnery, 1976.

Acitelli, Tom, *The Audacity of Hops*, Chicago Review Press, 2013.

Avery, Zak, *500 Beers*, Apple Press, 2010.

Baillie, Frank, *The Beer Drinker's Companion*, David and Charles, 1973.

Barber, Norman, *Century (Plus Plus) of British Brewers 1890 to 2012*, Brewery History Society, 2012.

Blais, Denis and André Plisnier, *The Belgo Cookbook*, Orion, 1998.

Boston, Richard, *Beer and Skittles*, Fontana, 1976.

Brown, Mike and Brian Wilmott, *Brewed in Northants*, Brewery History Society, 1998.

Brown, Pete, *Man Walks Into a Pub*, Macmillan, 2003; paperback, Pan, 2004.

— *Three Sheets to the Wind*, Macmillan, 2006; paperback, Pan, 2007.

— Introduction, *Michael Jackson: A Special Issue of the Journal of the Brewery History Society*, Brewery History Society, 2011.

Campbell, Andrew, *The Book of Beer*, Dobson, 1956.

Campaign for Real Ale, *The Good Beer Guide*, edns from 1974 to 2013.

Cooper, Derek, *The Beverage Report*, Routledge and Kegan Paul, 1970.

Cornell, Martyn, *Amber, Gold and Black*, History Press, 2010.

— *Beer: The Story of the Pint*, Headline, 2003.

Cottone, Vince, *Good Beer Guide: Breweries and Pubs of the Pacific Northwest*, Homestead, 1986.

de Moor, Des, 'The Language of Beer: A Long Journey', in *CAMRA at 40*, ed. Roger Protz, CAMRA Books, 2011.

Dredge, Mark, *Craft Beer World*, Dog and Bone, 2013.

Food Standards Committee. *Report on Beer*, House of Commons, 1977.

Glover, Brian, *CAMRA New Beer Guide*, David and Charles, 1988.

Green, Martin and Tony White, *Guide to London Pubs*, Sphere, 1965; revised 1968.

— *Evening Standard Guide to London Pubs*, Pan, 1973.

Hieronymus, Stan, *Hops*, Brewers Publications, 2012.

Hutt, Christopher, *The Death of the English Pub*, Arrow, 1973.

Jackson, Michael, *The English Pub*, Quarto, 1976; repr. Arlington, 1989.

— *The World Guide to Beer*, Mitchell Beazley/Quarto, 1977.

— *Pocket Guide to Beer*, Muller/Quarto, 1982.

— *Pocket Beer Book*, Mitchell Beazley, 1986.

— *New World Guide to Beer*, 1988; paperback, Apple Press, 1991; repr. 1993.

— *Great Beer Guide*, Dorling Kindersley, 2000; repr. 2005.

— 'The Color Purple', in *Slow*, August/September 2003.

Janes, Hurford, *The Red Barrel*, John Murray, 1963.

Koch, Greg and Steve Wagner, *The Craft of Stone Brewing*, Ten Speed Press, 2012.

Line, Dave, *The Big Book of Brewing*, 1974; repr. Special Interest Model Books, 2004.

— *Brewing Beers Like Those You Buy*, 1978; repr. Argus Books, 1993.

Mackey, Ian, *Twenty-five Years of New British Breweries*, Ian Mackey, 1998.

Mass Observation, *The Pub and the People*, 1943; repr. Faber Finds, 2009.

Monopolies Commission, *Beer: A Report on the Supply of Beer*, 1969.

Monopolies and Mergers Commission, *The Supply of Beer*, House of Commons, 1989.

Mulchrone, Vincent, 'The Glory that is Beer', in *Pub*, ed. Angus McGill, 1969.

Nairn, Ian, *Outrage*, Architectural Press, 1955, repr. 1956.

— *Nairn's London*, Penguin, 1966.

Protz, Roger, *Pulling a Fast One*, Pluto Press, 1978.

Protz, Roger and Tony Millns, eds, *Called to the Bar*, CAMRA, 1991.

Redman, Nicholas, *A History of The Society of Independent Brewers 1980–2005*, SIBA, 2005.

Richards, Timothy M. and James Steven Curl, *City of London Pubs*, Drake, 1973.

Schumacher, E.F., *Small is Beautiful*, Blond and Briggs, 1973; repr. 1980.

Sheen, David, ed., *British Beer and Pub Association Statistical Handbook 2012*, Brewing Publications, 2012.

Spicer, John, with Chris Thurman, John Walters and Simon Ward, *Government Intervention in the Brewing Industry*, 2011/2013.

Steele, Mitch, *IPA*, Brewers Publications, 2012.

Thornbridge Brewery, *Craft Union*, Regional Magazine Company, 2012.

ACKNOWLEDGEMENTS

Apart from those who were kind enough to submit to interrogation by interview or correspondence, and whose contributions are acknowledged in the text, we owe pints to many people.

Adrian Tierney-Jones was unfailingly supportive and generous in sharing items from his personal library, putting us in touch with Michael Hardman, among others, and sharing knowledge, gossip and experience gained through dedicated pubmanship. Pete Brown, Des de Moor, Leigh Linley, Alan McLeod and Ron Pattinson were also great sources of inspiration and encouragement. Stan Hieronymus helped us find sources of information about Michael Jackson's career and provided copies of some rare articles, as well as giving excellent advice about the use of sources.

Ian Mackey responded to numerous queries about the sources for his *Twenty-five Years of New British Breweries*, and very kindly sent copies of vital cuttings from his own collection. Brian Glover was similarly generous with his time when we asked about his 1988 *CAMRA New Beer Guide*. Alaric Neville of the revived Phipps-NBC put us in touch with Elspeth Urquhart, and was extremely helpful in reviewing and correcting material on the Litchborough Brewery with reference to his own extensive scholarship. Between them, Adrian Hilton and Ed Wray provided us with copies of CAMRA's *Good Beer Guide*, without which this project would have been impossible. Ed was also an invaluable source of guidance on the history of hops and questions of brewing science.

Tom Fozard at Rooster's, Alice Grier at Peyton and Byrne, Deborah Lyons (Terry Jones's PA), Mike McGuigan, Phil Mellows, John Porter, Guy Sheppard at Exe Valley Brewery, George Thompson, Sarah Warman at BrewDog and Ian Worden were all vital in putting us in touch with key interviewees, or at least trying. Rod Jones at Meantime not only put us in touch with Alastair Hook but also answered supplementary questions about Meantime, as well as giving moral support at various points.

Peter 'Tandleman' Alexander helped us with contacts in Manchester and within CAMRA, but we also owe him particular thanks for highlighting the importance of Passageway Brewing.

Though we didn't quote from them, we learned a lot from conversations and correspondence with Don Burgess of Freeminer, Rainer Dresselhaus (formerly of Freedom), Richard Morrice at People Solutions, Glyn Roberts from Utobeer, Richard Sutton at Pictish Brewing, Jim Turner at the Euston Tap and Ian Ward (also formerly of Freedom).

Tony Badger answered numerous questions about Durden Park Beer Circle and provided copies of out-of-print publications. Robin Allender, John Clarke, John Green, Darren Norbury, Steve Williams and Steve Wright also shared books, articles and papers from their private collections.

Tom Stainer and his colleagues at CAMRA head office gave us access to their archive and responded with great patience to endless follow-up queries. Roger Jacobson at the Society for the Preservation of Beer from the Wood was something of a co-conspirator, as eager as we were to uncover the history of an often overlooked organisation.

Sarah Millard at the Bank of England, Stephen Ayre at *Which?* and Kerryn Woollett at Heriot-Watt University very kindly dug out and supplied copies of essential articles from their archives. We also relied upon the expertise and patience of librarians and archivists at the London Metropolitan Archive, Westminster Archive, the British Library Newspaper Collections at Colindale and at Cornwall Libraries.

Per Nielsen gave us permission to use extracts from a series of detailed interviews with key figures in 'craft beer' from his blog, The Evening Brews. Rebecca Johnson was kind enough to allow us to use a substantial extract from her late husband's blog – the book wouldn't have been the same without Simon's voice.

At Aurum Press, Sam Harrison has been a collaborator almost as much as an editor, saving you, the reader, from being either mired in detail or lost without it, and guiding the shape of the story with an expert hand. Jenny Page was an excellent and considerate copy-editor who made many improvements to the text. We are also grateful to both Charlotte Coulthard, who worked hard to track down some extremely obscure pictures, and Lucy Warburton who provided much-needed guidance in practical matters as we struggled to the finish line.

Finally, though we can't mention everyone by name, screen name or @handle, we have also appreciated all the nuggets of advice and intelligence received through comments on our blog, and via Twitter and Facebook.

INDEX